W9-APO-168

UNNECESSARY
= CHOICES =

UNNECESSARY
═CHOICES═

The Hidden Life of the Executive Woman

Edith Gilson with Susan Kane

PARAGON HOUSE
New York

90-1046

First paperback edition, 1989

Published in the United States by

Paragon House
90 Fifth Avenue
New York, NY 10011

Reprinted by arrangement with William Morrow and Company, Inc.

The authors gratefully acknowledge permission to reprint excerpts from the following:

Mary Lou Weisman article, copyright © 1983 by Mary Lou Weisman. Reprinted with permission of the author.

Powerplay: What Really Happened at Bendix by Mary Cunningham with Fran Schumer. Copyright © 1984 by Mary Cunningham. Reprinted by permission of Linden Press, a division of Simon & Schuster, Inc.

Too Smart For Her Own Good: The Impact of Success on the Private Lives of Women by Dr. Conalee Levine-Shneidman and Karen Levine. Copyright © 1985 by Conalee Levine-Shneidman, Ph.D., and Karen Levine. Reprinted by permission of Doubleday Publishing Company.

Library of Congress Cataloging-in-Publication Data

Gilson, Edith.
    Unnecessary choices : the hidden life of the executive woman / Edith Gilson with Susan Kane. — 1st pbk. ed.
      p.   cm.
    Bibliography: p.
    Includes index.
    ISBN 1-55778-199-0 (pbk.)
    1. Women executives—United States. I. Kane, Susan. II. Title.
[HD6054.4.U6G55   1989]
658.4'09'088042—dc19   88-28612
                                            CIP

Manufactured in the United States of America

TO MY MOTHER, EDITH ROOS,
WHO LOVED ME AND LET ME GO

ACKNOWLEDGMENTS

Now that this book is finished, I realize the enormous debt I owe to so many. It gives me great pleasure to thank them now.

Almost a decade ago I sought the help of a psychoanalyst and was lucky enough to meet Gloria Marmar Warner, M.D. I felt dissatisfied with my career and was searching for a better, less painful way to grow professionally. It was Gloria who urged me to write about the problems I and so many other career-women were grappling with. She died of cancer just before the manuscript was written, but her impact on my life continues. This book is hers as well as mine.

Gloria and her closest friend, Anne Bernstein, M.D., have contributed greatly to the field of women's psychology. Dr. Bernstein continued to corroborate my findings, and I am very grateful for her help.

I am in debt to my agent, Wendy Lipkind, who was willing to take a big risk and who offered a calm, supportive place of nourishment during the writing of this book; and to my editor, Harvey Ginsberg, whose work on the manuscript was invaluable.

I want to thank my sister, Ursula Roos, who spent hours listening while I tried to articulate my ideas; my secretary, Agnes Doherty, who willingly gave of her time; Madeline Nagel, who constantly challenged my ideas and helped me reach important conclusions; and my friend Mary Sachs, who lovingly watered my flowers in the Berkshires while I spent weekends writing in New York City.

I want to express my appreciation to my colleagues at J. Walter Thompson, particularly to the members of the Consumer Behavior Group, whose moral support meant a lot and saw me through some difficult times. I also wish to acknowledge Nancy Friday, whom I greatly admire. Had she not written *My Mother/ My Self*, I couldn't have written this book.

Most of all, I want to thank all those women who took the time to complete a lengthy questionnaire and those who in personal talks opened their lives to us so generously.

CONTENTS

INTRODUCTION

This book is about successful women and their challenging but painful task of integrating career-oriented, traditionally masculine priorities with their feminine identities. It is about the high price we pay for emulating men.

So that we could give life to the facts we discovered in our national survey of executive women, we conducted lengthy interviews with twenty-five individual executive women. The six women whose stories are revealed in these pages are composites of those twenty-five. Many of the women who were interviewed are prominent in their fields, and some are well known to all of us. The women shared intimate details about their relationships with bosses, husbands and lovers, fathers and—in what were often astonishing revelations—their mothers. In return for their candid disclosures, the women were promised anonymity.

In the course of the interviews, we found that women whose childhood experiences were similar were often surprisingly alike in terms of their present temperaments and their attitudes toward people, work, and life in general. Three or four women of similar backgrounds were therefore merged into one figure to create each of our six characters. While we have taken artistic liberties in portraying the women's appearances, environments, and professions, our portraits reflect the spirits of very real women and their actual life-styles. Most important, the words they speak are exact words recorded in our interviews. These are the voices of America's executive women.

The opinions I express in this book are my own, and do not reflect the views of my employer, J. Walter Thompson.

THE
QUESTIONNAIRE

I f you would like to learn how you can improve your chances for career success—and would like an opportunity truly to get to know yourself—take the time now to answer the questionnaire on the following pages. Whether you are male or female, whether you are on the top or the bottom of the corporate ladder, your responses can teach you about yourself and your potential.

This is the same survey we sent to our executive women. You don't need to fill it out to understand the book, but if you do so after reading the book, your answers will be biased.

There are no right or wrong answers in the questionnaire; what matters is how you feel about the issues raised. Answer the questions in the order in which they appear, because if you read ahead, you will lose objectivity.

THERE ARE NUMEROUS THEORIES ABOUT THE FAMILY ENVIRONMENT THAT IS CONDUCIVE TO SUCCESS. IT IS OUR WISH TO VERIFY SOME OF THESE THEORIES. THEREFORE, THIS FIRST SECTION DEALS WITH YOUR FAMILY BACKGROUND.

1. **How many brothers do you have?** *(Check one.)*
   None ☐   One ☐   Two ☐   Three ☐   Four or more ☐

2. **How many sisters do you have?** *(Check one.)*
   None ☐   One ☐   Two ☐   Three ☐   Four or more ☐

3. Are you the: (*Check one. If you are the only child, skip to question 4.*)

The oldest child .... ☐
The youngest child .... ☐
Neither the oldest nor the youngest .... ☐

4. Now think back to the time when you were about 10 years old —how would you describe the neighborhood you lived in? (*Check all that apply.*)

Rural .... ☐
Urban .... ☐
Suburban .... ☐
Lower income .... ☐
Middle income .... ☐
Upper middle .... ☐
Upper income .... ☐

5. During your early childhood, was there a favorite among the children? (*Check one. Answer this question only if you have one or more brothers or sisters; otherwise, skip to question 6.*)

No ..... ☐
Yes .... ☐ → **My father favored:** → **My mother favored:**

Me .... ☐	Me .... ☐
A brother .... ☐	A brother .... ☐
A sister .... ☐	A sister .... ☐
No favorite .... ☐	No favorite .... ☐

6. At that time (until you were about 10 years old), what was your father's profession? Was he in: (*Check one.*)

Finance/Accounting .... ☐
Marketing/Sales/Advertising .... ☐
Personnel .... ☐
Professional/Technical .... ☐
Production/Manufacturing .... ☐
General management .... ☐
Education .... ☐
Medicine .... ☐
Legal .... ☐
Publishing/Writing .... ☐
Consumer Affairs/Public Relations .... ☐
Self-employed .... ☐
Other (*Please specify.*) _____ ☐

THE QUESTIONNAIRE

7. Was his job: *(Check one.)*

Clerical .... ☐
Managerial .... ☐
Professional .... ☐
Other *(Please specify)* ———————————————— ☐

8. Did your mother work outside the house? *(Check no or yes for each part—a, b, and c.)*

	No	Yes	*What did she do? (Please explain.)*
a. Prior to her marriage	☐	☐	————
			————
			————
b. After her marriage	☐	☐	————
			————
			————
c. After having children	☐	☐	————
			————

9. Would you say your mother considered her work: *(Check one.)*

Just a job .... ☐
A career .... ☐

10. What kind of education did your parents have?

Father		*Mother*	
High school .... ☐		High school .... ☐	
Some college .... ☐		Some college .... ☐	
Finished college .... ☐		Finished college .... ☐	
Finished graduate school .... ☐		Finished graduate school .... ☐	

11. In your opinion, all things considered, how would you compare your parents' education?

Was your *mother* better educated than your father? .... ☐
Was your *father* better educated than your mother? .... ☐
Or would you say they both had about *an equal* education? ☐

12. Which parent were you closest to?

Father .... ☐
Mother .... ☐
Neither .... ☐
Both .... ☐

13. Which of the following statements best describes your view of your father when you were a child?

My father was ...	Most of the Time	Some of the Time	Never
—Nervous	☐	☐	☐
—Angry	☐	☐	☐
—Insecure	☐	☐	☐
—Flirtatious	☐	☐	☐
—Worried	☐	☐	☐
—Self-conscious	☐	☐	☐
—Confident	☐	☐	☐
—Happy	☐	☐	☐
—Special	☐	☐	☐
—Creative	☐	☐	☐
—Distant	☐	☐	☐
—Healthy	☐	☐	☐
—Accessible	☐	☐	☐
—Conservative	☐	☐	☐
—Attractive	☐	☐	☐
—Successful	☐	☐	☐
—Outgoing	☐	☐	☐
—Playful	☐	☐	☐

THE QUESTIONNAIRE

My father was ...	Most of the Time	Some of the Time	Never
—Nurturing	☐	☐	☐
—Selfish	☐	☐	☐
—Intelligent	☐	☐	☐
—Demanding	☐	☐	☐
—Liberal	☐	☐	☐
—Giving	☐	☐	☐
—Authoritative	☐	☐	☐
—Reserved	☐	☐	☐
—Affectionate	☐	☐	☐
—Warm	☐	☐	☐

(Rank each of the statements you checked "Most of the Time," giving the lowest number to the item that describes your father most and the highest number to the item that describes him least. If you have ten statements checked, your rank should be from one to ten.)

14. **And how about your mother? Which statement best describes how you felt about her?**

My mother was ...	Most of the Time	Some of the Time	Never
—Conservative	☐	☐	☐
—Attractive	☐	☐	☐
—Successful	☐	☐	☐
—Outgoing	☐	☐	☐
—Playful	☐	☐	☐
—Nervous	☐	☐	☐
—Angry	☐	☐	☐
—Insecure	☐	☐	☐
—Flirtatious	☐	☐	☐
—Worried	☐	☐	☐
—Self-conscious	☐	☐	☐
—Confident	☐	☐	☐
—Happy	☐	☐	☐
—Nurturing	☐	☐	☐
—Selfish	☐	☐	☐
—Intelligent	☐	☐	☐

My mother was . . .	Most of the Time	Some of the Time	Never
—Demanding	☐	☐	☐
—Liberal	☐	☐	☐
—Giving	☐	☐	☐
—Authoritative	☐	☐	☐
—Reserved	☐	☐	☐
—Affectionate	☐	☐	☐
—Warm	☐	☐	☐
—Special	☐	☐	☐
—Creative	☐	☐	☐
—Distant	☐	☐	☐
—Healthy	☐	☐	☐
—Accessible	☐	☐	☐

(Rank each of the statements you checked "Most of the Time" in the same manner you did for the preceding question.)

15. Which statement best describes the kind of relationship you feel your parents had with each other when you were a child? *(Record one response for each group.)*

a. Closeness
    Very close ☐
    Fairly close ☐
    Not at all close ☐

b. Affection
    Very affectionate ☐
    Fairly affectionate ☐
    Not at all affectionate ☐

c. Respect
    Very respectful ☐
    Fairly respectful ☐
    Not at all respectful ☐

d. Passionate
    Very passionate ☐
    Fairly passionate ☐
    Not at all passionate ☐

e. Loving
    Very loving ☐
    Somewhat loving ☐
    Not at all loving ☐

16a. **Until you were about 21 years of age, did your parents:** *(Check one.)*

Stay married .... ☐ → *(Skip to question 17.)*
Get divorced .... ☐
Get separated .... ☐
Become widowed .... ☐

At that time was your age:
Under 10 .... ☐
10 to 16 .... ☐
17 to 21 .... ☐

16b. **If widowed, which parent survived?**

Mother .... ☐
Father .... ☐

17. **Now, just a few questions about yourself. Think back to the time when you were a teenager—which of these statements best describes what you were like and how you felt about yourself?**

	Very Much Like Me	*Somewhat Like Me*	*Not at All Like Me*
—Inhibited	☐	☐	☐
—Afraid	☐	☐	☐
—Nervous	☐	☐	☐
—Worried	☐	☐	☐
—Self-conscious	☐	☐	☐
—Having a close relationship with my father ...	☐	☐	☐
—Having a close relationship with my mother .	☐	☐	☐
—Overweight	☐	☐	☐
—Getting along well with girls	☐	☐	☐
—Happy	☐	☐	☐
—Hated studying	☐	☐	☐
—Liked going to school ...	☐	☐	☐
—Getting along well with boys	☐	☐	☐
—Healthy	☐	☐	☐
—Having many friends ...	☐	☐	☐

	Very Much Like Me	Somewhat Like Me	Not at All Like Me
—An excellent student	☐	☐	☐
—Athletic	☐	☐	☐
—Social	☐	☐	☐
—Attractive	☐	☐	☐
—Popular	☐	☐	☐
—Lonely	☐	☐	☐
—Outgoing	☐	☐	☐

(Rank these as before.)

18. At the time you were about 21, how important was marriage to you? *(Check one.)*

Extremely important .... ☐
Very important .... ☐
Somewhat important .... ☐
Not at all important .... ☐

19. And how important was a career to you? *(Check one.)*

Extremely important .... ☐
Very important .... ☐
Somewhat important .... ☐
Not at all important .... ☐

20. Which statement best describes how you started your professional life? *(Check as many as apply.)*

I planned it very carefully .... ☐
I just kind of fell into it .... ☐
It was luck .... ☐
I had a mentor who believed in my talents .... ☐
It was a good place to meet men .... ☐
I followed my father's career .... ☐
I followed my mother's career .... ☐

THIS NEXT SECTION DEALS WITH YOUR PROFESSIONAL EXPERIENCES, YOUR VIEWS ON SUCCESS, AND SO FORTH.

21. **In the early years of your career did you have a mentor?**

    No .... ☐ ⟶ *(Skip to question 22.)*
    Yes .... ☐ ⟶ Was your mentor:
                                               Female .... ☐
                                               Male .... ☐

22. **In the early years was there a professional person whom you admired very much or wanted to be like?**

    No .... ☐ ⟶ *(Skip to question 23.)*
    Yes .... ☐ ⟶ Was that person:
                                               Female .... ☐
                                               Male .... ☐

23. **Please use the space below to indicate in your own words the single most important trait a person must have in order to be successful:**

    _____

    _____

24. **The following is a list of personality traits. We'd like you to indicate how important you think each trait is to the successful career of a woman:**

	Extremely Important	Very Important	Somewhat Important	Not at All Important
Attractive	☐	☐	☐	☐
Young looking .	☐	☐	☐	☐
Sexy	☐	☐	☐	☐
Feminine	☐	☐	☐	☐
Elegant	☐	☐	☐	☐
Romantic	☐	☐	☐	☐
Mature	☐	☐	☐	☐
Outgoing	☐	☐	☐	☐
Warm	☐	☐	☐	☐
Nurturing	☐	☐	☐	☐
Humorous	☐	☐	☐	☐
Fun-loving	☐	☐	☐	☐
Aggressive	☐	☐	☐	☐
Assertive	☐	☐	☐	☐
Intelligent	☐	☐	☐	☐

UNNECESSARY CHOICES

	Extremely Important	Very Important	Somewhat Important	Not at All Important
Well-read	☐	☐	☐	☐
Masculine	☐	☐	☐	☐
Affectionate	☐	☐	☐	☐
Accessible	☐	☐	☐	☐
Outspoken	☐	☐	☐	☐
Cheerful	☐	☐	☐	☐
Generous	☐	☐	☐	☐
Even-tempered	☐	☐	☐	☐
Thin	☐	☐	☐	☐
Competitive	☐	☐	☐	☐
Empathetic	☐	☐	☐	☐
Selfish	☐	☐	☐	☐
Reserved	☐	☐	☐	☐
Conservative	☐	☐	☐	☐
Creative	☐	☐	☐	☐
Talented	☐	☐	☐	☐
Giving	☐	☐	☐	☐
Well-disciplined	☐	☐	☐	☐
Well-connected	☐	☐	☐	☐
Likable	☐	☐	☐	☐
Thoughtful	☐	☐	☐	☐
Independent ...	☐	☐	☐	☐
Demanding	☐	☐	☐	☐
Healthy	☐	☐	☐	☐
Playful	☐	☐	☐	☐
Hardworking ...	☐	☐	☐	☐
Idealistic	☐	☐	☐	☐
Smart	☐	☐	☐	☐
Loyal	☐	☐	☐	☐
Concerned with results	☐	☐	☐	☐
Concerned with people	☐	☐	☐	☐
Well-educated ..	☐	☐	☐	☐
Happy	☐	☐	☐	☐

(Rank as before.)

THE QUESTIONNAIRE

25. **Now, for each of the following personality traits, check the one phrase that best describes how important, in your view, these personality traits are to the successful career of a man:**

	Extremely Important	Very Important	Somewhat Important	Not at All Important
Likable	☐	☐	☐	☐
Well-connected	☐	☐	☐	☐
Well-disciplined	☐	☐	☐	☐
Giving	☐	☐	☐	☐
Talented	☐	☐	☐	☐
Happy	☐	☐	☐	☐
Well-educated ..	☐	☐	☐	☐
Concerned with people	☐	☐	☐	☐
Concerned with results	☐	☐	☐	☐
Loyal	☐	☐	☐	☐
Smart	☐	☐	☐	☐
Idealistic	☐	☐	☐	☐
Hardworking ...	☐	☐	☐	☐
Creative	☐	☐	☐	☐
Conservative	☐	☐	☐	☐
Reserved	☐	☐	☐	☐
Selfish	☐	☐	☐	☐
Empathetic	☐	☐	☐	☐
Competitive	☐	☐	☐	☐
Thin	☐	☐	☐	☐
Even-tempered	☐	☐	☐	☐
Generous	☐	☐	☐	☐
Cheerful	☐	☐	☐	☐
Outspoken	☐	☐	☐	☐
Accessible	☐	☐	☐	☐
Affectionate	☐	☐	☐	☐
Masculine	☐	☐	☐	☐
Well-read	☐	☐	☐	☐
Intelligent	☐	☐	☐	☐
Assertive	☐	☐	☐	☐

	Extremely Important	Very Important	Somewhat Important	Not at All Important
Aggressive	☐	☐	☐	☐
Fun-loving	☐	☐	☐	☐
Humorous	☐	☐	☐	☐
Nurturing	☐	☐	☐	☐
Warm	☐	☐	☐	☐
Outgoing	☐	☐	☐	☐
Mature	☐	☐	☐	☐
Romantic	☐	☐	☐	☐
Elegant	☐	☐	☐	☐
Feminine	☐	☐	☐	☐
Sexy	☐	☐	☐	☐
Young looking .	☐	☐	☐	☐
Attractive	☐	☐	☐	☐
Playful	☐	☐	☐	☐
Healthy	☐	☐	☐	☐
Demanding	☐	☐	☐	☐
Independent ...	☐	☐	☐	☐
Thoughtful	☐	☐	☐	☐

(Rank as before.)

26. Now, please indicate how you would describe yourself at this point in time—for each of the following items, check the box that best describes how you feel:

	Very Much Like Me	Somewhat Like Me	Not at All Like Me
Empathetic	☐	☐	☐
Selfish	☐	☐	☐
Reserved	☐	☐	☐
Conservative	☐	☐	☐
Creative	☐	☐	☐
Talented	☐	☐	☐
Giving	☐	☐	☐
Well-disciplined	☐	☐	☐
Well-connected	☐	☐	☐
Likable	☐	☐	☐
Thoughtful	☐	☐	☐
Independent	☐	☐	☐

THE QUESTIONNAIRE

	Very Much Like Me	Somewhat Like Me	Not at All Like Me
Demanding	☐	☐	☐
Healthy	☐	☐	☐
Playful	☐	☐	☐
Hardworking	☐	☐	☐
Idealistic	☐	☐	☐
Smart	☐	☐	☐
Loyal	☐	☐	☐
Concerned with results	☐	☐	☐
Concerned with people	☐	☐	☐
Well-educated	☐	☐	☐
Happy	☐	☐	☐
Attractive	☐	☐	☐
Young looking	☐	☐	☐
Sexy	☐	☐	☐
Feminine	☐	☐	☐
Elegant	☐	☐	☐
Romantic	☐	☐	☐
Mature	☐	☐	☐
Outgoing	☐	☐	☐
Warm	☐	☐	☐
Nurturing	☐	☐	☐
Humorous	☐	☐	☐
Fun-loving	☐	☐	☐
Aggressive	☐	☐	☐
Assertive	☐	☐	☐
Intelligent	☐	☐	☐
Well-read	☐	☐	☐
Masculine	☐	☐	☐
Affectionate	☐	☐	☐
Accessible	☐	☐	☐
Outspoken	☐	☐	☐
Cheerful	☐	☐	☐
Generous	☐	☐	☐
Even-tempered	☐	☐	☐
Thin	☐	☐	☐
Competitive	☐	☐	☐

(Rank as before.)

27. People set different priorities as to what is or is not important in how they choose to live—in both their professional and their personal lives. Please check the phrase that best describes how much importance you personally place on each of the following.

	Extremely Important	Very Important	Somewhat Important	Not at All Important
Having control	☐	☐	☐	☐
Being successful	☐	☐	☐	☐
Expressing what you really think	☐	☐	☐	☐
Being independent .	☐	☐	☐	☐
Having a mentor	☐	☐	☐	☐
Developing close personal relationships with men	☐	☐	☐	☐
Being a mentor	☐	☐	☐	☐
Developing close business relationships .	☐	☐	☐	☐
Being a leader ..	☐	☐	☐	☐
Taking a stand .	☐	☐	☐	☐
Getting to know your co-workers	☐	☐	☐	☐
Understanding the needs of others	☐	☐	☐	☐
Being the best one can be ...	☐	☐	☐	☐
Knowing who is in power	☐	☐	☐	☐

THE QUESTIONNAIRE

	Extremely Important	*Very Important*	*Somewhat Important*	*Not at All Important*
Being part of a team	☐	☐	☐	☐
Being visible	☐	☐	☐	☐
Being better at my job than anyone else ...	☐	☐	☐	☐
Keeping busy ...	☐	☐	☐	☐
Doing my job as best I can	☐	☐	☐	☐
Developing close personal relationships with women	☐	☐	☐	☐
Having time to be alone	☐	☐	☐	☐
Having sufficient time for family activities	☐	☐	☐	☐
Reading things other than business materials	☐	☐	☐	☐
Setting goals	☐	☐	☐	☐
Taking risks	☐	☐	☐	☐
Being flexible ...	☐	☐	☐	☐
Being consistent	☐	☐	☐	☐
Being liked by others	☐	☐	☐	☐
Being admired by others	☐	☐	☐	☐

(Rank as before.)

28. Now, look at these statements again and for each one please indicate your opinion as to what you think might be more important to men than to women or vice versa.

	Much More Important To Men	Much More Important To Women	No Difference
Being admired by others	☐	☐	☐
Being liked by others ...	☐	☐	☐
Being consistent	☐	☐	☐
Being flexible	☐	☐	☐
Taking risks	☐	☐	☐
Setting goals	☐	☐	☐
Reading things other than business	☐	☐	☐
Having sufficient time for family activities	☐	☐	☐
Having time to be alone	☐	☐	☐
Developing close personal relationships with women	☐	☐	☐
Doing a job as best one can	☐	☐	☐
Keeping busy	☐	☐	☐
Being better than anyone else	☐	☐	☐
Being visible	☐	☐	☐
Being part of a team ...	☐	☐	☐
Knowing who is in power	☐	☐	☐
Being the best one can be	☐	☐	☐
Understanding the needs of others	☐	☐	☐
Getting to know your co-workers	☐	☐	☐

	Much More Important To Men	Much More Important To Women	No Difference
Taking a stand	☐	☐	☐
Being a leader	☐	☐	☐
Developing close business relationships	☐	☐	☐
Being a mentor	☐	☐	☐
Developing close personal relationships with men	☐	☐	☐
Having a mentor	☐	☐	☐
Being independent	☐	☐	☐
Expressing what you really think	☐	☐	☐
Being successful	☐	☐	☐
Having control	☐	☐	☐

(Rank as before.)

29. This time please check how well you feel you're doing on each of these priorities:

	I'm Extremely Satisfied with Myself	I'm Somewhat Satisfied with Myself	I'm Not at All Satisfied
Having time to be alone	☐	☐	☐
Having sufficient time for family activities .	☐	☐	☐
Reading things other than business materials	☐	☐	☐
Setting goals	☐	☐	☐
Taking risks	☐	☐	☐
Being flexible	☐	☐	☐
Being consistent	☐	☐	☐
Being liked by others .	☐	☐	☐
Being admired by others	☐	☐	☐
Having control	☐	☐	☐

UNNECESSARY CHOICES

	I'm Extremely Satisfied with Myself	I'm Somewhat Satisfied with Myself	I'm Not at All Satisfied
Being successful	☐	☐	☐
Expressing what you really think	☐	☐	☐
Being independent ...	☐	☐	☐
Having a mentor	☐	☐	☐
Developing close personal relationships ..	☐	☐	☐
Being a mentor	☐	☐	☐
Developing close personal relationships with men	☐	☐	☐
Being a leader	☐	☐	☐
Taking a stand	☐	☐	☐
Getting to know your co-workers	☐	☐	☐
Understanding the needs of others	☐	☐	☐
Being the best one can be	☐	☐	☐
Knowing who is in power	☐	☐	☐
Being part of a team .	☐	☐	☐
Being visible	☐	☐	☐
Being better at my job than anyone else	☐	☐	☐
Keeping busy	☐	☐	☐
Doing my job as best I can	☐	☐	☐
Developing close personal relationships with women	☐	☐	☐

(Rank as before.)

THE QUESTIONNAIRE

30a. All things considered, would you describe yourself as: *(Check one.)*

Highly successful .... ☐
Very successful .... ☐
Quite successful .... ☐
Moderately successful .... ☐
Not very successful .... ☐

30b. Why do you feel that way? *(Please explain.)*

_____

_____

_____

_____

31. When it comes to making important business decisions, do you feel you have: *(Check one.)*

Complete authority .... ☐
Adequate authority .... ☐
Too little authority .... ☐

32. To what degree do you feel your financial compensation reflects your performance and contributions? *(Check one.)*

It's more than what I deserve .... ☐
It's in line with my performance .... ☐
It's a little below what I think I deserve .... ☐
It's much lower than what I deserve .... ☐

33. Is your current position: *(Check one.)*

As high as you want to go .... ☐
A little lower than where you want to be .... ☐
Much lower than the level to which you aspire .... ☐

34. All things considered, how satisfied are you with your career? *(Check one.)*

Extremely satisfied .... ☐
Very satisfied .... ☐
Somewhat satisfied .... ☐
Not at all satisfied .... ☐

35. To what degree, if any, would you say young women who plan to have a career like yours have to sacrifice some aspects of each of the following:

	Major Sacrifices	Minor Sacrifices	None
The number of children to have	☐	☐	☐
The amount of time spent with friends	☐	☐	☐
The amount of time spent on hobbies/leisure-time activities	☐	☐	☐
The way one expresses oneself as a woman (clothes, makeup, etc.)	☐	☐	☐
The time and involvement required to maintain a good love life	☐	☐	☐
The smooth running of a household	☐	☐	☐
The amount of time spent with family	☐	☐	☐

36. And in your view, how do you feel young men who aspire to a career like yours compare with young women in terms of the sacrifices they have to make for each of the following:

	Women Have to Give Up More	Men Have to Give Up More	No Difference
The number of children to have	☐	☐	☐
The amount of time spent with friends ...	☐	☐	☐
The amount of time spent on hobbies/leisure-time activities ...	☐	☐	☐
The time and involvement required to maintain a good love life	☐	☐	☐
The smooth running of a household	☐	☐	☐
The amount of time spent with family	☐	☐	☐

37. Which of the following obstacles may have hurt you in your professional growth?

	A Lot	A Little	Not at All
Simply being a woman	☐	☐	☐
Lack of confidence	☐	☐	☐
Jealousy of male bosses/peers	☐	☐	☐
Anxiety from too much pressure	☐	☐	☐
Jealousy of female boss/peers	☐	☐	☐
Difficulty relating to/understanding peers	☐	☐	☐
Difficulty relating to/understanding superiors	☐	☐	☐
Not controlling my emotions well enough	☐	☐	☐
Not being demanding enough	☐	☐	☐
Being too outspoken	☐	☐	☐
Being too aggressive	☐	☐	☐

38. In your view, are the professional women you know: (*Check as many as apply.*)

	Most of the Time	Sometimes	Not at All
Unnecessarily competitive with each other	☐	☐	☐
Supportive of each other	☐	☐	☐
Threatened by each other	☐	☐	☐
Manipulative of each other	☐	☐	☐
Understanding toward each other	☐	☐	☐
Fearful of younger, more attractive women	☐	☐	☐

39. In your experience, are there any differences in the ways men behave on their jobs as compared with the ways women behave? (*Check one.*)

There are a lot of differences .... ☐
There are some differences .... ☐
There are no differences .... ☐

40. Based on your own experience, would you say that men: *(Check all that apply.)*

Admire successful women .... ☐
Are distrustful of successful women .... ☐
Are attracted to successful women .... ☐
Are supportive of successful women .... ☐

41. Do you believe that women have to work harder than men to achieve the same status? *(Check one.)*

Yes ☐ No ☐

42. Do you believe that women today have equal job opportunities compared with men? *(Check one.)*

Completely equal .... ☐
Somewhat equal .... ☐
Not at all equal .... ☐

43. Are you currently actively involved in any feminist organization or activities? *(Check one.)*

Yes .... ☐→ *(Skip to question 44.)*
No .... ☐→ Have you ever been actively involved? *(Check one.)*
Yes ☐ No ☐

44. Do you consider yourself to be a feminist? *(Check one.)*

Yes ☐ No ☐

45. What are your opinions on the following feminist issues:

a. Do you favor the ERA?
Yes ☐ No ☐

b. The free choice of abortion?
Yes ☐ No ☐

c. Legislated maternity leave?
Yes ☐ No ☐

46. How effective, in your view, are female networking groups? *(Check one.)*

Very effective .... ☐
Somewhat effective .... ☐
Not at all effective .... ☐
Don't know .... ☐

47. Much has been written about the pros and cons of sexual involvements on the job. Based on your personal experience and feelings, how would you advise a woman just starting out in her career on this issue? *(Check as many as apply.)*

Stay away from it .... ☐
Only get involved with men who are your professional
  equals .... ☐
It's an experience that's unavoidable .... ☐
Never get involved with a man higher up than you .... ☐

Women always suffer more in this situation than men ..... ☐
It will always affect your performance and growth
  negatively .... ☐
It can be an exciting experience .... ☐

48. Have you ever had an affair with someone you worked with?

No   ☐
Yes   ☐ → a. How did that affect you professionally? *(Check one.)*
                Positively .... ☐
                Negatively .... ☐
                Not at all .... ☐

            b. Was he *(Check one.)*
                At the same level as you .... ☐
                At a higher level .... ☐
                At a lower level .... ☐

49. Which of the following books have you heard about? Or read?

	Heard About	Read
The Feminine Mystique	☐	☐
Unfinished Business	☐	☐
The Managerial Woman	☐	☐

	Heard About	Read
My Mother/My Self	☐	☐
The Female Eunuch	☐	☐
In Pursuit of Excellence	☐	☐
Megatrends	☐	☐
The One Minute Manager	☐	☐
The Second Stage	☐	☐
The Color Purple	☐	☐

50a. How do you feel about getting older? *(Check as many as apply.)*

Hate the idea .... ☐
I'm afraid of it .... ☐
Try not to think about it .... ☐

It's okay .... ☐
It's something I've come to accept .... ☐
I'm planning for it .... ☐

I plan to retire early .... ☐
I'm actively investing money for my old age .... ☐
I'm taking good care of my health .... ☐

I worry a lot about getting older .... ☐
I do not talk about my age .... ☐

50b. And how do you think men feel about getting older? *(Check as many as apply.)*

They are actively investing money for their old age .... ☐
They plan to retire early .... ☐
They are planning for it .... ☐

They do not talk about their age .... ☐
They worry a lot about getting older .... ☐
They are taking good care of their health .... ☐

It's something they've come to accept .... ☐
It's okay .... ☐
They try not to think of it .... ☐

They are afraid of it .... ☐
They hate the idea .... ☐

51. Now, a few questions on how you feel you are different from your mother when your mother was as old as you are now.

	More Than My Mother	About the Same	Less Than My Mother
Independent	☐	☐	☐
Fulfilled	☐	☐	☐
Affectionate	☐	☐	☐
Successful	☐	☐	☐
Assertive	☐	☐	☐
Loving	☐	☐	☐
Outgoing	☐	☐	☐
Controlling	☐	☐	☐
Outspoken	☐	☐	☐
Active	☐	☐	☐
Intelligent	☐	☐	☐
Attractive	☐	☐	☐
Happy	☐	☐	☐

52. How openly can you discuss your feelings about most things with your mother now? *(Check one.)*

Very openly .... ☐
Somewhat openly .... ☐
Not at all .... ☐
Don't know .... ☐

NOW, JUST A FEW MORE QUESTIONS FOR CLASSIFICATION:

A. How long have you been with your current employer? *(Check one.)*

Less than 1 year .... ☐   7 to 8 years .... ☐
1 to 2 years .... ☐   9 to 10 years .... ☐
3 to 4 years .... ☐   Over 10 years *(Please specify.)*
5 to 6 years .... ☐   _____ ☐

B. What is your title? *(Check one.)*
Manager .... ☐   Executive Vice president .. ☐
Vice president .... ☐   Other *(Please specify.)*
Senior Vice president ..... ☐   _____ ☐

C. What is your current yearly compensation (including types of compensation such as profit sharing, yearly bonus, etc.) *(Check one.)*

Under $15,000 .... ☐
$15,000 to under $25,000 . ☐
$25,000 to under $35,000 . ☐
$35,000 to under $45,000 . ☐
$45,000 to under $55,000 . ☐
$55,000 to under $65,000 . ☐
$65,000 to under $75,000 . ☐
$75,000 to under $85,000 . ☐

$85,000 to under
  $95,000 .... ☐
$95,000 to under
  $105,000 .... ☐
$105,000 to under
  $115,000 .... ☐
$115,000 to under
  $125,000 .... ☐
$125,000 and over ☐

D. In which of the following brackets does your age fall? *(Check one.)*

Under 25 .... ☐
25 to 29 .... ☐
30 to 34 .... ☐
35 to 39 .... ☐
40 to 44 .... ☐

40 to 49 .... ☐
50 to 54 .... ☐
55 to 59 .... ☐
60 to 64 .... ☐
65 and older .... ☐

E. What is your education? *(Check one.)*

High school .... ☐
Some college .... ☐
Completed college .... ☐

Some graduate school ... ☐
Completed graduate
  school .... ☐

F. What is your current marital status? *(Check one.)*

Single .... ☐
Divorced .... ☐
Married .... ☐

Separated .... ☐
Widowed .... ☐
Living with someone .... ☐

G. Have you been married? *(Check one.)*

Only once .... ☐
Twice .... ☐

Three times or more .... ☐
Never married .... ☐

THE QUESTIONNAIRE

(Answer question H only if you are separated or divorced; otherwise, skip to question I.)

H. Did your career play a role in your separation or divorce? *(Check one.)*

    Was a major reason .... ☐
    One of the reasons .... ☐
    Not a reason at all .... ☐

I. How many children do you have? *(Check one.)*

None .... ☐	Three .... ☐
One .... ☐	Four .... ☐
Two .... ☐	Five or more .... ☐

J. Have you ever taken a leave of absence from your career? *(Check one.)*

    No ..... ☐→*(Skip to question K)*
    Yes ..... ☐────────────→ For which reasons? *(Check all that apply.)*
    Maternity leave .... ☐
    Continued education . ☐
    Health reasons .... ☐
    Other *(Please specify.)*
    ────────────── ☐

(Answer this question only if you have children; otherwise, skip to question L.)

K. Do you feel you have been able to spend enough time with your children? *(Check one.)*

    As much as they needed .... ☐
    A little less .... ☐
    A lot less .... ☐

L. Which of the following best describes the type of profession you currently have? *(Check one.)*

Finance/Accounting .... ☐
Marketing/Sales/Advertising .... ☐
Personnel .... ☐
Professional/Technical .... ☐
Production/Manufacturing .... ☐
International .... ☐
General Management .... ☐
Education .... ☐
Medicine .... ☐
Legal .... ☐
Publishing/Writing .... ☐
Consumer Affairs/Public Relations .... ☐
Other *(Please specify.)* _____ ☐

M. Are you: *(Check one.)*

White ☐   Black ☐   Asian ☐
Other *(Please specify.)* _____ ☐

N. Is your religious background: *(Check one.)*

Catholic .... ☐
Protestant .... ☐
Jewish .... ☐
Other *(Please specify.)* _____ ☐

O. How many hours' sleep do you get on an average night? *(Check one.)*

Less than four .... ☐   Seven .... ☐
Four .... ☐   Eight .... ☐
Five .... ☐   Nine .... ☐
Six .... ☐   More than nine .... ☐

P. Do you generally take all the vacation time due you? *(Check one.)*

Yes ☐   No ☐

THE QUESTIONNAIRE

(Answer the following questions only if you are married or living with someone.)

Q. What is your yearly combined household income? *(Check one.)*

Under $15,000 .... ☐
$15,000 to under $25,000 .... ☐
$25,000 to under $35,000 .... ☐
$35,000 to under $45,000 .... ☐

$45,000 to under $55,000 .... ☐
$55,000 to under $65,000 .... ☐
$65,000 to under $75,000 .... ☐
$75,000 to under $85,000 .... ☐

$85,000 to under $95,000 .... ☐
$95,000 to under $105,000 .... ☐
$105,000 to under $115,000 .... ☐

$115,000 to under $125,000 .... ☐
$125,000 and over .... ☐

R. Would you say your husband (or lover) is: *(Check one.)*

A lot more successful than you .... ☐
Somewhat more successful than you .... ☐
Equally successful as you .... ☐
Less successful than you .... ☐

S. Do you contribute: *(Check one.)*

More than 50 percent of the household income .... ☐
About 50 percent of the household income .... ☐
Less than 50 percent of the household income .... ☐

T. With respect to the household chores, would you say you have: *(Check one.)*

Major responsibility .... ☐
Most responsibility .... ☐
Equal responsibility .... ☐
Minor responsibility .... ☐

U. Do you employ household help?

Full-time .... ☐
Part-time .... ☐
Not at all .... ☐

C H A P T E R

I

THE STRANGER BESIDE ME

These women [of the new generation], each thinking she is alone with her personal guilt and pressures, trying to "have it all," having second thoughts about her professional career, desperately trying to have a baby before it is too late, with or without husband, and maybe secretly blaming the movement for getting her into this mess, are almost as isolated, and as powerless in their isolation, as those suburban housewives afflicted by "the problem that had no name" whom I interviewed for *The Feminine Mystique* over 20 years ago.

—BETTY FRIEDAN,
"How to Get the Women's Movement Moving Again,"
The New York Times Magazine, November 3, 1985

At 7:30 on a raw February morning in 1982, I entered the glass-and-steel skyscraper on Lexington Avenue in New York that houses my office in the J. Walter Thompson advertising agency. I rode up a noiseless elevator, stepped out onto a carpeted floor, and walked down a corridor lit only by the red glow of Exit and Emergency signs. I had come into work early to get a head start on what promised to be a particularly hectic day, and the heat in the building, at that hour, was barely perceptible. Once at my desk, I sat, coat on, and looked at my calendar: a meeting to untangle some pressing administrative problems, a review of a draft of a presentation my staff had prepared and that was to be delivered to a client in three days, a Strategy Review Board session, and to end the day, a new-business presentation. I switched on the radio for some relaxing music, and the advertising news, a regular feature on WQXR, came on.

"Marie Luisi, a senior vice president of the J. Walter Thompson Company, has been suspended, pending an investigation of financial irregularities in her department."

Astonished, I turned up the sound.

"Luisi is the head of JWT's very successful television syndication unit," the announcer continued. "Apparently, the company's computer shows some six million dollars in revenue for her department for the year 1979 that management cannot find. Although dollar amounts are entered as profit into the computer, no clients appear to have been billed for the corresponding sales."

Marie suspended? An investigation into her department? Neither allegation could be true! Marie and I were two of only four senior-level executive women at J. Walter Thompson. She had started as a secretary in the company at age seventeen and had worked her way up into one of the most powerful positions in the advertising world. Marie was a legend on Madison Avenue.

Her job entailed buying commercial time from local television and radio stations throughout the country and reselling this time to our clients. So successful had she been at meeting— and exceeding—her profit goals that her nickname at JWT was "The Godmother." And over the last few years, counting on Marie's continued success, management had poured millions of dollars into the expansion of her department.

Marie Luisi was vivacious, dynamic, and a magnetic public speaker. Her reputation was that of a tough negotiator, and virtually everyone in the media world knew and respected her. At 9:30 that morning, the president called a conference for all department heads. He quietly confirmed Marie's suspension and the investigation into her department. Shocked faces surrounded the conference table.

During the company's ensuing investigation the so-called "phantom" sales were found to have begun appearing on the computer in 1978, when Marie apparently first fell short of her revenue targets. Six million dollars of fictitious profits then reached $30 million over the following four years. The money JWT had invested in the syndication unit seemed to have been wasted. Marie's suspension became a termination, thus abruptly ending one of the most dramatic success stories in the history of the female (or, for that matter, the male) executive.

Marie Luisi disappeared, leaving us all to wonder: *Why?* What had spurred an intelligent woman like her to allegedly concoct such a scheme? Certainly she was under pressure to perform . . . but we all were. Why might she have cracked? Because Marie and I had been among the few top women at J. Walter Thompson, I felt closer to the case than I would have had a man been involved. I wanted to understand what had happened, yet I also realized I had barely known her in the eight years I'd been with the company. While we hadn't worked closely together, we had shared the podium in many new-business presentations; somehow, though, we had never become more than acquaintances. She'd always seemed pleasant; at my last promotion, she'd sent me an expensive bottle of champagne. I'd tried to reciprocate by taking her to lunch, but we'd been unable to arrange a date.

The more I thought about Marie, the more I realized how little I knew about her or *any* executive women in my company or in other large companies; this in spite of the fact that many of us interact professionally or are at least aware of one another—not surprising when you consider that while women comprise half the country's workforce, when you get to the level of vice president or above, that figure shrinks to 5 or 6 percent. I realized I had worked with some of these women for over ten years without knowing a single thing about their private lives!

This revelation hit me hard, because a recent crisis had made me painfully conscious of my distance from the women at JWT with whom I worked most closely, women both at and near my peer levels. A year before Marie's dismissal, I had begun to hemorrhage vaginally. The doctor found a benign tumor in my uterus, which he couldn't safely remove. He advised me to wait; sometimes the uterus adapted itself to such a growth.

My condition grew worse. I began running out in the middle of meetings, missing work, and canceling business trips. Having such a female experience in a male environment made me feel extremely vulnerable, and I was frightened for my health and my career. Since I had no family in this country, no man in my life, and few friends, I felt a great need to talk about what I was going through with my female colleagues, but they seemed hesitant to listen or respond. One did advise me not to "tell management what was really wrong" and, as she phrased it, "not even to tell them [I had] 'female problems.' "

Finally, after six months of anguish, I went to the hospital for a necessary hysterectomy and was once again hurt and dismayed by the reactions of the women in my office. I had expected to receive the most sympathy from them; instead, I heard more often from my male associates.

Shortly after I returned to work, Marie Luisi was fired, and for months she was the subject of many casual conversations in the office. As we deliberated among ourselves as to what her possible motives had been, I became aware that I wasn't the only one who had failed to communicate with her. Clearly, Marie had closed herself off from nearly everyone she had worked with. And only then did it dawn on me: I had done the very same thing! My self-exile was part of the reason the women had been so reticent with me. I couldn't suddenly—in a time of crisis—ask for the kind of empathy and support that can be built only through a history of friendship and sharing. I had been as guarded as Marie. Was our behavior typical among executive women? For the first time in my career I took a hard look at the high-level women I knew and realized that many of them took no part in office camaraderie. And, as I would soon discover, many of them—like me—were secretly frightened, angry, insecure, and lonely.

My hysterectomy and Marie's firing were two entirely separate events. Both, however, left me grappling with the same question: What really went on in the minds, feelings, and lives of us executive women? I grew intrigued, disturbed, and finally compelled to find out. I read everything I could find on women in managerial positions, but none of the literature answered my question in a satisfying way. I was convinced that a story remained to be told, one well worth uncovering. As a researcher, I felt challenged professionally to find the answers that I sought, and I decided to conduct my own study into what I came to call the "hidden" or undocumented, lives of the women at the top.

Before I could design the study, the newspapers began to

uncover some interesting information about Marie Luisi.* First, they made it clearer than ever that she had been hard to get to know. Apparently Marie had devoted most of her time to a division of her department called the television syndication unit, which had its own staff. This unit produced and bought TV programs, which were traded to stations for advertising time; the ad spots were then sold to clients. Management gave Marie money to develop programming, and she was left on her own to create the barter deals. It was my impression that she never discussed the unit's operations at length with her superiors or peers.

Newspaper articles also indicated that Marie had a side to her few of us had seen. To me, she had always been a role model. When she had given speeches at new-business presentations, I had been mesmerized by her confidence and her friendly, almost jolly face. Now her staff—which was made up mostly of women—indicated to reporters that her nickname, "The Godmother," had been to them little more than a bitter joke. They said she had subjected them to intense pressure and verbal assault. One former West Coast employee was quoted in *The Wall Street Journal* as saying, "We would get a wire from [Marie] on a Friday night saying 'You bitches will not be allowed to leave this office until this work is done.' "

In light of Marie's distant or strained relationships with her colleagues, let's look again at what she was accused of doing. The dazzling sums she is said to have presented as profit were estimated figures, which presented how much she hoped her syndication unit *would* make. Marie now hints that management knew she was presenting the figures as actual profit. As of this writing, the case still hasn't come to trial; but even if management did know about the discrepancies, she clearly set herself up for a fall. She appears to have been unknown to, or unreachable to, almost everyone in the company. When financial shenanigans were discovered, she seems to have had no one to attest to her innocence.

I contend that Marie, through her seclusion, destroyed her-

---

*The following discussion of Marie Luisi's case is based not on personal knowledge but on published accounts. See Notes and Sources.

self professionally. In one way or another, she needed help and wasn't able to reach out for it. Had she been part of a business team, sharing her problems with co-workers, she couldn't have remained so long in the dangerous position of portraying projected profits as actual revenues. With others' counsel and support, she would have rectified the situation long before it escalated into the scandal known as Luisigate.

The news stories about Marie were jarring enough, but as I read them, I was further disconcerted by a sense of *déjà vu*. Then I remembered the stories written on Mary Cunningham when she had resigned from the Bendix Corporation only a year and a half before. I went to the library to reread those and was immediately struck by parallels.

As most of us know, Mary Cunningham rose rapidly in the Bendix hierarchy. But when she was promoted to the executive level, co-workers protested that it was more because of her boss's, William Agee's, feelings for her than for her professional expertise. Cunningham and her former boss are now married, but their relationship, past or present, doesn't reveal whether or not she was qualified for a promotion. There is a reason why so many *perceived* her as unqualified: As writer Gail Sheehy and others noted, Cunningham didn't make a single business friendship (save that with Agee) during her tenure at Bendix. Cunningham verifies this in her book *Powerplay: What Really Happened at Bendix*. Even if she was executive material, nobody trusted her enough to believe it. She also seems to have had particular problems with a female colleague. By her own account, her worst detractor was Nancy Reynolds, Bendix's vice president for national affairs.

The fact that both these "celebrity" female executives were isolated from others in the company and had unique problems with other women was no coincidence. These same patterns, and a number of others, recur in the lives of many executive women but remain invisible to the women who aspire to positions like ours. The ambitious young women in our companies are very much aware of who we are. They see that we have lavish offices and that we always fly first-class. They know we are part of senior management and realize that we wield power. What they don't see is our alienation, loneliness, and fear. And if our careers take nosedives—even fatal ones—they certainly don't comprehend what has led us to self-destruct.

Because these conditions and behaviors stay hidden, the public's impressions of executive women remain false. The media adds to the misconceptions by stereotyping those portrayed. In novels and on TV shows, powerful businesswomen are shown to be sexy, glamorous, and confident. In magazine profiles, executive women are similarly depicted: Those we read of are invariably attractive, outgoing creatures who "have it all": happy marriages, well-adjusted children, and fulfilling, successful careers.

My study shows that the life of the female executive, far from being ideal, is rife with problems that her male counterpart doesn't share. I have not focused in this book on the legitimate and well-documented problems that men and sexist conventions create for businesswomen. Rather, I have explored the reasons why certain executive women find happiness and professional success, whereas others become alienated from people in their business and private lives—*and* from self-understanding and true success.

Because the difficulties executive women face exist for women at all career levels, women aren't moving into positions of real power. Over the past twenty years, they have made significant inroads into middle management: In 1965, women held only 14 percent of managerial jobs, whereas in 1985 they held a third of those jobs (the U.S. Bureau of Labor Statistics). Yet the percentage of women in *senior* management, as well as the number who are members of corporate boards (women hold only 4 percent of the seats), has barely changed in twenty years. What's more, only one woman, Katharine Graham, has become president of a major corporation.

The women nearest the top don't see the tide turning. The *Harvard Business Review* polled managerial women in 1965 and again in 1985, and the number who felt that women had equal opportunities for advancement within their own companies *dropped* from 40 percent to 33 percent.

A sign of the times is that more new businesses are being started than ever before—the majority of them by women, often women who dropped out of corporate jobs. Newspaper and magazine articles about such women proliferate, sporting titles such as "Women in the Law: Many Are Getting Out" and "The Pink Parachute: Some Women Who Rise to Executive Heights Find It Hard to Breathe and Are Bailing Out."

Most people believe that senior-level men's penchant for working with male peers is responsible for both the small number of women in senior management and the large number dropping out of the business world, but until we learn how we prevent ourselves from entering the topmost levels—and from being happy when we do—where we are in the corporate hierarchy in the year 2000 will be almost exactly where we are right now.

CHAPTER

II

WHO IS THE EXECUTIVE WOMAN?

A vice-president since 1979, [Mary Constance Beck of
InterFirst Bank Dallas] counts John Hancock, Cigna, J. C.
Penney, and Zale Corp. among her accounts. . . . She and
her husband . . . decided not to have children. "In my mind
it was career vs. children," she says.
—"WOMEN: THE NEW STARS IN BANKING,"
Fortune, July 12, 1982

When I began my search for information on the executive
woman, what I found, after going through the past ten
years of books, magazines, and newspaper articles, was a dis-
maying lack of hard data. Articles and even a best-selling book
(*The Managerial Woman*) had been written about women with
executive titles, yet none of them presented comprehensive data
on who those few female pioneers were. More important, little
was known about their attitudes, opinions, feelings, and fears.
To better understand why I felt there was an urgent need for
firsthand research, let's look at some of the studies I found and
how they distorted important facts.

On June 21, 1976, *Business Week* published an article entitled
"100 Top Corporate Women," which, according to its subtitle,
was "A comprehensive survey of women with corporate clout
—and their routes to the top." What followed were brief blurbs
on one hundred women from large U.S. corporations that gave
the women's executive-sounding titles and synopses of their job
histories, but not their salaries, job responsibilities, or anything
else of real relevance. The article concluded by saying that "the
top female executives are indistinguishable from their male

counterparts in how they came to their present business eminence."

This statement is nonsense. Women's routes to the top have been both different from and more difficult than men's. What's more, when it comes to salary, those women were all too distinguishable from their male peers. An article in *Working Woman* (January 1980) criticized the *Business Week* piece, quoting one of the nation's leading headhunters as saying he had "placed a good percentage of those women, and not one . . . was making more than $35,000 in 1976." The *Working Woman* article rightly stated that "those 100 women . . . were chosen for their titles rather than for their corporate responsibility, for their presence rather than their impact." Still, the *Business Week* story gave a wide audience of readers the impression that women were buoyantly rising to the top ranks of the business hierarchy and that those with executive titles were being well paid.

On July 17, 1978, *Fortune* ran a story called "The Top Women in Big Business." Here were profiles of the ten most highly paid women in the Fortune 500. Seven of them began their careers with the help of family connections, with Katharine Graham of the *Washington Post* as a good example: Her family owns the controlling share of the corporation. Although *Fortune* didn't purport to show that these women were typical, the article inadvertently misled readers into thinking so. Actually, the typical woman has no help from connections and has far less professional support from people overall than her male peers.

For years, the most frequently quoted data available on the executive woman were from a survey done in 1977, and then repeated in 1978 and 1979, by the executive-search firm Heidrich and Struggles. The results of those surveys, which offer a profile of the "corporate woman officer," are still being cited in books and articles, yet only three out of ten of the women earned over $50,000 a year. The women's average salary was well below the known or expected level for an executive position in 1979.

Finally, I heard news of a survey done in 1982 by the executive-search firm Korn/Ferry International. A questionnaire had been sent to women executives at the Fortune 1000 companies. Its results had been compared to those of a similar study conducted in 1979 on male executives in Fortune 500 companies. (There weren't enough women for the study in the top five hundred largest U.S. companies; Korn/Ferry therefore had to go to the top one thousand.) I sent for the survey, and within a week I was reading it—with great excitement! For the first time, I was seeing evidence to confirm my own hypotheses.

But the survey, while of high quality, was designed to compare male and female executives; the questionnaire was therefore essentially the same for both groups. Korn/Ferry was unable to explore issues uniquely relevant to women, such as their opinions on maternity leave and whether or not they thought women had equal job opportunities. Moreover, the study gave us facts but no conclusions. For example, it revealed statistics on the women's family backgrounds but didn't say whether one or both parents had influenced their success. Korn/Ferry told what the women earned but not if they felt underpaid. Also, some of their facts were puzzling, contradicting my empirical observations and the patterns I'd discerned throughout the books and articles I'd read.

My own research on executive women was done in three phases. In the first stage, I conducted personal, in-depth interviews with twenty-five executive women. In the second, I sent a survey to a large group of executive women. And in the third, I consulted with a psychiatrist about the data I'd found. My definition of an executive was someone who earned, on the average, a salary of $75,000 and worked at the level of vice president or above for a major corporation.

The women I personally interviewed came from a diversity of cultural backgrounds, regions of the country, types of professions, and life-styles (single, married, and divorced; mothers and childless women). Each interview lasted about three hours, each was tape-recorded and transcribed, and some women were interviewed more than once. The interviews probed the women's childhoods and their personal experiences as daughters, students, teenagers, lovers, mothers, friends, and wives. The women spoke about everything from childhood traumas to their first sexual encounters, from past professional trials and triumphs to their present careers and future goals. Six women who are composites of the twenty-five will be featured in this book: Laura, the executive editor of a popular women's magazine; Annie, the executive in charge of movie development for a TV network; Rose, the marketing director for a commercial-chemical company; Sara, the head of new-product development for a computer and electronics company; Jennifer, the executive art director for a major cosmetics firm; and Katharine, a financial analyst for a large investment house.

The second and most important part of the research involved a survey of women who currently hold executive positions in top U.S. corporations. The names of the women were acquired from the *Million Dollar Directory*, published by Dun & Bradstreet, which catalogs the largest, most financially successful companies in the country: utilities, transportation companies, banks and trust companies, industrial concerns, mutual and stock insurance companies, publishers, wholesalers and retailers, manufacturers and ad agencies. Noncorporate career areas, such as medicine, the arts, and education, are not represented in this book. I chose to do my study on businesswomen, not on entrepreneurial or professional women (women whose professions —medicine and education, for example—require specialized training but generally don't involve managerial duties) because I felt that, as President Coolidge said, "The business of America is business," that the corporate world is where the money and power lie.

I began with the names of 1,700 women with executive titles and started the selection process through which I could represent America's top businesswomen. First I eliminated the names of those I believed didn't earn the salaries or have the responsibility that fit my criteria for an executive; for example, I excluded "corporate secretaries" for all companies but the largest ones. Then, when a company listed several female executives, I selected only the most senior women so that my results would reflect a diversity of environments rather than those of just a few corporate giants.

I now had a roster of eight hundred names. Almost half the women were in the Northeast, and most of that group worked in or near New York City. The rest were about evenly divided between the West Coast and the Midwest, with an additional few located in the Southeast and Southwest. My research team telephoned each of these eight hundred women to confirm her title, tell her about the project, and ask for her commitment to participate in the survey.

In most areas, nine out of ten women agreed to fill out the questionnaire, but in New York City the number dropped to seven in ten. Some bore out the stereotype of the abrupt, time-pressed New Yorker, saying they weren't interested in the survey, didn't have time to fill it out, or, as one woman put it, "didn't get involved with women-things."

Other of the eight hundred women were never reached despite five or six phone calls, and some had left their jobs, were on vacation, or on long business trips. This second screening left us with five hundred women, to whom questionnaires were mailed.

For those of you who didn't fill out the questionnaire, it covers all the standard demographic information: age, race, religion, length and type of employment, income, and number of children. In addition, we asked the women how much sleep they got, if they took their earned vacation time, what their marital status was (and, if they were married, which spouse earned more money and which did more of the housework). We asked about their family backgrounds: how many sisters and brothers they had and what professions their parents were in.

But the majority of the questions concerned the women's attitudes, opinions, and feelings, since these perceptions were missing in the studies that had previously been done. We began with their *childhood*. Which parent were the women closer to? Had they been either parent's favorite child? How did they view their fathers—as confident, giving, and creative, or as authoritative and demanding? What about their mothers? Were they distant and insecure, or happy, outgoing, and self-assured? We also solicited the women's impressions of their parents' marriages. Were the relationships respectful? Reserved? Or were they loving and passionate?

Next, we asked the women about their *adolescence*. Were our nation's top corporate women good students as teenagers, or were they more interested in going to parties and meeting boys? Did they consider themselves popular, or did they feel unattractive and lonely?

The most extensive section of the survey dealt with the women's *professional lives:* how they began their careers, and which behaviors and traits they believed led to their (and other women's) success. How hardworking and aggressive must a woman be to become an executive? Must she be attractive? Should she be feminine? We then asked the women how men should behave to reach the top. Must a man be more aggressive than a woman? Does he have to work as hard? Do his looks matter as much as a woman's in determining how far he'll advance?

The women told us what *priorities* they set in their careers and personal lives and which of these priorities they believed their male peers shared. How much weight did the women place on taking risks and setting goals at work? Did the women put more stock in spending time with their families? Were the men more interested in running their companies someday?

We quizzed the women on how their success had affected their *private lives.* Had their sex lives suffered? Had they given up hobbies? Friends? Did they believe their male peers made as many sacrifices as they did?

We next explored what *obstacles* inhibited the women's careers. Had they been more hurt by their own lack of assertiveness or by the sexist actions of male colleagues? Did they feel their female co-workers were generally supportive of them, or that they were often threatened and manipulative? Had the women ever had office affairs; and, if so, had the relationships harmed or helped their careers?

The women were then asked to *describe themselves:* their looks, personalities, and skills. In their own eyes, were they attractive and sexy? Aggressive? Competitive? Or did they consider themselves more thoughtful, empathetic, and feminine? Finally, where did they stand on *major feminist issues,* such as the ERA, abortion, and legislated maternity leave?

The survey was long (twenty pages) and—as some of you are acutely aware—took at least an hour and a half to fill out, but an impressive 250 questionnaires were returned. To understand the significance of that number, just consider that the Nielsen ratings are based on 1,700 interviews representing 85 million U.S. households. On the strength of those polls, advertising rates are set and TV shows are either canceled or renewed. My 250 women represent only 5 million executive women in the country, making the survey the most representative ever conducted of executive women.

After the survey results were tallied, the third and final phase of the research began. To verify the psychological patterns that emerged from my data, I consulted with Anne E. Bernstein, M.D., a prominent New York psychoanalyst who has analyzed many executive women in her private practice and is the co-author of the book *Women Treating Women: Case Material from Women Treated by Female Psychoanalysts* (International Universities Press, 1984).

We're now going to review the survey's demographics to get the basic facts about the women's personal and career lives. First, what family influences, if any, predispose women to business success?

The one characteristic shared by all the women is their race, which is white—a distressing but less-than-surprising fact. Setting race aside, the women are different in several significant ways: They weren't raised in one type of locale and they don't come from similar kinds of homes. Roughly a third were reared in suburbia, another third in urban locales, and two in ten in rural areas.

The women are also from dissimilar economic backgrounds. Half are from middle-income families, and the rest are almost evenly divided between lower- and upper-income backgrounds. The women's religious upbringings also followed an average pattern. Sixty percent were Protestants, about the same percentage of Protestants in the general population (54 percent). Of the remaining women, 23 percent were raised Catholic; 10 percent Jewish; and the rest (7 percent) in various other faiths. These ratios correlate with the national percentages, where Catholics are the second largest group (38 percent), Jews the third largest (4 percent), and all other religions the smallest (4 percent all together).

Statistically, 75 percent constitutes a majority, and a solid majority of our women (80 percent) grew up with both parents living at home. One is tempted to deduce that executive women come mostly from two-parent homes, but actually our women don't deviate from the norm. The high ratio only serves to point out that divorce was a rare occurrence in the recent past. Only one in ten women had parents who divorced, and another one in ten suffered the death of one parent. Intriguingly, in each case of death, the mother survived the father. This number represents a "skew," a percentage not large but significant, since it is twice as large as the number for executive men (Korn/Ferry). Clearly, these widowed mothers set strong examples for their daughters in terms of learning how to support themselves.

Something of a pattern also emerges in our women's birth order. The single largest group grew up as either the eldest or the only child. Psychologists believe that successful people of both sexes are often firstborn, since the birth of a couple's first child is a major event, and the special attention the child receives promotes his or her self-worth. Also, the firstborn often learns to defer to the needs of younger siblings, adapting at an early age to both sacrifice and competition.

Still, the number of firstborn women in my study is nowhere near as dramatic as I had been led to believe by *The Managerial Woman,* in which twenty of the twenty-five women profiled were firstborn. Just 40 percent of our women were the "oldest" children in their family. Only one in ten was an only child; most came from families of three children. Thirty percent of the women were someplace in the middle, and the remaining 20 percent were "youngest" children. So, younger sisters, take heart! Contrary to popular opinion, a full half of the nation's executive women are apparently the "youngest" or "neither the oldest nor the youngest" in their family.

Where distinct differences emerge between our women and most women is in the educational and job statuses of their parents. Both the fathers and mothers attained higher levels of education and job responsibility than was typical during the period when our women were raised. When we compare the women's fathers with the average man in 1950, over three times as many of the fathers had more than high school educations. Fifty percent either attended or graduated from college, as opposed to only 16 percent of most American men.

Similarly striking differences exist between our women's mothers and their female peers. Forty percent of the mothers went to college or obtained college degrees as compared with just 12 percent of all women in 1950. The mothers' educations had a strong impact on many of the women I interviewed. "I was very conscious that my mother wasn't like my friends' mothers," said Laura, a beautiful executive editor for a well-known women's magazine. "She graduated first in her class from a prestigious university. Most of my friends' mothers married right out of high school."

"My mother was very well educated," said Annie, the spirited executive in charge of TV-movie development for one of the networks. "She was an intellectual and a feminist—nothing at all like the other mothers in my neighborhood."

The women's parents were also professionally upscale. A third of the fathers worked as managers, a much higher number than the national average (17 percent in 1950). Otherwise, the fathers fit no mold in terms of what they did for a living and worked in a variety of fields including finance, sales, manufacturing, production, general management, and law.

The mothers were equally exceptional. The majority (75 percent) were employed before getting married, and about a third were professionals (mostly nurses and teachers)—twice the percentage of an average group of women in 1950 (16 percent). After they had children, only a third (33 percent) of the mothers continued to work, but their numbers were still much higher than was typical in 1950, when only 13 percent of women with young children worked outside the home.

Let's now turn to the demographics that tell us about the women themselves: their age, education, and the major facts about their lives. First, how old are our women? About three out of ten (28 percent) are from thirty to thirty-nine years old; another three in ten (31 percent), between forty and forty-nine; and the remaining four in ten (41 percent), fifty and older. That puts their average age at forty-seven—quite a bit older, no doubt, than the average age for men at their levels. "The men I work with are all at least ten years younger than I am," said an exasperated fifty-five-year-old bank executive. "Sometimes my male peers treat me like the office grandmother." Later we'll explore the reasons for this age discrepancy.

Our women, like their parents, were unusually well educated. Eighty percent had had some college, and almost 60 percent received diplomas—a stark contrast to most American women age thirty and up, only a third (35 percent) of whom went past high school. Thirty-five percent of the women also went on to graduate school. I had thought that a much larger number would have pulled themselves up by the bootstraps like Marie Luisi, advancing from high-school-educated secretaries to the executives they are today. But that trend is apparent only among the oldest women, who are the least educated.

Today, America's female executives work in a great variety of professions, yet certain career areas show the highest concentrations: finance/accounting; marketing/sales/advertising; and general management. Other fields in which we find women in significant numbers are personnel, technical fields, corporate law, publishing, and consumer affairs.

The women's job titles are impressive: Fifty percent are corporate vice presidents and 12 percent are senior or executive vice presidents. The rest are senior managers, treasurers, directors, and assistants to the president. In line with their distinguished titles, the women's salaries are high; their mean income (including all types of compensation such as profit sharing and yearly bonus) is about what I'd expected: $72,500. Viewing the figures a little differently, one third of the women make below $55,000, another third earn between $55,000 and $95,000, and the final third have incomes of $95,000 and more, with the majority in this group earning $125,000 or more. But while our women are unquestionably successful in financial terms, they are frequently unhappy with the size of their paychecks. Fifty-two percent insist that they aren't paid what they deserve. Even among the group of women that earns the most money ($95,000 and more), 50 percent believe they aren't adequately compensated.

The census shows that women at all levels, across all professions, don't make as much money as men, a fact that accounts in part for the women's dissatisfaction. "I work harder than most men I know, I'm very good at what I do, and I'm committed to my job and my company," said an irate Sara, the executive for the computer and electronics company. "My bosses give me glowing evaluations, but they don't put their money where their mouths are. If a man got such evaluations, he'd make twice the salary I do."

Regardless of why the women aren't earning what they think they should, their salaries strongly affect their self-image. First, the good news: The majority say that, "all things considered," they judge themselves to be successful. Just one in five (20 percent) sees herself as "highly" successful, but 55 percent view themselves as "very" successful, and only 25 percent report that their achievements are "moderate." The women who feel the most successful, however, are those who earn the most money. The women who make $95,000 or more were *ten times* more likely to say they were highly successful than were those who make $55,000 or less.

The bad news is that while our women feel they are successful in the world's eyes, they are generally unhappy with their careers. A near majority (70 percent) are "not very" pleased with their careers!* Again, salary emerges as the major factor in determining how satisfied they are. In general, only three in ten say they are happy with their job; but among the women in the high-income group, twice as many feel gratified.

Besides their feelings of being underpaid, a key reason for their discontent lies in the degree of authority granted them. When asked if they had sufficient authority to carry out their responsibilities, 70 percent replied that theirs was "barely adequate." A few women (14 percent) believed they had as much say as they needed, but just as many said they "[didn't] have nearly enough" (16 percent).

All together, then, an astounding 86 percent of our women feel they don't have the authority they need to accomplish their tasks! Katharine, an attractive but plump vice president and financial analyst, shook with anger when she spoke about the small amount of clout she exercised. "I have recently been assigned to make an ineffectual division of my company profitable within six months' time. To carry out that goal, I need the power to hire and fire whom I please, to apportion my budget as I see fit, and to make decisions autonomously. Because I haven't been given that power, the fate of the division *and my own fate*

---

*If you filled out the questionnaire, you'll note that I occasionally alter the wording of its questions in the book. These changes reflect my analyses of the data. In this case, I collapsed the numbers of women who were "somewhat" and "not at all pleased" with their careers into the new category "not very pleased."

aren't in my hands." The degree of control a person has over what he or she is accountable for is a serious matter in any career and a crucial concern at the executive level.

The trend that shows the high-salaried women to be the most content with their careers reverses dramatically when it comes to the issue of authority: The sense of having too little clout is the strongest among the women who earn the most. The women who make six-figure salaries have the clearest view of what power is and are the most painfully aware of how much more they could have.

When we turn to our women's private lives, we see more reasons for distress. Surely, some of their career frustrations could be offset by the emotional support of husbands and children . . . but for a startling number of the women, marriage and children are comforts they live without. According to this study, the odds that an executive woman will never marry are four times greater than for the average American woman. Only 5 percent of most women age thirty and up have never wed (the 1985 Census), whereas 21 percent of our executive women have never been brides.

Even if our women do marry, the probability of their divorcing is twice as great as the norm. Thirty percent are currently divorced, and another 10 percent are on second or third marriages. Forty percent of all our women have therefore been divorced—compared with just 20 percent of most women in their same age range.

The differences between our women and their male peers are even more striking. Less than half (48 percent) of our women are currently married—compared with a whopping 96 percent of executive men (Korn/Ferry). What's more, just 11 percent of the men have been divorced, compared with nearly four times as many of our women.

Many of the women I interviewed felt that men couldn't handle being married to women as or more successful than they. "Here we've gone and sweat blood to become independent, to become women the men can have intelligent conversations with—and they don't want us!" lamented Laura, the pretty magazine editor.

Since so many of our women either don't get married or

don't stay married, the fact that less than half of them are mothers is inevitable. Forty-seven percent are parents, giving the women a bleak one-in-two chance at mothering. By contrast, 87 percent of American women age thirty and older have children, giving most women a nine-in-ten chance at being parents. The differences between our women and male executives is greater still: Every last one of Korn/Ferry's men is a father! Finally, even if our women do have children, they have fewer than in the average American family (1.3. versus 1.8) and less than half as many as in the average male executive's (1.3 versus 3.0).

The demographics reveal several very important truths. First, the features of their past that make them stand out from other women are the high levels of education and job status their parents attained—factors that influenced the women to distinguish themselves at school and at work. The second truth is that many executive women are strongly dissatisfied with their career. And the third, unpleasant but indisputable, truth: Women aren't at, or even near, the point where they can "have it all" —a lasting marriage, children, and a satisfying, successful career.

CHAPTER

═III═

THE EARLY YEARS

"Who, with her own body, with what she did and didn't say, provided us with our most enduring image of how to be a woman?"

—NANCY FRIDAY,
My Mother/My Self

Can our women's childhoods explain why some of them made more money and felt more satisfied with their careers than the rest? The prevailing theory as to why certain women succeed claims that as children they were closer to their fathers than their mothers and that the fathers' influence endowed them with qualities necessary for corporate success—a liking for competition and achievement, assertiveness, a capacity to take risks. *The Managerial Woman* found that all the women it studied had close early bonds with their fathers:

"Shared in essence by all the women . . . [was] a very special relationship between the young girls and their fathers. Fathers and daughters shared interests and activities traditionally regarded as appropriate only for fathers and sons." They hiked, climbed trees, fished, played baseball, and went to the fathers' offices together. By contrast, the women's "memories of their mothers were not as rich in detail, and the mother-daughter relationship was the most elusive to capture and characterize . . . the women's recollections [of their mothers] were vague and generalized. They consistently reported that their mothers were 'typical' . . . and had done 'the right mother-type things.'"

The authors of *The Managerial Woman* conclude that the father-daughter bond was "the most important source of support and confirmation of these women's developing self-concepts" and that that relationship "helps explain why [the women] were later able to challenge the male world of management in ways that enabled them to enter that world themselves."

To test this theory, I asked our women to think back to their childhood and to tell us if they had been particularly close to one parent. In response, only two in ten reported being closer to their father, while four in ten asserted that they were closer to their mother. One in ten felt no special closeness to either parent, while the remaining three in ten said they were equally close to both. On the surface, then, the mothers seem to have been more involved in our women's lives. But while the word *closeness* indicates that two people are emotionally attached, the description reveals little more about the nature of the bond. People can be closely tied in many ways, including destructive ones. To use an extreme example, children pulled away from abusive mothers often feel so "close" to them that they beg to go back home.

A more reliable measure of a positive parent-child bond is whether or not the child felt like a "favorite" in the parent's eyes. Studies of family environments show that in an optimally healthy family, each child—when asked privately—will say that he or she is a favorite. That's how it should be; all of us need to feel uniquely loved. But when I asked the women if their father had a favorite child, just one in four (25 percent) felt that she had been her father's pet.

The women's descriptions of their fathers help us to understand why so few felt close to or special to them. The picture that emerged of the average father was that of a typical "macho" man: vigorous, commanding, and confident—but extremely emotionally reserved. "Intelligent" and "healthy" were the two traits on which the fathers received the highest ratings. The women also saw their fathers as very "attractive" and "self-assured," as well as highly "conservative" and "authoritative." Half the women recalled their fathers as "happy," but only a minority described them as "affectionate," "giving," "nurturing," or "warm"; and the fathers were almost never deemed either "playful" or "creative."

Since most of our women were unable to form strong attachments to their fathers, why did *The Managerial Woman* say that their women had been able to? First, because their women came from a different generation. The "managerial women" reached top management in the early 1970s and needed strong bonds with their fathers to have started in business when they did. "Despite the Depression all of the twenty-five found jobs after college," the authors report, and "almost all of them got their jobs because of their fathers' connections or through friends of the family." Also, these women were the true trailblazers, entering an all-male executive sphere. Having been close to their fathers may have helped them be at ease in that world, but whether their "drive to achieve" was inherited from their fathers is debatable.

The second reason the "managerial women" presented their fathers as the parent they loved more is probably that the questions they were asked didn't probe deeply. On the surface, the trend of special closeness with fathers bore out remarkably in my own interviews. Just beneath that surface, a far more significant truth was revealed. Although the women liked or adored their fathers, they had barely spent any time with them; their positive feelings derived less from reality than from idolatry. As was the case with most children, the mothers were their prime caretakers, whereas the fathers were away at work most of their daughters' waking lives. The women saw their fathers as exciting and exotic and, as many daughters do, they romanticized them.

Katharine, the vice president and research analyst for a brokerage firm in Chicago, provides a good example of how daughters glorify their fathers. I interviewed her at my New York apartment when she was in town on business. On meeting her, I was struck both by her lovely features and skin and by the fact that she did little to play them up. Katharine's hazel eyes are fringed with black lashes, and her complexion is the proverbial peaches and cream. She wore no makeup, however, and her dark brown hair was pulled tightly back from her face. She was overweight and wore a plain, beltless navy dress.

Katharine's personality also presented a paradox. She acted as if the interview, and life itself, were burdensome; she frequently "tsked," fretted, scowled, pouted, and let out heavy sighs. When she entered my living room, she selected a chair and wearily sank into it. She complimented me on the decor, but made no effort to explore the room. Appearances to the contrary, she was a sensitive, feeling woman. Her eyes were extremely expressive, flashing with anger one moment and glistening with tears the next. When she spoke about difficult times in her life, her unease was obvious: She toyed with the barrette in her hair or smoothed her dress out over her knees. Eventually, Katharine revealed a good sense of humor. Something weighed upon her that she hadn't the strength to shuck off, but her humor and even her brooding showed that she had spirit.

Katharine, forty years old, was raised in rural Illinois. When I asked how she'd felt about her father as a child, her eyes sparkled with warmth. "I thought my father was wonderful. I believe he was an emotional person but that he found it difficult to express his feelings. I suspect his hesitation was due to my mother's example. She didn't laugh or show her emotions very much."

She then told me about some letters her father had written to his parents shortly after her birth (she was bequeathed the letters after her grandparents' deaths). "The proof I have of my father's love for me is in those letters. He wrote them as if they were letters from me. Long, handwritten letters, all 'from me.' They say, 'Today I did this and my daddy did that and I think my daddy is so silly.' They're wonderful." She flushed with pleasure. "I feel so loved when I read them."

When I asked how she'd spent time with her father, a long, uncomfortable pause ensued. "That's a hard one," she finally replied. "He worked late all week, and on the weekends he always worked in the yard. I thought that he was wonderful, but to tell you the truth, I hardly knew him."

In an extreme but telling example of how daughters idealize their fathers, Laura avowed special love for hers in spite of the fact that he beat her. Laura, the magazine editor, is thirty-six years old and, by anyone's standards, is gorgeous. She has jet-black hair that falls to her shoulders, a stunning figure, and compelling sapphire-blue eyes. The day I met her, she wore a silk pantsuit with a long coat-jacket that swirled out when she walked. Laura's extreme nervousness was as obvious as her beauty. She chain-smoked, and her hands continually shook. Again and again she jumped up from her seat to pace about the room, look out the window, or fetch a cigarette from the pack on her desk. Deep furrows on her forehead marred her otherwise beautiful face. The lines were from worry—and, I soon realized, from anger.

This lady was *angry!* Her voice was tough, defensive, and her speech was peppered with swear words. She yelled a lot, and even her normal speaking voice was painfully loud. When she barreled down the corridor with her silk train flying, I saw fear in the eyes of her staff. Like Katharine, she was somehow psychologically trapped, but she wasn't taking her confinement at all quietly. She was like a wild animal raging in its cage—and she was spellbinding.

I met Laura in her spacious New York office, where a wicker couch and chairs had magazines and layouts spread all over them. Her desk, made of a blond wood, groaned beneath stacks of papers. On a coffee table, a glass bowl held yellow and white gladioli. Around this floral arrangement were two overflowing ashtrays and several empty, lipstick-stained Styrofoam cups.

When I asked Laura about her father, she loudly asserted, "I loved my father desperately. I never felt much affection for my mother. He was a strict disciplinarian, but a funny, charming man. He was also extremely handsome, unbelievably handsome. He looked like Cary Grant up until the day he died." I asked her how she had spent time with him. "Isn't that funny," she remarked, "I can't remember spending time with him."

Now Laura's tale took a bizarre twist, as she stated matter-of-factly: "My father hit me throughout my childhood. His picking on me was ridiculous, because I was a well-behaved girl. He beat me if I was one minute late or if I didn't make my bed. I knew my father loved me because after he thrashed me, he'd go to his bedroom and stay there for hours. He didn't know how to discipline children. I was the eldest, and he went overboard with me."

Both Katharine and Laura are able to deduce only by inference that their fathers loved them—Katharine by the letters she cherishes and Laura by the remorse her father suffered after hitting her. Their fathers, like the other fathers in our survey, didn't openly show affection. Since the women had so little positive or genuine interaction with their fathers, it's not surprising that the fathers didn't influence their careers. When we isolate the women surveyed who were closer to or favored by their fathers, they are no more apt than any of the others to be well paid or happy with their careers.

Like the fathers, the women's mothers were seen as good-looking and smart, but they were also depicted as loving and available. They received the highest marks for being "intelligent" and "attractive." They were then rated very "accessible," "giving," "creative," "nurturing," and "warm." As with the fathers, half of them were described as "happy," but they were seen as far less "self-assured" and far *more* "worried" and "insecure" than the men.

Despite the fact that the mothers were perceived as warm, the women viewed their parents' relationships as very reserved. Fifty-three percent said the word "respectful" fit the marriages well, but "loving" or "close" was used less often (40 percent), "affectionate" by just 23 percent, and "passionate" by a mere 4 percent. We can safely assume that many of the fathers—restricted by society's notions of "manly" behavior—were unable openly to display affection to their wives.

The differences in the women's perceptions of their parents show that the women must have had more intimate, emotionally potent bonds with their mothers. But before we conclude that all was well between them and their mothers, the next fact must give us pause. Only one in twenty (5 percent) of the women were their mother's favorite! How can it be that the mothers were caring and accessible yet the women felt favored five times more often by their fathers? Dr. Bernstein explains:

"Our mothers took care of us; almost by default, they were much more available and giving than our fathers. They were also far more nurturing, since society encourages this behavior in women alone. What the women are saying in their descriptions of their mothers is simply that they behaved like mothers. They aren't saying they felt unconditionally loved by their mothers. Feeling loved no matter what is how a favorite child feels.

"Mothers often find it difficult to love daughters uncritically because they unconsciously see themselves in daughters. If a mother doesn't believe *herself* worthy of unconditional love, she won't be able to make her daughter feel a favorite no matter how much she loves the girl. Unfortunately, many women suspect they aren't deserving of consistent love because of the psychological legacy of their second-class citizenship. For centuries, women were taught to defer to others—taught that their own needs and desires weren't as valuable as those of their parents, husband, and children. Women came to feel unworthy, and these feelings were passed on to their daughters."

Another reason for the low ratio of women who felt "special" to their mothers is that most of the mothers who had favorites favored sons. In fact, the mothers preferred sons twice as often as the fathers did! "Fathers don't tend to choose favorites on the basis of sex," Dr. Bernstein finds, "but a mother will almost never favor a daughter when she has a son. Many women—for good reasons—believe that men are more privileged than they; having a son gives them a vicarious feeling of having power and confidence. People like to associate with winners, and in our society men are usually the winners."

The terrain of being a favorite—or not—carries an explosive charge: It can make the difference between a happy childhood and a very painful one. To comprehend the impact that "feeling like a favorite" can have, let's compare the childhood memories of three of our executive women.

Sara, at age forty-seven, is the senior vice president in charge of new-product development for a computer company in Silicon Valley. She came to my apartment when she was in New York on business, and her charisma was evident from the moment she walked in my door. Sara is an avid windsurfer, and her skin is tanned a warm toast color. Her green eyes are flecked with gold, and her sun-streaked hair is a halo of loopy curls. Her facial features are strong—a prominent nose and an outthrust jaw—and her body reminded me of ancient statues of Greek goddesses: proud, full-figured, and with an athlete's muscle tone.

Sara was extremely direct, speaking her mind without qualifying her words. She had a dry sense of humor, but when something struck her as particularly funny, she tipped her head back, shut her eyes, and let out a lusty guffaw. Today she wore a bright yellow dress with a fitted waist and full skirt. On her feet were a pair of flat yellow shoes, and around her neck was a string of seashells.

Sara was intrigued by my apartment's view of Central Park and, after greeting me, strode to my window to look out. Spring had arrived and late-afternoon sun flooded the room. With her hands deep in her skirt pockets, she looked healthy and completely at ease. That's how I remember Sara—steady, strong, at peace with herself.

She grew up outside Stockbridge, Massachusetts, in the countryside of the Berkshire Mountains. She felt she was her mother's favorite but said she was willing to "bet that both her sister and brother would make the same claim. For years, we went to three different schools and got up at three different times. My mother sat with each of us while we had our cereal. She made sure each of us had some private time with her. Still"—she smiled slyly—"I know I was her favorite one."

Sara accepted a glass of wine and continued speaking of her mother. "I liked being around her. She was affectionate, generous with her love. She was sensitive to children and never patronizing. One winter, the family business wasn't doing well and I had to wear the same winter coat I had worn for years. It was out of style; also, I had grown quickly and the sleeves were too short. I was upset"—Sara shrugged to indicate she had been silly, young—"and told my mother I was afraid the kids at school would make fun of me. That winter, she walked me to and from school every day so that nobody would dare say a word about my coat."

Annie, the head of movie development for a TV network, also saw herself as her mother's favorite. Forty-nine-year-old Annie was the most ingenuous person I've ever met. She spoke her mind so uncalculatedly that her words shot out at a rapid-fire pace, and her feelings were instantly apparent on her fine-boned face. She sat as she pleased—in the Indian position or hugging her knees up close to her chest. She was obviously a happy person, with a ready grin and twinkling eyes. Her artless, lively manner reminded me of the heroines played by Katharine Hepburn in 1940s movies; she also looked the part. She's very tall (five feet eleven inches), coltishly slender, and, on the day we met, was casually elegant in blue jeans, low heels, and a lavender silk blouse. She wore her brown hair in a loose bun, which fell down twice during our interview.

Annie's office, where we spoke, offers a panoramic view of Los Angeles. A rose-and-blue oriental carpet covers the floor. A round wooden table serves as a desk, and around this are several comfortable tweed chairs. By one wall is a couch with a crocheted blanket folded in one corner, and pictures of Annie's husband and children and their weekend home fill the room. Today, a vase of lilacs stood on a wooden chest of files.

Annie poured us cups of coffee and sat with one foot up on her chair. She told me she grew up the younger of two girls in Lynn, a working-class suburb of Boston. She had no doubt at all that she had been her mother's pet. Why, I asked her? "I don't know," was her lightning-fast reply. "I knew I was the favorite. I always knew. My mother was a very busy woman, but she made sure to be home when I got home from school. She was home for my sister, too, but my sister visited friends a lot. So I'd come home, and my mother would serve me cookies or cake with milk and then she'd sit and ask about my day, ask all about what I'd learned in school. I was very attached to my mother, very *emotionally* attached. I'd make her cards and things at school, and she would treat them like works of art."

Now let's see what life was like for the nonfavorite child.

On a cold November day, I drove to the large home in a New Jersey suburb that Rose shares with her husband and daughter. Rose is the vice president and marketing director for a commercial-chemical company in New Jersey. When I contacted her for our interview, she told me she was forty-six years old, so I was thunderstruck by how young she appeared. She was five foot two and small-boned, with a big bust and shapely legs. Her complexion was fair and unlined, and her chin-length hair was carrot red. Her clothes were flattering, if outdated: a beige cashmere sweater with a plunging V-neck; a tight, straight skirt, and high heels.

As our interview progressed, I repeatedly had the feeling I was talking to someone much younger than Rose. Her red hair and smooth skin made her look no more than thirty-five, but it was her manner that made her seem so young. She had great, luminous brown eyes that were as innocent and appealing, and as fearful and vulnerable, as a child's. Her soft voice, round shoulders, and the way she dipped her head when she talked made her look as if she were always on guard against attack. When she spoke of painful memories, she cringed. Because she was so tiny, she seemed especially fragile, and I found I couldn't help but feel protective toward her.

In Rose's sunny living room, a cream-colored satin couch and two matching armchairs faced a marble fireplace. Above the mantel hung a Klee, a numbered lithograph. Along one wall, French doors led out to a garden patio, and a mahogany grand piano stood nearby.

Rose grew up in Queens, New York. Her father died in World War II when she and her brother were babies, and her mother had since worked as a cashier. When I asked if her mother had had a favorite, she smiled anxiously. "I'll say. My brother was the apple of my mother's eye. There were countless times when her preference was clear. To give you an example, he and I had our tonsils out just a few months apart. I was a year older, so I went first; I was six years old. One of the days I was in the hospital, my mother didn't come to visit at all. She didn't come to visit at all," Rose repeated softly. "When she arrived the following day, a nurse told her I had cried. My mother was very angry. She scolded, 'Don't be a baby! Act your age!'

"Then it was my brother's turn." Rose's smile turned wry. "My mother took time off from work, something she almost never did. She gave him lollipops, soda, toys—all kinds of goodies I hadn't received. But it wasn't the obvious things that hurt the most. It was the little things—like the way her voice and face brightened up when he entered a room. I still get upset when I think of how she acted toward him. They were always laughing together, going for walks, playing cards. I grew up hoping my mother's face would light up like that when she saw *me*, but it never did." Rose looked down at her hands to hide the emotion in her eyes.

"One big, sad, terrifying moment from third grade comes back. My mother didn't pay much attention to me, and so I was never dressed very well. She seemed annoyed if I asked for help, so I went to school in all kinds of things. One day the teacher called me to the back of the room and said, 'Look at you! Your arms are streaked with dirt up to your elbows. Your hair isn't combed with a part in it. Your blouse is ripped.' The whole class heard and started tittering." Rose shuddered and shrank back against her satin chair. "I'm forty-six years old and I still have nightmares about that day."

Since the mothers were the constant figures in the women's lives, whether the *mother* favored them or not was far more meaningful than whether the father did. When I isolated those few surveyed (5 percent) who were their mothers' favorites, they were the most likely to be well paid and happy with their salary and career. No other factor in the twenty-page survey correlated as highly to the women's contentment with their income and job!

For additional analysis, I would have liked a larger group of women who were favored by their mothers. Statistically, the 5 percent of those surveyed is too small a sample from which to draw detailed conclusions; too large a possibility exists that any differences between that 5 percent and the other 95 percent of women surveyed are just the result of chance. To further explore how the nature of the mother-daughter relationship affected our women, I therefore established what we researchers call an analytical surrogate group—a larger body of women whose relationships with their mothers predicted the women's incomes and career contentment.

To find my surrogate group, I looked at the responses to each survey question pertaining to the women's mothers to see which correlated with the women's salaries and career satisfaction. The measure that emerged was the women's reaction to the question "Do you feel that your mother had a successful life?" As we'll see, the women who strongly agreed with the statement differ significantly from those who did not. Analytically, the size of the group is sound; roughly half (46 percent) the women fell into it. The differences between the women with "successful" and "unsuccessful" mothers are therefore not the product of chance, but are real.

What do our women mean when they say their mothers had successful lives? First, these mothers—even if they didn't always favor their daughters—were viewed as more consistently loving than the other mothers were. The "successful" mothers were described as much more "affectionate," "giving," "warm," "nurturing," and "accessible" than were the "unsuccessful" mothers, and their daughters were twice as likely to have felt closer to them than to their fathers.

One reason the "successful" mothers were more emotionally available to their daughters is that these mothers had active, fulfilling lives. They were twice as likely as the other mothers to have worked while raising their children (half of them worked as opposed to one quarter of the "unsuccessful" mothers) and were also more likely to have been professionals. Whether or not they worked, they set positive examples for their daughters: They had good marriages and enjoyed being mothers. *These mothers, in other words, believed that life itself had not failed them.* Their daughters saw them as more "outgoing" than the other daughters saw their mothers; as twice as "intelligent," "happy," and "attractive"; as three times more "playful" and "creative" and—importantly—as three times more "self-assured."

Of the six women you will get to know in this book, Sara and Annie made the most money and were the most satisfied with their careers. Each painted a vivid portrait of the "successful" mother who raised her. Sara earns $150,000 a year and loves her work developing new computer and electronic products. "My mother was wonderful in all the traditional ways," the tanned, curly-haired woman told me. "She loved to cook and she loved us kids. She used to brush my hair at night until I tingled with pleasure. But my mother was also an individual." Sara fumbled in her pocketbook, found her wallet, and strode over to where I was seated to show me a photograph. "Look," she said eagerly, "that's my mother with some friends when she was twenty-one. See how everyone else in the picture is wearing a long coat and gloves? My mother is the one with the short coat and muff!"

Sara's parents ran a restaurant; her father handled the business end, and her mother the cooking and menus. I asked her if her mother had spent a lot of time away from home. Sara walked to the window, and her seashell-necklace glittered in the sunlight. "My parents worked very hard to make the restaurant a success, so my mother naturally couldn't be home as much as other mothers were. That was okay; her mother—my grandmother—lived with us and took care of us. My mother taught each of us how to ski. If we needed her, she was always there, like the winter I wore the too-small coat." Sara tilted her head and crinkled her nose; she was thinking of how to express something. After a moment, she smiled. "We have a family joke about the time my mother left me at a friend's house. I was two. She had taken me along while she visited and put me in a bedroom to nap. When she got home, my father asked, 'Where's the baby?' She cried, 'Oops!' She had forgotten me." Sara leaned her head back and laughed heartily. "My point is, she was a great mother and we all adored her, but she had too much of a life of her own to be doting or smothering. She was vivacious; she loved people and parties. My mother loved life."

As a creator of TV movies, with a salary of nearly a quarter of a million dollars, Annie is one of the most highly paid women in the country, but she loves her work so much she says that she'd "gladly do it for free." Her mother, like Sara's, was warm, independent, and lively. She didn't have a job (half the successful mothers didn't) but was extremely involved in her community.

"My mother was a maverick, highly aware, ahead of her time," Annie said animatedly. "I grew up on words like *chauvinist* and *imperialist*. My mother was an activist for women's rights and a passionate Democrat. She was also involved in every war organization that she could be—Russian War Relief, Civil Defense, the Red Cross, the Air Raid Patrol. Every night she was out at meetings or holding meetings at our house."

Annie jumped up to fetch the coffeepot from its portable burner on the shelf. In her blue jeans, she looked right at home, and her step was jaunty and light. She refilled our cups, replaced the pot, and plopped back into her tweed chair. "The most vivid memory I have of my mother is of seeing her run up the street with two bags of groceries in her arms to be with me after I came home from school. My mother was a beautiful woman." Annie's face shone with love. "She was also a great cook, and she loved to entertain. Saturdays and Sundays she held court for every one of my uncles and aunts. Ours was a very colorful household!"

The "successful" mothers had happier marriages than the other mothers: more "respectful," "affectionate," "loving," and "close." "I always knew there was something special between my parents," Sara mused, "that they loved each other in a way that was different from how they loved us kids. They're almost eighty years old and they still hold hands."

There was electricity, not mere affection, between Annie's parents. "They adored each other. They loved what was different about the other. He was uneducated, sexy, street-smart. She was elegant, classy, aware. My parents used to argue about politics when the relatives were over. They would pretend to be mad at each other but were clearly having the time of their lives."

Laura's description of her mother affords us an example of an "unsuccessful" mother—a woman relatively unfulfilled in her marriage and her life. Today Laura, the magazine editor, makes a large salary ($125,000) but feels she lacks the authority and recognition she needs. "My mother was a negative person, always unhappy, always complaining." Laura rose from her wicker chair and crossed to the window with her long coat-jacket billowing behind her. "My mother was brilliant. She graduated from college first in her class, but as a person, she was just a mess. She used to walk around the house dressed like Lucy and Ethel. I'm not kidding!" Laura moved toward her desk and took a cigarette from the pack on it. "She was an awful cook and an awful housekeeper and she was always screaming and yelling about how much she hated every minute of her life. She hated living in Milwaukee and never having the money to go to a play or concert or anything. I never liked being affectionate with her. I never liked kissing and hugging and all of that gushy stuff. My mother's parents didn't pay a fucking bit of attention to her. She didn't have any self-esteem and," Laura added bitterly, "she didn't instill any in me."

I asked her to tell me about her parents' relationship, and she shouted her reply: "They never should have gotten married! They fought all the time!"

I also asked our women if they felt their fathers had been "successful." Half answered affirmatively, but having had a "successful" father had no effect on their careers. Also, the "successful" fathers, instead of being judged as fulfilled, became caricatures of the average father—tough and brusque, yet appealing, like the Marlboro Man. The "successful" men were regarded as more "attractive" and "intelligent" than the "unsuccessful" fathers were. At the same time, they were seen as twice as "authoritative" and "demanding" . . . and as no more contented, affectionate, happily married, or close to their daughters.

Over the last decade, the role of the mother in a daughter's development has been recognized as far more important than was acknowledged by the "fathers" of psychology. In Freudian thinking, a girl's development devolved upon her relationships with men; specifically, with the resolution of her Oedipal attachment and her supposed penis envy. Now experts believe that the mother-daughter bond is a more critical factor and may even be the most emotionally potent of all family ties.

The stages of a girl's development reveal why her mother plays such a large role in her life. First, a powerful bond is forged between a mother and daughter at the moment of the daughter's birth. When a woman bears a son, she perceives him as dissimilar to herself; she knows he'll grow up to lead a life totally different from her own. But when a woman has a daughter, she creates a tiny replica of herself. Although she may favor a son, she will never be able to identify with him as strongly as she does with her daughter, because she doesn't share a gender with her son.

From the start, girls are kept physically closer to their mothers. Mothers hold their baby girls nearer to themselves, because they perceive the girls as more vulnerable. This notion that girls need more attention is socially learned; experiments show that people cuddle babies in pink blankets more often and for longer periods of time than they do babies in blue blankets.

In the first major developmental stage for infants, called separation-individuation, the tie between mothers and daughters is strengthened. The major trauma for all babies is being separated from their mothers. To a helpless baby, a mother's leaving the room is terrifying, a death threat. As the baby learns that mother will return to provide comfort and care, he or she slowly develops what psychologists call basic trust—a sense that the world is okay and that he or she is okay when alone. This process of separation-individuation forms the core of a person's sense of self (ego) and self-esteem.

Daughters experience more difficulties in the stage of separation-individuation, not only because they have been held closer to their mothers for longer periods of time but because they are given less opportunity than boys to be on their own. When a baby girl cries, a mother is much more likely to go to her and pick her up. Boys are allowed to experience more frustration, which increases their ability to become independent. Girls "almost always have difficulties separating from their mothers," Dr. Bernstein says, and these difficulties have strong effects upon their development, making them more anxious about their ability to take care of themselves. As girls grow up, mothers take the lead in raising them and continue keeping them nearer than sons. Perceiving her daughter as fragile, a mother is more likely to pull her away from a perceived potential danger than she is a son, which increases the girl's view of herself as vulnerable and in need of protection.

If a little girl can form a stable relationship with her father, can spend time with him and feel secure in his presence, she can become more independent of her mother. Unfortunately, many fathers are unavailable to their daughters, as the survey data made clear. By contrast, little boys can usually count on playing sports with their father. Boys are also aided in giving up their dependency on their mother by their recognition that they are physically more like their father than their mother. In the normal process of identification, children relate to their same-sex parent and model their behavior on that parent's own.

Because a dependent tie is such a common feature of the mother-daughter bond, the need for consistent affection from mother to daughter is crucial to the girl's psychological health. A mother who is sometimes affectionate but frequently distant and uncaring will raise a daughter who feels she is unlovable —and who is secretly angry that she didn't get the love she wanted and needed.

Today, Katharine is very unhappy with her $60,000 job as a financial analyst; she thinks she is grossly underpaid and unappreciated by her boss. Not coincidentally, her mother believed herself a martyr to her husband and children. While the pretty, plump executive tried to present her mother objectively, her assertions of how "good" a mother hers was soon deteriorated into descriptions of how—for all her mother's "sacrifices"—she, Katharine, felt cheated of love.

"She was a very good mother." Katharine sighed deeply. "She was always there. She did everything a mother was supposed to do. She ran the local Girl Scouts and was a member of the PTA. However, she wasn't affectionate in terms of kissing and hugging. I think she sacrificed her life for the family because that's what mothers were supposed to do. Once, when I was five or six, she bought a new suit and blouse and was so happy to have those new clothes. At first, I remember thinking, 'Why didn't she spend the money on me?' Then I felt guilty. Even then, I knew she never spent money on herself.

"I think my mother was depressed." Katharine's hazel eyes grew reflective. "She graduated from college *summa cum laude* and was extremely intelligent. She grew up in Chicago, where there were lots of interesting things to do. I've heard from my aunts that she was fun and popular before she met my father and moved out to the sticks of Illinois with him. She was too smart to live in a dinky town and raise a bunch of kids. Out where we lived, people were narrow-minded and uninterested in culture. She kept to herself. We never had company. She never made any friends."

Katharine frowned and smoothed the folds of her dress over her knees. "My mother *made* things," she said in a tone that warned that a *but* was impending. "She made clothes for us, and she baked cookies and cakes sometimes, but she wasn't a mother who cooked a lot. She was handy with sewing and crafts—things to keep you busy and out of her hair—but she wasn't one of those mothers who enjoyed being domestic. She made soup because there were bones left from dinner and you *should* make soup with bones. You always had the feeling that she'd rather be somewhere else."

Many mothers "project" feelings onto their daughters. These mothers can't view their daughters as separate persons with separate needs and desires. Instead, they perceive their daughters as extensions of themselves. Through messages subtle and overt, they insist that their daughters be the people they want them to be. Psychologists call such mothers narcissists after the Greek myth about the boy who was punished by the gods for loving no one but himself. Narcissus was condemned to love only his own image.

If a little girl gets angry or cries, comes home with dirt on her dress, or is slow at being toilet-trained, a mother who "lives through" her daughter reacts as if the girl has shamed her personally. Throughout the daughter's life, the mother perceives the daughter's failures and successes as reflecting directly on her.

Held close to her mother from infancy and hypersensitive to her mother's moods ("Daughters know their mothers' true feelings like they know the inside of their pockets," says psychiatrist Mio Fredland), the daughter of the mother who projects comes to understand that only by acting in certain ways will she be eligible for love and approval. As she grows up, she learns that if she behaves like a "good girl"—that is, as mother wants her to—she will be able to win care and love. But the daughter of the narcissistic mother gets a raw deal. "The sometimes-affectionate mother, who offers love on condition, holds her daughter forever in the vise of a push-pull relationship," Dr. Bernstein explains. "The promise of love is held out only to be withdrawn. Hope springs eternal in the daughter's heart, and hope is also eternally crushed."

A mother plays Pygmalion with a daughter for two reasons: (a) Her own mother offered love only on condition. She herself is desperate for approval and needs to make sure that everything about her—including her daughter—is acceptable. (b) Unconsciously, she yearns to be tied to the all-giving mother of her infancy. Because she is "raging [for the kind of love] infants need," as psychotherapist Elizabeth Hauser says, she unconsciously fuses her identity with that of her daughter.

The sixth and final woman you will get to know in these pages portrayed her mother as a narcissist—self-conscious, insecure, and only "sometimes-affectionate." Today Jennifer earns $80,000 as an executive art director for a cosmetics manufacturer but doesn't feel successful or fulfilled in her career or private life. I interviewed her in her high-tech office in a busy Connecticut city. There, a streamlined black leather couch faced a low black table. Steel-and-black-canvas director's chairs were artfully scattered about the room. Gray carpeting matched gray walls, and beside a black Lucite desk a cactus towered six feet high. The dark room was brightly lit by several rows of track lights.

Jennifer looked shockingly out of place in this environment. She is ghostly pale, wears little makeup, and has boyishly short platinum-blond hair. The day I met her, she was dressed in a fitted gray suit and high-necked white blouse—very conservatively for a person in her field and completely out of keeping with her office's modern style.

Jennifer sat with the posture of a strictly bred private-school girl (which I later learned she had been) and held her hands folded on her lap for most of the interview. Her jaw was set so firmly that when she smiled, her mouth muscles moved but the rest of her face stayed motionless. Her light-green eyes were intelligent within her wire aviator frames, but were otherwise almost spooky in their expressionlessness.

Jennifer was able to analyze her life with uncanny perceptiveness, but she had deadened herself to her own feelings. She showed no sadness when discussing painful parts of her life. Her tone of voice was drily sarcastic, which made her seem even more detached. The only thing in her office that revealed her sensitivity and originality was a framed award that hung above her desk—a prize given her for one of her many famous makeup ads.

She was born thirty-nine years ago into a wealthy Connecticut home. "My mother came from a poor family," she said in a surprisingly deep voice. "My father came from a rich family, so she dropped all her friends when she married him. She couldn't have friends who didn't meet her new standards. She was very hung up on status, and she played the *grande dame* morning and night. She loved to cook before marrying, but stopped cooking afterward; she thought hiring servants to cook was an impressive thing to do. I always used to hear her say, 'I am not a servant.' After she married, my mother quit working, although she had loved her job, and I think that left her angry and depressed. My father didn't want her to work—he didn't think it looked right, you see, and my mother wanted to do only what was right.

"My mother was intelligent, but all she had to do with her days was to order the servants around. She was a harsh taskmaster, and most servants quit after just a few months. The house was immaculate. She went crazy if I made a mess, so I never played at home and I never had friends to my house.

"When I was seven, my father began having an affair. My mother knew, but she never confronted him. Appearances meant everything. She didn't want to threaten her status as a rich man's wife, so she kept her mouth shut and took out her anger on the servants and me."

Jennifer paused, weighed a decision, and then began to speak again. "I just found out that my mother's brother lived nearby until he died a few years ago. Their parents were dead, and he was the only person in the family left. I had been told that he was dead too. Can you believe that?" Her voice rose in pitch. "My uncle lived right here. I could have gone to see the guy. I mean, he lived right here in this state, and my mother was so—darned ashamed of her past she disowned him and never told me that I had an uncle. That was a shocker, I tell you."

Jennifer colored slightly, but her voice quickly resumed its low pitch. "My mother wanted me to be a little lady. She liked to pick out all my clothes. When we visited my grandparents— my father's parents—she made me get all gussied up. I remember once wearing this scratchy wool sweater on the way out to their house. I complained from the backseat of the car, and my mother gave me a *murderous* glare.

"At times, I felt very close to my mother. She could be warm and lots of fun. I remember our going for drives in the country and the joy I felt being with her. But then suddenly she would be critical, and it seemed I couldn't do anything right. For example, she was a talented artist, and her standards were high, and I once entered a painting contest at the local museum. The first prize was a hundred dollars, and I wanted desperately to win. I worked on my painting for four months. The day before I was going to bring it to the judges, I unveiled it for my mother. She looked at it and pronounced, 'Jennifer, that is *not* art. You don't want this seen in public.' I ran into the bathroom and threw up. I was only ten years old." Jennifer stared straight in front of her, and her pale-green eyes betrayed no feeling.

All of us suffer to some degree from having to bend to our parents' wills. Each of us has what psychologists call narcissistic injuries to overcome, wherein we must eventually defy our parents and assert our individual selves. But daughters suffer much more often from these slights than do sons. When a mother allows her daughter to have almost no say of her own, that daughter will tailor herself to her mother's measure and push her own feelings and wishes—which she comes to perceive as flawed—aside until she loses touch with who she is and what she wants. This pattern will be repeated in all her future relationships. Busy doing what other people want her to do, she won't be able to pursue her own dreams.

Jennifer, Katharine, Laura, and Rose all had "unsuccessful" mothers—mothers too preoccupied with their own problems to be consistently loving or to set positive examples for their daughters. From here on, I will be referring to the two groups of women in the survey with "successful" and "unsuccessful" mothers as the "nourished" and "undernourished" women, because a mother who likes herself and is happy with her life is more able to give her daughter the emotional nourishment she needs to achieve happiness and success in her own life. Sara and Annie were emotionally nourished and, as we will demonstrate, were much more able than the other four women to get what they wanted from their careers and lives.

The mother is the most powerful force in a woman's destiny. A mother's own self-image, her relationship to her daughter, and her fulfillment in her marriage, sexuality, and life will determine the daughter's feelings about herself, her ability to relate to women and men, her sexuality, the choices she makes, the goals she sets, and her ability to reach her goals.

Kim Chernin, in her book *The Hungry Self: Women, Eating and Identity,* provides a pungent example of how a non-nourishing mother can cripple her daughter from becoming all she can be. Chernin counsels women with eating problems that often render them incapable of living normal lives. She asked one of her patients to discuss her mother's life:

" 'My mother's life? You want me to talk about my mother's life? It's a disaster area. When I go to visit her it feels to me as if I'm walking into a bomb shelter. You know? Where the bomb already fell? It's a wasteland. A camp for displaced victims. You get the point? My mother's a victim. A sacrificial victim.'

"Would we expect a woman who feels like this to skip out happily into those new opportunities made available in this generation?" Chernin asks.

CHAPTER

=IV=

THE TEENAGE YEARS

I worked very hard through junior high school. At first I studied hard to incur favor, but as I got older, it became a convenient excuse to avoid going out.
—MARY CUNNINGHAM,
Powerplay

In a woman's adolescence, the major conflicts of her childhood are replayed. As a child, she had to learn about her body's basic functions and needs; now she undergoes great physical changes and must adjust to menstruation and sexuality. As in childhood she turned to her father to become more independent from her mother (successfully or not), she now turns to boys her own age. One of the most difficult tasks for the adolescent woman is pushing away from her mother—not only emotionally, as she asserts her adult identity, but physically, when she leaves home.

Whether a woman was nourished or not, leaving home can be a trial. When Katharine, the financial analyst, left Illinois for college in Boston, she developed shingles, a virus triggered by anxiety. "I felt as though no one was there for me anymore," she explained. Annie, the television executive who was "very emotionally attached to her mother," insisted that her mother spend her first night at college in her dorm room with her. Afterward, she phoned her mother daily.

Sara, the computer executive, left her Berkshires home for California. "My mother thought it important that I strike out on my own, so she encouraged me to go away to college, although she knew she'd miss me. I didn't realize how much I missed *her* until my first visit home. I woke up and there she was in my room opening the windows to let in the fresh air.

She looked so happy and alive! I was overcome with homesickness, and I stuck my head in the pillow and cried."

Most women feel apprehensive or sad about leaving home, but being nourished helps them adjust with a minimum of pain. A nourished woman adopts her mother's confidence and sociability, whereas an undernourished woman—without a secure, outgoing maternal model—has trouble building relationships and dealing with everyday problems.

In adolescence we form the self-images and ways of interacting with others that stay constant through our adult lives. For this reason, I thought it crucial to understand our women as teenagers. I asked those surveyed to think about themselves between the ages of thirteen and twenty and to describe what their home, school, and social lives had been like: how they related to their parents, what activities they enjoyed, and how they felt about themselves physically, emotionally, intellectually, and socially.

First, I asked, how did they feel about their looks? In reply, a dismally small number—only 27 percent—said they saw themselves as "attractive." Why is obvious. In America, the social pressure on women to be attractive is insane. The magazines we read, the movies and TV shows we see, bombard us with images of gorgeous models, singers, and actresses. Advertisers regale us with promises that beauty brings love and happiness. In no other country is such a premium placed on a woman's being flawlessly pretty—having perfect skin, a taut body, and breasts that are neither too big nor too small. I grew up in Germany, and until I came to America, I felt fine about my looks. After I observed the efforts that American women made to look good, my self-doubts geometrically increased. I came to believe that I was overweight and that without makeup I was ugly; I *learned* American women's anxieties about their appearances.

"At what age does a girl child begin to review her assets and count her deficient parts?" asks Susan Brownmiller in her book *Femininity*.

> When does she close the bedroom door and begin to gaze privately into the mirror at contortionist angles to get a view from

the rear, the left profile, the right. . . . When is she allowed to forget that her anatomy is being monitored by others, that there is a standard of desirable beauty, of individual parts, that she is measured against by boyfriends, loved ones, acquaintances at work, competitors, enemies and strangers? How can she be immune to the national celebration of this season's body, to the glamorous model in the high-fashion photograph, to the chance remark of a lover, the wistful preference of a husband, the whistle or unexpected hostile comment heard on the street?

This cultural emphasis on beauty affects all women. As teenagers, our nourished women were insecure about their looks as often as the undernourished women were. "When I was a kid, my parents were always kissing my arms and legs," Annie said. "They thought I was gorgeous. Not just pretty, *gorgeous*. Do you know what a shock it is to find out you're not gorgeous after a whole life spent with parents who constantly told you that you were?" The willowy executive laughed good-naturedly. "At fifteen, I was skinny as a rail and I had no bust. Those were the days when you were supposed to be thirty-six–twenty-four–thirty-six. I wore an undershirt in gym when every other girl in school had a bra. We had 'spots' in the gym instead of lockers; we had to change our clothes in front of the entire school. And I had this *undershirt*!" Annie threw up her hands exasperatedly. "I was so humiliated! They didn't make junior bras back then. Finally, I made my mother buy me a bra, cut out the cup, and sew it back up so that I could at least wear *something*. I was also very tall—five-eleven, the same height I am today. I thought I was going to grow right through the ceiling and never get a guy."

The undernourished woman's insecurities were far more severe than those expressed by the nourished woman. "I thought I was ugly and fat," financial analyst Katharine stated. "When I was thirteen, I used to pray that I would wake up looking like the head cheerleader at my school. She had a slim, petite body and straight hair with these cute little bangs. I had a mop of wavy hair and a big, clumsy body. I used to beg God to make me more like her; I would pray until the tears rolled down my face. I felt like a complete reject." Katharine sighed heavily.

"Once, in high school, I went to a party in a new white dress I loved. I walked into the party and a boy yelled out, 'Oh, oh, it's a cumulus cloud!' Anyone else would have sassed him back; he was pimply and a jerk. I left the party and stayed in bed crying the whole next day."

Jennifer, from the wealthy, unhappy home, also felt very insecure. "It was not cool to be as palefaced as I am when I was a teenager," she said in her deep, sardonic voice. "I had colorless eyelashes and pasty skin. I was tall and thin and wore glasses. The popular girls were all tanned, bouncy, and buxom. When I think of myself at that time, I see myself looming around groups of people hoping to be noticed and failing."

Some of the undernourished women's lack of confidence stemmed from their feelings about their periods. "Menstruation officially marks our entrance into womanhood, and how a woman reacts to it will in part determine how much she likes her body and femininity overall," Dr. Bernstein states. "If she views menstruation as dirty or shameful, she won't have a good body image. How her mother deals with the subject will be pivotal to her view."

Katharine's martyrish mother saw her daughter's menarche as a nuisance. "I had sort of heard about periods at school, but when I got mine the first time, I was very scared. I had no idea of what to do. I burst into tears and called out, 'Mommy! There's blood all over my underpants!' And then she said—this still makes me mad—'Hasn't anyone told you about that yet?' She brought me a napkin and said, 'Pin it on.' I said, 'Can I do gym and can I—' and she said, 'Oh, yeah.' Just 'Oh, yeah,' and then she never uttered another word on the subject. I realize now that she was embarrassed to buy Kotex and things, and that I still associate something shameful with my periods."

Sara's nourishing mother treated her daughter's first period as a happy event. "I was young—eleven—and my mother hadn't yet explained menstruation to me. I was in bed one cold New England morning when I saw the blood on the sheets. I was sure that I was a goner. I yelled to my sister in the other bed, 'Jessie! Get Mommy! Tell her I'm dying!' " Sara plunked down her wineglass and clutched her breast in mock alarm. "I showed her the blood, and poor Jessie took off screaming like a bat out of hell. I'll never forget the smile my mother had on her face when she entered my room. I was outraged! How could she smile when I was dying? Then she hugged me and said, 'Welcome to womanhood!' and explained everything to Jessie and me."

"Teenage girls turn to their mothers, the parent most physically resembling themselves, for validation that their bodies and appearances are okay," explains Dr. Bernstein. "What a mother does or doesn't tell her daughter about her attractiveness and physical adequacy is vital for the completion of the daughter's mental picture of her body. If a mother constantly criticizes, she'll confirm her daughter's worst fears that something is wrong with her."

As teenagers, the nourished women I polled were twice as close to their mothers as the undernourished women were (neither group felt close to their fathers now). Sara and Annie could confide their fears to their mothers and count on receiving their support. "I got my period at sixteen, much later than my girlfriends did, but my mother kept me from worrying," Annie said. "She told me over and over that she had also gotten it late and that we were lucky for being late bloomers. She'd mention a girl in my class who had big breasts and say, 'She'll sag to her waist someday!' "

Sara's mother also helped her through an awkward phase. "When I was in high school, I went through a chubby stage. My mother helped me shop for slimming clothes and assured me that I looked okay. She took me to a diet doctor and made me all the meals he told me to eat. Since I was athletic, I lost the weight quickly."

The undernourished women received no signs from their mothers that they were attractive or even okay. "I don't think my mother thought I was *homely*," Katharine said testily, "but she certainly never said I was pretty. When I look at myself in old pictures, I realize I was very cute. I was a little chubby, but cute. I didn't think so at the time."

Jennifer's narcissistic mother castigated her. "I think she couldn't bear that I was getting out from under her thumb. No matter how I styled my hair, no matter what I wore, she was critical. No, not critical; she was downright cruel. Whenever she saw me, she'd say, 'Fix your hair up! You look terrible!' Or 'Don't you know that the color green makes you look like you're going to be sick?' "

In our culture, a woman's physical insecurities often foster social insecurities. Only about a third of our women said they were "popular" (34 percent), "outgoing" (39 percent), or "social" (37 percent). Many were "inhibited" (64 percent). Half were "lonely" (52 percent), "nervous" (47 percent), and "worried" (47 percent), and only half (50 percent) were "happy" as teenagers.

On the whole, the nourished women viewed themselves as far more popular, social, and happy than the undernourished women did; however, both groups lacked confidence when it came to boys. In general, the women made female friends easily (61 percent) but didn't get along well with boys (only 43 percent). The nourished women got along better both with girls (71 percent versus 57 percent) and with boys (53 percent versus 33 percent), but a good half of them felt awkward around the opposite sex.

Forging a comfortable heterosexual tie is much more difficult for adolescent women than it is for men. For most teenage women, a goal (as well as a sign of adjustment) is to have a close, caring relationship with a male peer; this bond allows her to replace the mother as her primary love object. But most children, male and female, grow up receiving more affection from their mothers than from their fathers. Now, as they sexually develop, males turn to other females for love. As Nancy Friday notes in *My Mother/My Self*, a man's "primary, straightline involvement is always with women. First his mother, then girlfriends, later his wife, etc." Women "must make this extremely complicated shift to the male sex." This switch is made all the more difficult because so many girls grow up with fathers who aren't easy to get to know; they therefore assume, somewhat rightly, that all men will be hard to get close to.

In high school, Annie didn't feel at all comfortable with boys. No wonder: Her father worked two jobs when she was growing up. "I don't know why, but I couldn't be myself with boys. I dated, but I couldn't get a steady relationship going. Maybe I was too self-conscious about my height and my flat chest."

The undernourished women felt even more awkward around boys. Dr. Bernstein believes they were particularly frightened of physical intimacy. "If a mother is comfortable with her sexuality and conveys this attitude through open affection to her husband, her daughter will tend to be comfortable with men and sex," she explains, "but healthy sexuality ultimately comes from successfully negotiating the early stages of closeness to and separation from the mother. The girl infant's ability to be close to her mother's body in an atmosphere of mutual comfort will be transferred to future love objects; first her father, then later her boyfriends. How she related to her mother will be duplicated in these relationships."

Katharine (whose mother "wasn't affectionate in terms of kissing and hugging") refused the one boy who asked her for a date in high school. "Clifford sat next to me in biology lab. He was cute and smart and he liked that I was smart. We were good friends, but after he asked me to a dance and I said no, he never spoke to me again."

"Why did you say no?" I asked.

Katharine shrugged. "I'm not sure. I remember being petrified that he'd try to kiss me good-night. We never talked about sex in my house, and we weren't a physical family. My parents had separate beds, and I never saw them in the same one."

Jennifer attended a private, all-girls high school and a coed dance class. The proper-looking blonde was ill at ease when speaking of sex. "I was kind of . . ." She blushed, and her sentence trailed off. "I was afraid of the guys," she said haltingly, "because I never saw any physical stuff going on in my house. My parents' relationship was . . . well, *wooden* is the word. They were like Noël Coward characters, too genteel to show affection. Also, my father was involved in a long, very serious affair. So I didn't know what to do around the boys at dancing school. I kept them at arm's length and became nervous if they got close. I couldn't understand all those feelings tumbling around in me."

Nearly every woman I interviewed had an upsetting experience the first time she had sexual intercourse, with the undernourished women's being especially unpleasant. A woman's sexual awakening is almost always complicated by fears—the real fears of pain and pregnancy, plus social and emotional fears. Many women fear that men will find fault with their bodies. Others have guilt feelings because of the old double standard that encouraged men to enjoy sex freely and discouraged women from doing so. Also, women who were overly dependent on their mothers (and many women are) often fear being used and abandoned by men. For all these reasons, while men usually long (and often beg) for their first sexual experience, women often approach it with something akin to trepidation. Men may look back on the experience as thrilling, but women often do so with regret. Here are our six women's responses to my question: "What was it like your first time?"

"Terrible." Katharine inhaled sharply and let out an angry breath. "I was nervous, and it hurt, and the guy was an insensitive clod. I did it the day a friend got married because I wanted a relationship. The guy pressured me. I gave in, but he never called again, and I was crushed. I was also kind of young, and so I felt guilty and cheap."

"No stars were shining," said Rose, the soft-spoken New Jersey executive. "I was brought up to believe that sex was a little unacceptable, and I didn't have any real experience until my wedding night. It took a while for us to get used to each other." She cast a furtive glance toward her living room's French doors to make sure her husband wasn't listening from the patio and then turned her liquid-brown eyes toward mine. "I enjoy sex, of course, but all that stuff you read about in books—the fireworks, the bells ringing—that sort of thing has never happened to me."

"It was okay." Sara, the computer executive, laughed. She was one of a handful of women who described their first experiences as at all benign. "I was fourteen, and I did it with the boy next door in his barn. In the Berkshires, lots of people had farms with horses, goats, and cows. We grew up seeing the animals do it, so we figured, why not us? He kept slipping out of me, which both of us found hilarious."

"Very bad," Jennifer said crisply. "I was twenty, and I vowed that I wasn't going to be a virgin by age twenty-one. I met somebody at a party and got smashed; I felt that I had to get drunk to get through it. I don't remember much of it. Well, I do remember one thing. The next morning, I looked at the guy beside me and said, 'You must think I'm disgusting.' "

"It was pretty bad." Annie walked over to her vase of lilacs, stuck her face in the flowers, and breathed in. "I felt something was wrong with me that I'd waited so long to do it. I also liked the guy a lot and hoped we'd have a relationship. He was a lovely guy, but our affair didn't last beyond two nights. I was devastated, and I carried the torch for him for a long, long time."

"Horrid, absolutely horrid! What was all this shit about it's being so beautiful? It was terrible! I'm serious!" Laura noticed the long ash on her cigarette and ran toward an ashtray; in her haste, she tripped on her long coat-jacket. She kicked it out of her way and crushed out her cigarette in fierce stabs. "I had been madly in love with a guy who was engaged. He dated me, but married his fiancée. I was heartbroken. I met some other guy and slept with him. I didn't give a damn about him. Yecccch! It was horrible!"

Since so many of our women felt badly about their social and romantic lives, what gave them satisfaction in their teenage years? The answer is clear: They were exceptional academically. Being good in school allowed them not only to stand out from their peers but to gain approval from their educated, intelligent parents. The two phrases the women said were most like them were:

- "Liked going to school" (77 percent)
- "An excellent student" (65 percent)

The nourished women believed they were even better students than the undernourished women (80 percent versus 60 percent), another manifestation of their greater self-esteem. But although they were concerned with doing well in school, other facets of their lives were also important.

"I was my high school's resident math whiz," Sara said. "I love numbers, that's why I love computers. I got the only eight hundred in the school on my math S.A.T., but I was not a grind," she assured me with a small smile. "I loved boys, and to my father's dismay, I loved boys with motorcycles. At sixteen

I dated a twenty-year-old guy with a Harley-Davidson, and my father hit the roof. My mother told him to leave me alone, that I could take care of myself. When I went to college, I made a lot of friends and discovered my passion—windsurfing. I worked hard in college, but I also had a blast."

After adjusting to college, Annie had a happy, well-balanced life. "I worked hard only in the subjects I liked," she said cheerfully. "In high school, I won awards in English but was mediocre at math. When I got to college and majored in English, I did very well. I finally grew into my height and had some very nice boyfriends. I loved college! I still missed my mother, though. I called her constantly, and she was always there for me."

For the undernourished women, excelling in school was an absolute necessity. They felt very unpopular and, frequently, the only positive attention they got from their mothers was for their good grades. As a result, they studied extremely hard and became reclusive.

"I was terrified that I might do poorly in school," Katharine said. "Luckily, I did well. I always figured that if I worked hard, I could at least be noticed for my grades." A desolate look stole over her face. "At high school parties, I was the one who changed the records while everyone else necked. Out east, at college, I felt even less popular. There, my *only* source of self-esteem was my grades."

"The only recognition I got at home was for getting A's on my report card or for getting awards like the National Merit Scholarship," Laura declared in her loud, tense voice. "My mother *paid* me for my A's. Can you believe that? And since I didn't get any attention from anywhere else, you had better believe I was an overachiever."

For a few moments Laura drummed her fingers on the arm of her chair. I heard car horns from the street and typewriters clacking outside the room. "As you can imagine, I was a very nervous, very neurotic teenager," she suddenly said. "Here I had this father who had hit me when I was a child and this mother who was miserable and had no self-esteem. I had a shitty life as a teenager. I had numerous physical problems. My eye had a tic. I had a bad lisp. And kids are very mean to each other. At school, they followed me around and imitated my tic and my lisp. Oh, and I thought I looked like a mouse!" Laura cried out with a hollow laugh. "That's an important fact for your record! I was timid, had big ears and only weighed about ninety pounds."

When Rose, the executive for the chemical company, spoke about her teenage years, she slipped off her heels, brought her feet up underneath her, and curled deep into her armchair. Once again, I had the strange feeling I was talking to a little girl. "As a teenager, I was short and thin and plain with straight brown hair," she said softly. "I thought nobody liked me and nobody cared for me—and nobody did. I was a loner; I read all the time. I read every book in the local library."

"Were you a good student?" I asked.

Rose looked at me as if I were mad. "Of course I was. I had to be. I didn't have any friends. Doing well in school was the only way I could be better than my brother. I was a straight-A student in high school and college."

In a recent interview for *Vogue,* Mary Cunningham revealed that schoolwork was the focus, and the refuge, of her teenage years. "There were girlfriends I really respected, but we'd do homework together," she said. "It was not the kind of thing where we went to dances or out on dates together. . . . I was the one you came to if you had a problem, but I wasn't the one you wanted to go jolly it up with on a Saturday."

According to her autobiography, this life-style didn't make her very happy. Raised as a strict Catholic, she was shy and conservative and "somewhat of a pariah" in high school. She rarely dated or socialized and was often lonely. "Mostly, I would stay in my room and study. . . . Even at midnight my light would still be on. . . . I found solace in my work."

While our average to-be-executive woman worked extremely hard at school and made considerable sacrifices in her social life, most of the successful men I know were well-rounded teenagers. They were often better at sports than at studies, and their ability to get along with others was the key factor behind their success. Our women's social adjustment left a lot to be desired. Here, in their teenage years, their isolation began.

CHAPTER
═V═

THE
EXECUTIVE WOMAN
TODAY

And so we leave home, we leave the apron and . . . put
on . . . tailored executive suits. . . . And now we take ourselves in hand, tailoring ourselves to the specifications of
this world we are so eager to enter. We strip our bodies of
flesh, our hearts of the overflow of feeling, our language
of exuberant and dramatic imprecisions. We cut back the
flight of our fancy, make our thought rigorous and subject
it (this marvelous rushing intuitive leaping capacity of ours)
to measures of demonstration and proof, trying not to talk
with our hands, trying hard to subdue our voices, getting
our bursts of laughter under control.
—KIM CHERNIN,
The Hungry Self

B oth the real and the fictional executive women portrayed
in the media have extremely well-rounded personalities.
They possess "male" traits that make them vital, confident
businesspeople (outspokenness, competitiveness) and "female"
traits that endear them to others (prettiness, sensitivity, warmth).
They are intellectually gifted, but "fun to be with. Their humor
is hilarious; their repartee quick and dry," as author Aasta Lubin says in her article on five executive women. Alexis Colby
from TV's *Dynasty* is exemplary. Self-assured and aggressive at
work, she is charming and witty, beautiful and—when she wants
to be—affectionate and warm.

Karen Valenstein, a first vice president of E. F. Hutton, was described in *The New York Times Magazine* as having a "killer instinct" that made her a powerful business adversary ("Against the Odds: A Woman's Ascent on Wall Street," January 6, 1985). She can "trade locker-room vulgarities, belt back stingers until dawn, and recite National League Football scores on Monday morning," but behind her tough exterior beats a very feminine heart. An attractive redhead, she loves clothes and goes on expensive shopping forays; she is also empathetic, nurturing, and thoughtful. She "plucks loose threads from the hems of other people's raincoats, carries matches even though she doesn't smoke and buys people little presents, like a silk tie for a boss on a trip to Paris or embroidered hair ribbons for her daughter after a painful trip to the orthodontist."

Are Alexis Colby and Karen Valenstein representative of executive women? Can the typical woman, as a well-known jingle assures us, bring home the bacon, fry it up for her family, and dazzle her husband with her sexiness? If so, our women have changed drastically from their teenage days.

I asked those surveyed to tell us about their appearance, personality, and working style today. Let's look first at how they assess their appearance.

Negative feelings about our bodies lodge deep in our subconscious. The fact that just a few more women see themselves as attractive today (35 percent) as when they were teenagers (27 percent) is therefore inevitable. Besides, many careerwomen—including 60 percent of our women—believe that they can't play up their looks at work. The theory goes that a woman who looks pretty calls more attention to her appearance than to her abilities and indicates to superiors that she doesn't care about her job. Without exception, the people who advise women how to dress for success tell them to downplay their appeal. "Some male comments can be tip-offs [about how not to dress]," says Betty Lehan Harragan in *Games Mother Never Taught You: Corporate Gamesmanship for Women.* " 'I see you're wearing a dress today—you look so pretty.' If a man says that to you at the staff meeting, never wear that outfit again"(!). Even academics have gotten into the act. A recent study out of New York University shows that pretty women are less apt to excel in business than plain women are.

"My field is computers," Sara reminded me. "Ten years ago,

when very few women were executives in the field, I was made a vice president. I felt that I had to start dressing in a certain way. I worked in a conservative corporation where all the men wore suits, so I lopped off my curls and wore suits myself. I couldn't wait to get out of those clothes! Finally, I woke up and said, 'Damn it, I'm a woman, not a man.' Women have a huge array of clothes that they can wear to the office. Now I choose clothes that are tasteful but feminine and colorful." Sara and I traded smiles; her yellow dress proved her point. "And I feel *much* better about myself."

Most women do have a wide choice of clothes to wear to work. Even in conservative fields such as banking and law women can wear suits with soft collars, dresses or even skirts and blouses, but many don't exercise these options and wear only "man-tailored" suits. As Amelia Fatt notes in her book *Conservative Chic,* man-tailored suits are cut to compliment a man's shape: wide at the shoulders and narrow at the hips. Women are generally built the opposite: slim at the shoulders and full at the hips. Women not only wear men's unflattering styles, they adopt men's dull color schemes. "Most of the women in my office wear only black, navy, brown, or gray," Sara observed.

"I hate wearing these uniform suits," Jennifer said, gesturing to her gray jacket and skirt. "But people associate competence and seriousness with business suits." Today I find that logic absurd, but I—like Sara—dressed in conservative suits for years, during which my opinion of my looks reached an all-time low.

Even more astonishing than the small number of women who say they are attractive is the tiny number who feel they are "sexy"—only 8 percent. This sad fact underscores how difficult it is even in the 1980s for a woman to have a positive sense of her sexuality. Since the percentage of women who feel sexy is so glaringly low, however, we must assume that some of them are trying to say they aren't *provocative*. Of course, suggestive actions and garb are inappropriate at work—but why can't being "sexy" merely mean for women, as it does for men, that we have a feeling of ease and pride about our bodies, that we exude a sense of being comfortable in our female skin? Why must "being sexy" for women translate into being seductive? Successful businessmen are always described as sexy, regardless of how ugly they are.

Our nourished women feel no prettier or sexier than the undernourished women do. But while the numbers of women who felt unappealing were the same in each group, the interviews again reveal how profound the undernourished women's insecurities are.

"I'm still a mouse inside," Laura said. "When I look in the mirror, what I see are a lot of wrinkles and sags and flaws. For about an hour after I put my makeup on and fix my hair I think I look okay. After that, I think I look terrible. In fact, if I run out of my apartment with no makeup on to get cigarettes and I see someone I know walking toward me, I'll turn around and run back home before I'll let them get a glimpse of me."

Like Laura, Rose spends a lot of time on her looks—not out of vanity, but in an attempt to hide what she fears is her ugliness. With her tight clothes, high heels, and bright red hair, she is as flashy as she can be without overstepping her bounds. In her teenage years, Rose thought herself very unappealing; then, her last year in college, she went to a beauty salon and had a permanent. She believed this made her more attractive. "At the same time, I filled out," she said, "and the boys at college began to flirt with me."

Exhilarated by their attention, Rose flaunted her body and her looks: She "dyed my hair fire-engine red and wore tight dresses and spike heels." Not unexpectedly, when she started working, her boss told her to "tone herself down." Rose heeded this warning—up to a point. "I darkened my hair and started to wear looser-fitting clothes, but gradually I went back to the tighter sweaters and redder hair. I'm just not comfortable unless I can look a little sexy and jazzed up."

Katharine and Jennifer also try to mask what they view as their ugly selves, but their methods are the other side of Laura's and Rose's coin. While Katharine's eyes are exceptionally pretty, she wears no makeup to accentuate them; she also pulls her hair back and shrouds her body in shapeless clothes. "I don't think I'm attractive at all. Maybe I could be if I lost weight, but I haven't been able to do that," she said unhappily. "As it is, I prefer to fade into the woodwork."

For a woman in the cosmetics field, Jennifer wears surprisingly little makeup, and with her pale skin and lashes, she looks washed out under her bright track lights. Like many of the women I interviewed, she wears suits she knows don't flatter her. She believes that "women in business should try to look inconspicuous. If you look too pretty, men will get the wrong idea. Of course," she added self-deprecatingly, "I could never look too pretty."

If they don't like their appearance, are our women self-assured in other ways? Do they display the strength-denoting "masculine" qualities so apparent in their counterparts in the media? Are they tough and ambitious? No-nonsense when it comes to firing lazy staff members or housekeepers?

No. Only every other woman (48 percent) told us that she was "outspoken" in business or anywhere else. Just half, again, said that they were "assertive" (52 percent). Only a few more (55 percent) are "competitive" when pursuing their goals. And while Alexis Colby may be a bold, dynamic executive, only 35 percent of our women say they are "aggressive."

Our nourished women are no more "outspoken," "assertive," "competitive," or "aggressive" than the undernourished women. Many of the women, as we'll see, are uneasy with these "male" qualities. One trait that might be considered traditionally "masculine" that the nourished and undernourished women do feel describes them is "independent" (82 percent in each group). By saying they are "independent," our women mean that they are financially sovereign and free to spend their money as they choose. Thanks to the feminist movement, they can make other choices as well: They can marry or stay single, have children or remain childless, be homemakers or executives without being viewed as odd.

On the surface, the *anima* (feminine side) of these women seems stronger than the *animus* (masculine side). The majority say they are highly loyal (75 percent)—a fact I don't find surprising, since loyalty to family and friends has long been a "female" value. The women go on to depict themselves as feminine in other respects. Many say they are considerate of others: They are "accessible" (68 percent), "thoughtful" (64 percent), and "warm" (65 percent). But lest we believe that they openly or consistently display this side to themselves, the following facts quickly dispel that notion. Only about half manifest their tender, caring sides by being either "empathetic" (55 percent), "generous"

(50 percent), or "giving" (49 percent). On the quintessentially feminine traits, the numbers dip even lower: Just 37 percent are "nurturing" and 32 percent, "affectionate." Most telling, less than four in ten (38 percent) say that they are "feminine"!

The women's dissociation from femininity lies in their belief that acting "female" impedes a woman's career. "Women in business don't want to be seen as frivolous or incompetent," Annie told me. "They're afraid that if they gush about a project or hug a staff member who's done a good job, their male colleagues will think they're not serious." As Annie spoke, she rummaged in her files and pulled out a bag of chocolate kisses. "I knew I had some candy in there. Here, have some! Anyway, when I began working in TV, I tried not to act like a typical female. I was scared to giggle at a joke or to show I was moved by a screenplay. I never touched anyone when I spoke to them, and I *never* rattled on about my kids."

Jennifer, like many I interviewed, was guilty of the stereotypical thinking that equates femininity with passivity, weakness, and even stupidity. She spoke so sternly on the subject that, with her rigid posture and glasses, she reminded me of a schoolmarm. "If you're too feminine, you'll look out for the other guy instead of yourself. You'll be a doormat, and you can't be a doormat in business. Femininity also means flightiness and spaciness, and in business you have to be calculating and rational. Feminine women get too emotionally caught up with colleagues. I made that mistake once, and I deeply regretted it. Now I'm very businesslike with all my co-workers."

When we compare our nourished and undernourished women on the "feminine" qualities, both groups rank themselves equally low on the adjective *feminine*, telling us that most executive women bring unfavorable interpretations to that word. The nourished women rated themselves higher on all the other feminine traits.

"Women who weren't sufficiently nurtured by their mothers have an unconscious reason for squelching their femininity—the wish not to be identified with their mothers," Dr. Bernstein says. "Being feminine, to all women, means being like mother. Most mothers are capable of being warm; very few mothers are complete ogres. But if a mother only loved us sometimes, we'll want to divorce ourselves from her. Women who suffer in their relationships with their mothers often repress their femininity as a defense mechanism. They don't want to remind themselves of their mother's positive, feminine qualities because too much pain and longing is attached." Also, as Kim Chernin suggests in her book *The Hungry Self,* women who perceive their mothers as unhappy failures feel compelled to be different from their mothers so that they themselves can survive and succeed. "Mother stands for the victim in ourselves, the unfree woman, the martyr. . . . We develop matrophobia and try to split ourselves off from her, to purge ourselves of her bondage; in a desperate attempt to know where mother ends and daughter begins, we perform radical surgery," Adrienne Rich wrote in *Of Woman Born.*

Jennifer is a good example of a woman who has cut off her femininity to distinguish herself from her mother. Her brusque, indifferent manner allows for no receptivity or warmth. When her secretary interrupted us to deliver a message, I was amazed at Jennifer's coldness. "Okay, Carol," she said in her deep, dismissive voice. She didn't introduce us, and Carol left as fast as she'd arrived. *All* Jennifer's working relationships seemed formal and stiff. She never joked or asked "How are you?" when a colleague popped his head into her office.

Because society permits women to show their emotions more than men, women generally use more body language and have a greater range of vocal inflections and tones. Jennifer's voice has none of the variety and expressiveness that normally characterizes female speech. Her short blond hair and tailored suit are mannish, and her body and gestures are stiff and controlled. Even her office is "unfeminine." Its color scheme—black and gray—is hardly welcoming. The Lucite surfaces and leather couch lend no warmth to the room; nor, certainly, does the six-foot cactus.

Laura, with her tendency to "swear like a man" and her conviction that kissing and hugging are "gushy," has also rejected her feminine side. She doesn't want to be anything like the mother who "screamed and yelled about how much she hated every minute of her life" and who didn't help Laura through an excruciating childhood and adolescence. Jennifer and Laura rarely show the gentleness, expressiveness, and sensitivity that are the special and wonderful legacies of femininity.

"Feminine" traits are people-oriented traits, because women's traditional role has been that of nurturer. Empathy and kindness draw people toward us, as does the ability to be charming, easygoing, or funny. Yet when other women were developing their social skills, ours were apt to be studying alone in their rooms. Consequently, only half of them now say that they are "outgoing" (53 percent). Less than half dub themselves "likeable" (47 percent), "even-tempered" (49 percent), or "humorous" (40 percent). The women are no "happier" now (52 percent) than they were as teenagers, and one reason is that they rarely kick up their heels. Less than four in ten are "fun-loving" (37 percent), and only 13 percent are "playful"! Again, the under-nourished women tip the scales: They are far more introverted and glum than the nourished women are.

So far, our average executive woman has told us that she is not good-looking, not feminine, not outspoken, and not much fun. What *is* she like? You guessed it. The characteristic that nearly all the women share is "hardworking" (92 percent). It follows that the vast majority are extremely "concerned with results" at work (89 percent) and very "concerned with people" at work (77 percent), that is, with maintaining good working relationships. The women additionally see themselves as very self-controlled: Seventy-six percent regard themselves as highly "disciplined."

The majority (75 percent) believe they are very "intelligent," but on other positive traits, they don't rate themselves nearly so high. I expected as many to say they were "well-educated" as said they were "intelligent," but only half (49 percent) did. Since 80 percent went to college, this discrepancy calls for an explanation.

We are seeing a reflection of the fact that, until very recently, the bastions of the Ivy League (Harvard, Princeton, and Yale) were open exclusively to men. Our women hesitate to make claims about their education because they were so often barred from attending one of the "right schools." Many of those I interviewed went to excellent women's schools—Barnard, Vassar, Radcliffe—but felt insecure about their education once they entered the business world.

"My parents were never prouder of me than when I was accepted to Bryn Mawr." Jennifer smiled cynically. "They considered having a daughter at Bryn Mawr the ultimate in status. In business, though, Bryn Mawr doesn't count. People assume that a man who went to Harvard has a strong economics background and that I have a meaningless liberal arts training. The old-boys' network is made up of men who went to the Ivy League schools."

Besides downgrading their education, only half the women portray themselves as "talented" (50 percent) and even fewer as "creative" (37 percent). This modest assessment of their innate skills derives, in part, from years of hard work in an environment where women have long been viewed as less competent than men.

The nourished women think they are much more intelligent, talented, and creative than the undernourished women feel they are. Additionally, they view themselves as far better educated, although in truth, they are only slightly better educated.

Our typical executive woman is extremely hardworking; that comes with the territory of being an executive. But again, the undernourished women are singlemindedly focused on gaining recognition for their achievements. I asked each of the women I interviewed to describe her average workday. Sara's and Katharine's replies highlight the dramatic differences between the nourished and the undernourished women.

"A day in my life? Oh God," Sara half-laughed, half-groaned. "I'm not sure I want to think about it. I get up at five-thirty A.M. and do yoga for twenty minutes. I have breakfast with my daughter, and that's a high point of the day. I'm in my car at six-forty-five and I listen to the news on the radio because I can only skim the newspaper later. I reach the office by seven-fifteen and I work until about seven P.M."

The vibrant blonde slipped off her shoes and began pointing and flexing her toes. "I work on between five and ten computer products at one time. My biggest project now is a robot for restaurant and industrial kitchens. All day I work closely with my staff and sell my bosses on my new ideas. Every hour I have to move on to a new project. It's a wild schedule." Sara shook her curly head, causing the shells around her neck to rattle. "Thankfully, I have a bright, creative staff I can depend on and who make the job fun. I also have a couple of bosses that I relate to very well.

"The need for constant discipline is the hardest part," Sara continued. "My calendar is so crammed that if someone wants an hour with me, they have to wait at least two weeks. I can't allow meetings to run over or I have people lining up outside my door. By the time seven P.M. rolls around, my body and brain are screaming, 'No more!' But chances are I have to work at home or have dinner with an associate.

"I plan very carefully to make time for my daughter. Her father and I are divorced, and he doesn't live nearby, so I try to be there for her as often as I can. I love to wind down by cooking dinner with Julie. She's only twelve, and she's a great cook. We inspire each other in the kitchen, and it gives us a chance to talk. That's my typical day." Sara smiled.

Katharine's depiction of her average workday contained few details about her job; instead, she discussed how little attention or thanks she gets for all her hard work. "I always get to work early, because I have to make sense of the mess on my desk before my boss starts in with his demands. In the mornings I write memos because I communicate best in writing. I like financial research, but I'm not a good people-person. Managing a staff I find just about impossible; even handling peer relationships is something I have a lot of trouble with. If people don't pay attention to what I write, they'll never understand me. If they don't read my memos—and a lot of people don't—the situation is hopeless."

Katharine sat brooding for a moment and then continued. "I do historical analyses of the performances of particular stocks and companies and make long- and short-term investment recommendations based on that information. I also research future trends; for example, I met yesterday with an economist who predicted what products are going to be needed in the year 2010, when the baby-boomers are senior citizens.

"I have real problems with the people in my office, especially the men. In meetings, I'll say something and the men will just ignore me and say what they want. I've gotten to the point where I come right out and say, 'I wish someone would listen to me, because I have something to say!' Sometimes I yell it." Katharine's hazel eyes radiated anger and hurt. "My boss is no help. He barely listens to me. He doesn't read my memos half the time and he's very disorganized. All day it's 'Stop working on the merger deal and start looking into this new company. Do this, do that, do this, do that.' I'm there until seven-thirty at night. By then I don't want to see anyone, so I go home and see my dogs. My dogs appreciate me."

When we look one last time at the profile of our average woman, an interesting fact comes to light. Although my question asked what they were like as people, not just as executives, the women described themselves in terms of their work personae. Why, if they don't believe they can be feminine or sexy at work, can't they be feminine or sexy outside of work? The answer is that for many women, who they are at work is who they are.

Men have always based their identity on a number of different roles. Men can be soldiers—and therefore killers—and at the same time be loving fathers. They can be shrewd businessmen, ardent lovers, and good husbands and sons simultaneously.

Women have never learned to play a variety of social roles comfortably because they traditionally had a single role in life, that of nurturer. Because of their difficulties shifting psychological gears, women find it hard to be one person in one situation and another in another. As teenagers, they feel that they can't be smart and pretty too. As adults, if their main source of identity is their careers, they believe their work persona to be inviolable.

When women began migrating into the workforce in the late 1960s, they had few female role models to show them how to retain their feminine attributes and add to these the professional qualities they saw in successful men. Metaphorically speaking, the women transferred all their eggs from one basket to another; they relinquished their femininity and became as "businesslike" as they could. Women still discuss the issue of office demeanor in black-and-white terms. Books that advise women on how to succeed at work tell them either to be impersonal and manlike (*The Right Moves, Games Mother Never Taught You*) or, more recently, to be nurturing and intuitive (*Feminine Leadership*).

Most executive women attempt to imitate men. In so doing, they relinquish some of life's most natural and important pleasures—self-expression and feeling proud and good about being female.

C H A P T E R

=VI=

ON THE JOB

Women tend to put on an unreal personality in the office.
I think women are trying so hard to be taken seriously that
they make life very difficult for themselves. They're afraid
that men will think they're kooky, silly, frivolous. Women
are so serious that most of the time they're dull. If you
have to be on guard and play a role, you're not going to
be happy at the office.

—LOIS KOREY,
president, Korey, Kay and Partners
advertising agency
("Life at the Top," *Vogue*, August 1983)

In this chapter we're going to look at our women's careers
from their start to the present. We'll learn how they rose to
executive positions and what their experiences, both positive
and negative, can teach women about success. First we'll examine how they began their careers and if and how they charted
out their paths. Second, we'll review who helped our women
in the early years—whether either of their parents guided them
or if they had role models or mentors.

In the third part of the chapter, we'll find out what behaviors
and skills led to their success and what weaknesses impeded
their growth. Then, because many people debate the pros and
cons of office romance, we'll find out if our women have had
office affairs and if these relationships helped or hindered them.
Finally, we'll learn how much our women's jobs mean to them
and which aspects of their jobs receive priority.

IN THE BEGINNING

When they were twenty-one, how much relative emphasis did our women place on establishing careers and on finding husbands? Since many of them were twenty-one in the late 1950s and early 1960s, when the home was considered a woman's proper sphere, their commitment to a career was impressive. Fifty percent said a career was "very important" to them, whereas only 40 percent found marriage as important. Many of our women, then, entered the business world as most men do—ready and eager to make their mark.

But in spite of the priority they gave to their professional lives, few thought seriously about the kind of work they wanted to do. A majority (73 percent) agreed they "just kind of fell into" their particular fields. A third said "a mentor who believed in [their] talents" gave them their start. Twenty-one percent cited "luck" as a major catalyst. Only 17 percent began their careers with goals in mind!

The women's ages (and, therefore, the social climate of the times) had no effect on the women's propensity to plan: The youngest group of women (age thirty to forty-five) also "fell" into their vocation. Nor did being nourished make a difference, because no generation of women had yet been raised to think they would choose to work for a living.

"I wound up as a financial analyst through a series of accidents," Katharine yawned. "I stayed in Boston after college and got a dead-end job as a secretary for a city planner. When I was twenty-five, a friend who worked for an investment firm told me of an opening for a research trainee. I applied and was hired and was lucky enough to have a boss who thought I was very smart. He pushed me to seek promotions. I wouldn't have budged if he hadn't pushed me so hard."

"Never in my wildest dreams did I think I'd be a businesswoman." Rose still sat curled in her satin armchair. "I majored in chemistry in graduate school because men had begun to notice me, and the chemistry department was full of men. I met my husband in a class and was married as soon as I got my M.S. Life as a housewife was boring, so I went to work. I became the secretary to the head of marketing for [a major chemical company]. My boss was impressed with my knowledge of chemistry, and with a lot of luck and hard work, I got to where I am today."

"My success is due to plain dumb luck." Annie's eyes twinkled merrily. "I got married after college and I had four terrific kids. I only went to work because my husband and I were strapped for cash. I met a fellow at a party who was a producer for a soap opera. He needed cheap labor, and I was desperate for a job. I was a very good production assistant, although I didn't even know what you called the work I did. Soon I was offered a better-paying job, and the rest is history." Annie pointed to a picture of her husband that stood by her vase of lilacs. "*He's* the one who encouraged me to take my work seriously. *He's* the one who's responsible for my success."

Laura knew what she wanted to do, but did nothing to speed the process along. "I wanted to be a writer and editor for a fancy woman's magazine. I came to New York after college because that's where the women's magazines were. I got a job as an editorial assistant for [a women's magazine] and worked my ass off. Finally they let me write a few features, and I slowly became a staff writer. I worked like a maniac and slowly got more responsibility. I used to get these teeny-weeny itty-bitty little raises. I was ambitious, but my career moved along at a snail's pace. I had no idea how to take the bull by the horns and plan my career path. If I had, I could have made it to where I am in half the time."

Sara is the only one of the six who set solid goals for herself. "I knew at college that I wanted to work with computers after graduation. The field was extremely new; this was way before the microchip. I graduated with high honors in mathematics, and [a major computer company] recruited me to work for them back East. I did think-tank work on the first models of computers, figuring out what programs corporations would need in the future. It was one of the most exciting times of my life. I was greedy to learn and I volunteered to help everyone who could teach me more. I learned very fast, and before I knew it, I was in way over my head: I was made head òf the think tank. I had people with Ph.D.'s in engineering reporting to me. It was sink or swim, and I've never swum so hard in my life."

"The success I've had in my field is a freak. I wanted to be a surgeon," Jennifer said. "I decided after Bryn Mawr to work and save money for medical school. I had minored in art in college, and I took a job in the art department at [her cosmetics company]. I learned how to do mock-ups for ads and how to use a darkroom. I liked learning, but the real reason I stayed is that the people who hired me *liked* me so much." Jennifer's stiff face broke into a smile. "For the first time in my life, I felt wanted and needed. They told me I was talented, and I put my fate in their hands."

Many of those interviewed sought the next step in their career because someone else—usually a boss or a husband—persuaded them to. The women's drive to achieve rarely originated from within. Just as when they were teenagers, they were working to win other people's respect.

Men, for the most part, begin their professional lives with distinct goals based on a knowledge of their fields. Our women's almost total lack of planning gave a strong advantage to the men with whom they would be competing for promotions and opportunities. This dramatic absence of control is a major reason why the women now find themselves working with men who are younger than they are.

MENTORS AND ROLE MODELS

Having a mentor has long been established as a factor behind success, and most ambitious men try to attach themselves to such a guide. The higher a person climbs, the less useful a mentor becomes, but in the early years, having a mentor is almost imperative. Mentors give a tremendous boost to a person's career, one that that person can't attain alone (Mary Cunningham's rise at Bendix was largely due to the patronage of William Agee). A senior person instructs a protégé on how to make intelligent career moves and also explains the corporation's hierarchical structure. In every company there are figureheads and people with real influence; a mentor teaches a subordinate which people are which and how to get closer to those in power. The association with a high-level person whom the company respects also gives a protégé a seal of approval that inclines management to take him or her seriously.

110

Our women's failure to plan a career started them out with a severe handicap, so having a mentor would have been extremely beneficial—but only every other woman (50 percent) had such a guide. In the majority of cases, the women's mentors were men; and with so few women in senior management, that fact comes as no surprise. Unfortunately, the dearth of women at the top inhibited our women from seeking mentors because they were uneasy about approaching men at high levels. Few of them, after all, were close to their fathers, nor had they learned to be comfortable with men in the teenage years. Women also tend to feel cowed before men in authority because, as they grew up, their doctors, police, and presidents were usually men.

"I was intimidated by the top men." Rose's eyes were wide with innocence. "People kept telling me, 'Find a rabbi!' I hadn't the slightest idea how. Was I supposed to make small talk in the hallways with the upper-level men? Why would those guys want to have anything to do with me?"

Making "small talk in the hallways" is not an effective way to establish a mentor relationship. A junior person must first excel so that her efforts are noticed by senior people. She can then volunteer to help her potential mentor on specific projects. A senior person sometimes initiates a relationship when he or she notices the quality of a person's work, but even in these cases, our women shied away.

"I didn't want anyone to see that I had shortcomings." Annie sat, Indian position, in her chair. "My husband was my only mentor when I started working, because I could admit to him that I wasn't sure of how to handle a tough problem. I didn't want to show my hand to anyone at work. A couple of the senior guys offered to help, but I didn't allow them to. I called my husband when I needed to discuss something."

Laura refused the support of a would-be mentor because she feared that the man expected sexual favors in return. "One high-level man offered to help me," she said wryly, "but he intimated that I turned him on. The bastard! I didn't want to be in a position where I had to compromise myself or face his vindictiveness when he discovered I wasn't going to put out. So I ignored him, and he concluded that I wanted him to leave me alone."

Laura's behavior in this situation was entirely correct. However, her fear that men would continue to take advantage of her prevented her from associating with someone who honestly wished to help her. "When other men were friendly, I was suspicious," she explained, "and so I avoided getting close with any of the senior guys."

What neither Laura nor Annie realized is that men build business relationships precisely by asking each other for help. Rose's low self-esteem was the major hindrance to her finding a "rabbi." She didn't understand that shrewd businesspeople always respond to the overtures of astute junior people. Being a mentor can be as important to one's career as having a mentor, as an example from my experience reveals.

Ten years ago I hired a man who had been working as a philosophy professor to fill an entry-level spot in the research department at J. Walter Thompson. Edwin was intelligent, ambitious, and very, very nice. He was also completely naive about the business world. Nevertheless, I took a chance on him, and my risk paid off handsomely. He was hardworking, eager to learn, and pleasant to be around. I promoted him within six months and, when he asked, gave him advice on how he could advance. In time my superiors realized he was a valuable asset. They offered him a good position in another department, which I encouraged him to take. When Edwin was later offered a high-level job at another company, I backed him in his decision to leave.

A few months ago Edwin rejoined JWT to head a new department, and today he is one of my staunchest supporters. He is the first to champion my ideas and offer his expertise on my projects. This *quid pro quo* system is at the heart of good business; yet our women radically underestimate the significance of mentor relationships. In a question that asked how much importance they attached to different aspects of their lives, "having a mentor" and "being a mentor" were two of the *lowest*-ranked!

Role models were even harder to come by for our women than mentors were. These professional people whom we admire or want to be like allow us to set realistic goals. They clarify the directions that we wish to take and give us a good idea of how to move in them, yet less than half our women (45 percent) had role models. Happily, the models were as likely to be women as men; still, that leaves less than one quarter of our women who patterned themselves after other women.

The first woman each female looks to in life is her mother. If we can incorporate elements of our mother into our "ideal self"—our mental picture of the person we want to be—we can also adopt positive aspects of other women. This "transference" signifies a healthy mother-daughter relationship, and the nourished women were therefore more likely than the undernourished women to have had female role models (30 percent versus 13 percent).

One problem many working women who seek female role models have to deal with (again, aside from the scarcity of women in high positions) is their own unwillingness to "split their egos," as Dr. Bernstein says. "A woman will generally not look to another woman solely on the basis of how she performs in her career," she explains. "She will regard the other's professional *and* personal life. If a woman 'wants it all,' she won't follow the example of a female colleague who is unmarried and childless; she'll try to find someone whose total life-style she can emulate."

Men can take for granted that the high-echelon corporate males they imitate will be married and be fathers too, but men also choose a variety of models for their different roles in life. A man might copy a famous baseball player's pitching style, a friend's mode of fathering, and a successful executive's business demeanor.

Men have the additional advantage of being able to grow up with a potential model at home. Casual observation shows that men often enter their father's profession. Almost none of our women were directly influenced by what either their father or their mother did for a living; only 4 percent followed their father's and 2 percent their mother's career. Most of those whose mother worked said their mother had seen her job as "just a job." Still, we can never underestimate the power of the mother-daughter bond. A solid skew (one third) of the women I interviewed entered or "fell into" careers their mothers had once wanted to be in themselves.

Laura, who said she "never felt much affection" for her mother, freely admitted her mother's part in her career decision. "My mother was an assistant editor for a book publisher before she married. I loved to read, so I thought that I might be an editor too, but my mother told me I'd never make any money in the book industry. She said, 'Go into magazines, that's where all the money is.' She said that if she were me, she would become a high-powered magazine editor. So," Laura grudgingly concluded, "I have to give her credit for my choice."

Jennifer's story was more representative of the rest of the skew. Before our interview, Jennifer—generally so astute—had never recognized her mother's role in her career decision. Premed in college, Jennifer was determined to be a surgeon. Before enrolling in medical school, she decided to get a job and save money. Today she is a vice president and art director for the company she started out with.

Earlier, Jennifer had told me her mother had been a graphic artist before marrying. Afterward, to comply with her husband's wishes that she be a woman of leisure, her mother painted and sketched only as a hobby. I asked Jennifer whether there was any connection between her mother's unfulfilled aspirations and the work she herself did. She was stunned by my suggestion. Slowly, her pale face turned bright pink. She took off her glasses and massaged her temples with the fingers of one hand. "You know," she said, "I never thought about the fact that my mother was a graphic artist. Part of the family lore was that she would have been very successful had she kept working. And here I am today, a hotshot art director." During the long pause that followed, Jennifer stared at her cactus plant. Finally she looked at me with a sheepish smile. "I just realized that what I'm doing is exactly what my mother wanted to do."

When my publisher offered me a contract, I called my mother to tell her the news. "Mother," I said excitedly, "I'm going to write a book!" When I began telling her the details of the deal, she broke into sobs. I was flabbergasted since she is not sentimental. Like anyone else, I don't like to hear my mother cry. "Why are you crying?" I asked anxiously. "Because," she wept, "I'm so happy for you. Writing a book was a great dream of mine, but the war and having you four children made it a pipe dream."

Although I had begun my interviewing and seen other women realize that they were living out their mothers' dreams, I had never thought that I might be doing the same thing. I still can't recall my mother ever saying she wanted to write a book.

THE TRAITS FOR SUCCESS

How, in the frequent absence of mentors and role models, did our women succeed? I asked them what behaviors (such as competitiveness or assertiveness) and what qualities (such as intelligence or creativity) they thought most important to their advancement. I posed this question for two reasons: first, to give readers an idea of what it takes to become an executive; second, to find out if the women were underemphasizing any qualities that are known to lead to business success.

The three characteristics considered most important by all the women were

1. Being concerned with results
2. Being intelligent
3. Being hardworking

That a concern for results is ranked number one is no surprise. In the high-stakes corporate game, you can't just talk, you have to deliver. As a senior manager, you have to show that your work contributes to the company's profits. Executives have stockholders to answer to and are held directly responsible for a company's failure or victory.

The need for intelligence (number two)—a discerning mind and a solid knowledge of one's field—is essential. Executives must make tough decisions quickly and often. They must also know their business inside out so that they can undertake only those projects that will reap rewards.

"Hardworking" seems a natural choice as the third major key to a woman's success. An executive career requires long hours; a lot of travel; business breakfasts, lunches, and dinners; and many nights and weekends spent poring over memos and reports. Earlier, Sara and Katharine described their typical workday. Now let's look at a day in Laura's life.

"I'm not a morning person." The beautiful editor sat on her wicker couch surrounded by mountains of paper. "I don't make it into the office until at least ten-thirty. By then, I have fifteen phone messages, and I ignore most of them. Five or six people are at my door clamoring to see me." Laura paused to sip coffee from a Styrofoam cup. "Yesterday, I found a staff writer near tears because of the comment I'd scribbled on her article-in-progress—it was a piece on nutrition, and I'd written, 'Where's the beef?'—a photographer with C-prints of the cover shot, an editor with a letter announcing a lawsuit for a story we ran that came down hard on those goddamned pro-life terrorists" (here Laura laughed) "and three or four others who needed my okay on copy or layouts. I use the *triage* method for dealing with the morning emergencies. The phone constantly, *constantly* rings. I have to take the calls from the guys at [the parent company] and from my best writers to hear their new story ideas. At noon I shoo everyone out and meet with my two secretaries. My office is by now in a state of utter chaos." Laura made a sweeping gesture around her messy office, and we both laughed.

"Then I'm hurtling out the door, late as usual, for my lunch date at the Four Seasons with some crackpot who claims to have discovered the secret of eternal youth or, if I'm very lucky, with Sam Shepard or Warren Beatty. I like to get my own questions in on the celebrity interviews; most writers don't have the guts to ask the tough, personal questions. The rest of the day I'm in and out of meetings, trying not to scream too much. At seven I'm working the room at a book publication party or an art opening, and at nine I'm in a restaurant brainstorming with a writer or two. By eleven or twelve I'm home, too keyed up to go to bed. I skim the day's mail—I subscribe to fifty magazines and ten newspapers. I dictate letters and memos and scribble down new story ideas. I never go to bed until two or three in the morning."

The next seven attributes that a majority of the women found important to their advancement were, in order:

4. Well-disciplined
5. Smart
6. Concerned with people
7. Even-tempered
8. Assertive

9. Loyal
10. Talented

The fact that "well-disciplined" (number four) follows so closely after "hardworking" is to be expected: An executive has immense responsibilities and can't get sidetracked when trying to live up to them. Being well-disciplined means doing the hardest tasks first and the easiest ones last and never giving in to the temptation to stay home when one is very tired.

"I'm the head of the marketing department, and that means I have to be constantly 'on,'" said Rose. "When my chemical company creates a new drug, I have to present it to the press and project energy and confidence no matter how late I stayed up the night before overseeing the printing of the press release. I have to force myself to be upbeat through days of travel and back-to-back meetings. Being truly disciplined is never saying die."

Discipline also means ordering one's priorities and adhering to a timetable; spending only an hour on an important memo because other tasks need attending to. An executive who moves from one crisis to another, as we've seen Laura do, lacks that element of discipline.

Besides having to be judicious with her time, a woman with high career hopes must also be very "smart" (number five). When we in business call someone smart, we mean that that person has good gut instincts, that she can react quickly and shrewdly to a challenging business problem. A smart marketing manager, for example, anticipates how a competitor will market a product and then institutes a campaign of her own that outstrips the competition's promises and claims.

As smart, intelligent, and hardworking as she may be, no corporate manager gets anywhere unless she can relate well to her co-workers and they to her. An executive spends as much as three quarters of her time in interpersonal relations and *must* be "concerned with people" (number six). She must first of all be aware of the delicate balance between the need to maximize her productivity and the necessity of maintaining good relations with her staff. Not working one's people hard enough is not wise management, nor is asking so much from them that unhappiness or dissension ensues, as Marie Luisi appears to have done.

The importance of how well a manager communicates with colleagues becomes clear when one considers the forms on which a company evaluates its managers in their annual performance reviews. The forms are similar regardless of the company, and easily half the standards by which executives are judged are people-related. These criteria include the abilities to motivate, instill respect in and delegate to subordinates, promote team-work within a staff and among a group of peers, listen to clients and establish rapport with them, and take direction from and respond to the criticism of superiors.

Concern for people also means showing that one cares—that one has empathy for co-workers' problems, can inject humor into the office environment, and can express appreciation and warmth to helpful staff and peers. Since our women rarely let themselves loosen up or display affection, we must raise a question as to how concerned with people they actually are.

The next trait was "even-tempered" (number seven), and I fully expected to see it as high on the list as it appears. Everyone in a high-level job suffers painful disappointments: Proposals are rejected, work is lambasted, and budgets are suddenly slashed. No executive can help but show some frustration, but men are taught to hide their emotions (the phrase "act like a man" *means* "don't be emotional"). Women are given more rein to vent feelings and therefore have more trouble suppressing them. Every woman I know has had to deal with the fear or actual embarrassment of bursting into tears during a tough confrontation at work. And, as many of us are aware from our personal relationships, men don't deal well with crying women.

A male peer told me how much he dreads criticizing a female staff member. "We've worked together for years, and she still cries when I find fault with her work," he said unhappily. "Maybe that's just the way she expresses frustration," I suggested. "Oh, no it isn't!" he replied. "Women use tears to manipulate men, to make us feel guilty!" This man likes women, but is angered and confused by tears—to the point where he won't further promote that particular woman. Our women understand the importance of keeping cool, but since only half said they were even-tempered, controlling their feelings is clearly a problem for a number of them.

The importance of the next trait—"assertiveness" (number eight)—can't be stressed enough. A corporate executive's most precious commodity is time; she can't afford to hedge or mince her words. Being clear and direct when she expresses herself to bosses, staff, and peers is essential. However, half our women told us they weren't assertive. Later, we'll consider the problems a lack of even-temperedness or assertiveness can create.

Right behind the need for assertiveness comes the importance of "loyalty" (number nine), a quality the women strongly ascribe to themselves. Loyalty is a wonderful attribute, but I have no doubt that our women, and most women, overrate its importance to their careers. Men remain devoted to people and corporations for as long as their allegiance is rewarded. Women remain faithful long after such bonds have ceased to offer them a chance for growth; they stay tied to bosses who "need" them and stuck in dead-end jobs.

Women's constancy derives from their social history as well as their psychology. Women's social roles were once wholly relationship-oriented; women were daughters, mothers, and wives. And because most women were dependent on husbands for financial security, loyalty was necessary to their very survival.

"I was blindly loyal to my first boss in movie development." Annie spoke with her typical candor and speed. "I went out of my way to do things for Joyce that I'd never do for a boss today. She was a lonely woman, and I had her over to dinner all the time. In the office, she was an impulsive decision maker, yet I rarely questioned her judgment, even if it meant too much work for me. If someone said a word against her, I became furious. I feel very uneasy about how I acted in that relationship."

Many women are faithful to others at far greater cost to themselves—so many, in fact, that the theme recurs throughout music and literature. Billie Holiday, in "My Man," sang that she would love her man in spite of his beating her and cheating on her. The character Julie Jordan, in the musical *Carousel*, sings "What's the Use of Wondrin' " if her husband is any good or not, since she's doomed to love him either way (meanwhile, he plots a robbery). In the musical *Oliver!* the character Nancy—

in "As Long As He Needs Me"—sings that she'll stay with her thieving lover no matter what (he kills her at the end of the play).

Self-destructive fidelity "always correlates with problems separating from the mother," Dr. Bernstein believes. "Women who are overly loyal act toward others in the same way they felt they had to behave with their mother. Their fear of abandonment keeps them from breaking free of a harmful relationship."

Katharine's career was badly hurt by her inflated belief in loyalty. It's relevant to remember how, even when Katharine could barely contain her anger toward her mother, she was compelled to enumerate all her good points.

"I once worked for a woman named Donna whom I absolutely adored. When I was thirty-one, I moved from Boston to Chicago, and she hired me to assist her in the research department of a brokerage firm. She taught me everything she knew and took me along on all her business lunches and dinners. She was a terrific person, a kind person, and we loved each other. Then the political climate grew ugly; top management wanted her out. They gave her impossible assignments and criticized her for not accomplishing them. It was a terrible time." Katharine fidgeted with the barrette that held her hair back. "Eventually, I realized that Donna made mistakes in her work, and in financial research, mistakes are the kiss of death. I knew I should find a new job, but I just couldn't seem to leave Donna. Finally, I was approached by someone in management who told me—confidentially—that she was being fired but that I could stay on if I chose to." Katharine drew in a labored breath. "Instead of saving my neck, I told Donna what the man had said. She made a terrible scene, and we were both fired. I hurt my reputation and spent a year on unemployment."

The last item on the list of important traits was "talented" (number ten). The women are saying that while having a "born" gift (such as a good head for figures) can help you in business, it's not as important as basic intelligence or the ability to bring in revenue. Still, there were more women who rated "talent" as being important than said that they considered themselves talented—further evidence of their insecurities in this area.

The next three qualities, the women tell us, are only moderately important:

11. Competitive
12. Well-read
13. Well-educated

Despite what they say, a competitive attitude (number eleven) is vital in business. How well a company leads the competition with its superior service or innovative product differences will directly determine its success. Every business plan, be it the decision to create a new personal computer or the commitment to publish a new Italian cookbook, is carried out only after an analysis of what's "out there."

Personal success calls for the same analytical thinking. How are we delivering as compared with those we consider our rivals? What are our relative strengths and how can we maximize them? What are our relative weaknesses, and how can we strengthen or compensate for them? All people in corporate careers are judged not only for their own performance, but vis-à-vis a group of peers.

Our women may be more competitive than they admit, for this adjective carries a "bitchy" connotation when applied to women. Another reason women underestimate the importance of competitive behavior is that they aren't socialized to compete. Much has been written about the fact that men are more comfortable with rivalry because they grew up engaging in friendly competition. Boys play aggressive games and team sports that teach them to gauge their strengths and shore up their weaknesses. More significant, boys *enjoy* pitting their abilities against one another. "Without the motivation of showing his friends and rivals how much he's improved his physical skills, it's a rare boy who would willingly spend hours practicing how to throw or catch a ball," observes Betty Lehan Harragan in *Games Mother Never Taught You*. "In the male culture, competition is the reward. Competition is the fun. Competition is what makes it all worthwhile."

Both nourished and undernourished women are often ignorant about how to compete at work. "I grew up skiing in the Berkshires and then windsurfing in California," Sara said. "Maybe because I never played *team* sports, I never learned to be competitive in the way my brother learned. For a long time I had no idea of what my assets and liabilities were. Was I better as a technician or as an idea person? It never occurred to me to figure it out."

Katharine resents the idea that a competitive attitude is required in the corporate world. "I don't understand why you can't just rest on your laurels awhile," she complained. "If you do good work, you should be promoted; then you should have a rest period where you can just do your job before you have to start proving you're ready for the next promotion. I can't warm to the fight; the mere thought of it makes me tired."

Katharine's low self-esteem also prevents her from competing effectively because she can't realistically weigh her positive and negative qualities. She overemphasizes her weaknesses—and then, to console herself, overrates her strengths. "I'm an excellent financial analyst," she stated imperiously. "I have come to realize that I'm smarter than most of the people I work with, but I'm a terrible manager. I can't get along with people at all. Also, I'm fat, and people don't like fat people."

Women whose mothers projected feelings onto them have additional problems being competitive, because this behavior carries a powerful taboo. "A narcissistic mother doesn't want her daughter to fail, but neither does she want her daughter to outdo her," Dr. Bernstein explains. "This mother's self-esteem is too low to handle her daughter's being prettier or smarter. Her praise for her daughter will always be tainted with spoken or implied reservations. The daughter of the narcissistic mother learns to tread a very fine line. She learns to perform, but she also learns that she can't be better than her mother. Unconsciously, she will always fear that the price she pays for winning something for herself is the loss of approval and love."

After only a few years in her art department, Jennifer was made an art director and awarded a vice presidency. "That's very unusual for such a short time," I remarked. "How did you react?"

"I never really thought about the fact that I had been recognized. I was glad that everyone liked me," the proper-looking woman said. In time, she realized that the other art directors were surpassing her. "They were becoming senior vice presidents and being voted onto the management committee. I should have been blowing my horn and asking for raises all along, but

I'm not the type to strut her stuff, probably because my mother always put me in my place. When we painted together, she had to show that she was the better artist. If my father paid attention to me, I would see daggers in her eyes. She needed to have all the attention all of the time. I always shrank back and let her hold center stage."

Two other characteristics our women said were of some significance to their careers were being "well-read" (number twelve) and being "well-educated" (number thirteen). Being well-read is indeed only moderately important, for while having a breadth of knowledge can be helpful, it isn't as essential as being smart and concerned with results. But because our women feel they became executives in spite of their inferior schooling, they don't give the role of education its due. In truth, their educations were by no means inferior—and the best-educated women among them are the most successful. Those with graduate degrees make nearly twice the salaries of those with only high school diplomas.

Next came eight traits that our women found of only minor importance. These characteristics add humanity and flair to a business personality:

14. Outgoing
15. Accessible
16. Happy
17. Thoughtful
18. Humorous
19. Creative
20. Cheerful
21. Likable

Let's think for a moment about how these terms apply to a manager. A "thoughtful" boss brings a secretary champagne when the secretary has worked late five nights in a row. She may, as Sara does, keep a record of her staff members' birthdates and give each a birthday card with a special, handwritten note on it. A thoughtful boss notices when one of her staff is in trouble with a project; if she is "accessible," she steps in and offers encouragement and advice. She is the person colleagues gravitate toward when they need to talk over thorny business problems.

Being "happy," "outgoing," "cheerful," "humorous," and "likable" make a manager nice to be around. Subordinates are inclined to work hard for her, peers to do her favors, and superiors to want her as part of their team. A "creative" manager, in my opinion, is the best manager there is. She can easily inspire a staff and solve complex business problems in original ways. Nevertheless, our women believe that being personable is not nearly so important as being doggedly hardworking.

They are wrong! We have already seen evidence of how our women isolate themselves by not having or being mentors. By downplaying the need to relate to colleagues on a human level, they sharply limit their chances to form close business friendships with anyone. Many of these former bookworms never learned basic social skills, and another factor compounds their tendency to withdraw: Since they are often the only women in their peer group, they feel self-conscious and curb their spontaneity. But the best managers are better at relating to people than at doing specific tasks. A person who works extremely hard but can't build strong allies will be able to rise to a certain level but will eventually reach a plateau. All CEOs were buoyed to the top by the strong support of staff, superiors, and peers. Predictably, the nourished women placed much stronger emphasis than the undernourished ones on the group of traits we just reviewed.

Now our women told us that three attributes were of little importance to their careers:

22. Well-connected
23. Aggressive
24. Demanding

In ranking "well-connected" (number twenty-two) so low, they are saying that, unlike men, they can't rely on an old-boys' network. But their lack of faith in connections is also linked to their philosophy that friendship (apart from loyalty to bosses) has no place in the business world.

Although our women don't want to be seen as feminine, they

don't think being "aggressive" (number twenty-three) can help them advance. Many of those I interviewed saw the word in a derogatory light. "Being pushy and ruthless is counter-productive," Rose said. However, aggressive need not mean being pushy. It can also mean being bold or daring to take the initiative, and such courage is essential to an outstanding performance in business.

Jeanette Kahn, the publisher of DC Comics, is known for her bright, feminine clothing, her openness and warmth—and her aggressiveness. When she took the reins at DC, the famous comic book company was in the red. To give the artists and writers who were the life's blood of the company proper incentive, Kahn initiated the first royalty program in the history of the industry, paying the creative people a share of the magazine sales. She also established the first marketing department in the comic book trade. By bringing DC into the black, Kahn is an example of how femininity and aggressiveness can healthily coexist in a woman.

If being bold in business is anathema to most of our women, being demanding (number twenty-four) ranks a notch lower. A demanding woman, to many minds, is a shrew or a nag rather than someone who's unafraid to lay claim to what's due her. But our executive women are very demanding of themselves. Don't they therefore have the right to ask a lot from the people they work with and for? We find this demanding quality admirable in successful men; shouldn't it be equally praiseworthy in women?

Next we come to a list of traits the women considered of almost no importance:

25. Empathetic
26. Warm
27. Generous
28. Giving
29. Nurturing
30. Affectionate

This belief that tender, traditionally "feminine" qualities can't contribute to our advancement is *the biggest mistake* we make.

We are raised to be sensitive and intuitive. Following our natural inclinations can give us an enormous competitive edge over men. Showing that she genuinely cares about her co-workers can enable an executive to gain greater productivity from her staff and to create a better working environment for all. A nurturing woman can build strong allies and be a topnotch mentor and team player. Women's repression of their warmth and receptiveness not only alienates them from others but prevents them from exploiting some of the most potent assets they could bring to their careers.

Finally, the traits the women felt were of least importance to their success were

31. Attractive
32. Sexy
33. Feminine

Yet doesn't feeling proud of her appearance give a woman self-confidence? And doesn't feeling good about being a woman do the same thing? Only 4 percent of the women told us that being "feminine" helped a woman get ahead! Later in the survey, 27 percent—almost seven times as many—said that "being masculine" aided a man in his ascent. Yet again, we see the extraordinarily pejorative meanings that executive women attach to the word *feminine*.

"Generations of women have done it before us. Generations of ethnic minorities have changed language, style of dress, and manner of expression to get into that exclusionary society of power and privilege," Kim Chernin writes. "Women are the new immigrants crossing the border from an old world. And meanwhile, as we make ourselves over into men, we are busily stripping ourselves of everything we have traditionally been as women."

CAREER OBSTACLES

We know what aspects of their personalities our women see as their professional strengths, for the traits they deemed most important to success are those they say they possess themselves.

But did other of their behaviors *hinder* their forward motion? The women's answers to that question come as no surprise.

Nearly two thirds (63 percent) told us that "not being assertive enough" had been a major obstacle to their growth. Women's difficulties with assertiveness have achieved wide recognition in the last decade. Their inhibitions about speaking their minds without temporizing or apologizing are a hangover from a long history of playing second fiddle to men. Traditionally, a husband ruled the roost and a wife deferred to him. Because an adult woman's role required that she be a "helpmate" and nurturer, women haven't been socialized to give clear voice to their own desires.

Virtually every woman I interviewed spoke of her difficulty —or even inability—to assert her need for a raise. The most striking example comes from Annie's experience. Annie is not a person one would guess had trouble asking for what she felt she deserved. As one of a handful of top women in network television, she works with million-dollar budgets and takes great risks with her movie ideas; she also usually says exactly what's on her mind. I asked her what she considered her greatest professional strength. "Creative people feel comfortable with me, and so I attract talent," the slender woman volunteered. "Some writers and directors are very sensitive people. I'm myself and I guess my manner puts people at ease. People seem to open up to me. I never consider acting any way, I just am who I am."

Although Annie is straightforward in many ways, witness what happened the last time this powerful executive asked for a raise. Some years ago, she was hired as a producer for a sitcom and told that after a year went by, she'd have a salary review. "And the date came and went," she told me, "and nobody said anything."

"Did you remind them of their promise?" I asked.

"I did," said Annie with uncharacteristic hesitancy, "but it took me two months to screw up the courage. When I finally decided to, I got laryngitis. Asking for that raise was very, very hard for me. Finally I dragged myself into my boss's office and croaked out a few words. He said, 'You know, you're right. You are up for a raise. How about if we give you such and such?'

The whole ordeal took one minute! I looked at my boss and said, 'You mean, I can get my voice back now?' I realized then that asking for money was a big problem for me, and now I have an agent negotiate my contracts."

The undernourished women's low self-esteem exacerbates their problems with assertiveness. Jennifer went to her art department's weekly meetings for a year without uttering a word. "I didn't dare speak up," the platinum-blonde explained. "I was convinced I'd say something stupid. My boss finally forced me to contribute my two cents. The first few times I did, I broke out in a drenching sweat."

Rose has difficulty making demands of her staff. "I want them to like me, so I don't push them as hard as I should. At one point, if a staff member wrote a press release that needed rewriting, I'd do it myself rather than tell that person to. Now I'm much better at giving direction, but I still often slip and say, 'I'm sorry, Maureen, but could you . . . ?' "

A serious problem shared by many of the undernourished women was their inability to put a foot down when bosses made unreasonable requests. "Daughters whose mothers were controlling have terrible problems saying no," Dr. Bernstein states. "Women are generally taught to be 'nice' and are discouraged from displaying anger. If their mothers never let them have their way, a wall of rage often builds within. Such women are usually acutely unconscious of their inner anger. For them, assertiveness is contaminated by the threat of what will be unleashed if they stick up for themselves. Rage is a physical reaction, a wanting to hurt someone. In our unconsciousness, the way to deal with an overwhelming mother is by murdering her.

"I have had passive women in analysis," Dr. Bernstein continues, "who were able to tell me the fantasies they had about what they would say or do to anyone who threatened their well-being. These fantasies indicated a very limited ability to assert themselves because they could never say merely, 'I can't help you with that,' but always something like, 'Drop dead.' In real situations, they therefore said nothing at all."

"I was a good girl all my life," Katharine sighed. "I always did what my teachers and my mother told me to. The problem is, since men are taught to delegate to the best workers, all the top men delegate to me. That's why I work so damn hard. I'm afraid to say, 'No, I'm not able to do that' or 'I can do it, but I can't have it ready until next week.' I'm a terrible sucker; I feel guilty saying no. And then I get so overworked I explode."

Katharine doesn't feel she has the right to oppose or even negotiate her superiors' demands, yet every employee must exercise these privileges to avoid being overwhelmed.

Obviously, the inability to say no to a boss can affect a person's private life. Rose and I sat now before a fire her husband had come in and built and drank tea from delicate bone china cups. "When my two children were young, I was the associate marketing director at my company," she explained. "My baby-sitter could stay until seven or eight at night, but for two months she needed to leave at six o'clock. My husband often worked nights, so I had to relieve her. When I told my boss I had to leave at five-thirty, I immediately qualified the statement. I said, 'Of course, if you *really* need me, I'll stay. You guessed it." Rose smiled helplessly. "He *really* needed me almost every night. Soon, the baby-sitter told me she'd quit if I was late again. I got hysterical and blew up at my boss. He said, 'Why didn't you tell me what a bind you were in? I insist you go home at five-thirty each night.' "

The inability to assert themselves at the right time caused many of the women to store up resentment that—as we'll see —often snowballed into a destructive force.

Another major barrier to these women's growth was a profound "lack of confidence" (60 percent). All the women I interviewed had developed insecurities from being one of few women, or the only woman, in a large peer group of men. When Annie was hired into the movie-development department of her TV network, she was one of only two women above the secretarial level. "At first, that made me so nervous I stayed in my office more than I should have," she explained. "I only gradually became friendly with my male colleagues and as a result I wasn't taken seriously for a while."

"There were almost no women in computers when I entered the field," Sara said. "I almost never had a woman as a yardstick to measure myself by. I felt like a stranger in a strange land. I couldn't always look to men to see if what I was doing was right.

I ran meetings differently than they did and I managed differently. And, after a while," Sara said in a deadpan manner, "I dressed differently too. It took a long time for me to feel confident about my performance."

The undernourished women's insecurities were severe. "I didn't trust my opinion on the best way to tackle a job," admitted Jennifer. "I'd have an idea on how to package a new mascara, but instead of running with it, I'd ask the men I worked with for their comments first. Sometimes, their reactions would cause me to junk an excellent idea." Jennifer frowned and gripped the sides of her director's chair. "Once we introduced a line of lipsticks inspired by the colors of tropical fruits, and I wanted to photograph our models in a rain forest I had been to. It was an intoxicating place, and the ads would have been spectacular, but the men's feedback was negative. I still get upset when I think about the ideas that I just threw away."

Many of the undernourished women spent inordinate amounts of time on their work. "I've never been able to keep a secretary long," Jennifer said, "and I only recently understood why. It took days to get a memo out, and I thought it was the secretary's fault. It was mine. I made so many changes it took five days for a page to leave my office. I changed whole paragraphs and then changed the changes. Since I held everything up, my secretaries lost momentum and assumed that nothing was urgent. They figured they'd have to retype what they showed me, so the letters and memos they gave me to sign were full of typos. I'm quite conscious now of my insecurities. I have to be; I can't deal with orienting a new secretary every six months."

"After twenty years in the business, I still rehearse over and over and over the marketing-strategy presentations I give to the president." Rose opened her hands in a gesture of appeal. "Also, I can't let a press release or a piece of ad copy alone. I write and rewrite, edit and reedit until the last second it's due at the printer's. If I could let go of things, I'd be a lot more productive."

The next hurdle the women cited was "not being able to control their emotions" (40 percent). Each woman I interviewed told at least one story about breaking into tears over a boss's reprimand or a seemingly unresolvable dilemma at work. The undernourished women had the greatest difficulties remaining composed. "I have yet to get through a performance evaluation without crying," Rose confessed. "Here I am, tops in my profession, and when I'm reviewed by senior management, I fall apart. Every year I tell myself that they'll inevitably find some areas for improvement. But you try so hard, you know? After all your hard work, it doesn't seem fair to be criticized." Rose's soulful eyes begged me to understand.'

Rose sought all her life to win her mother's approval—to no avail. Little wonder she has such a need for acceptance and such a problem handling criticism. Yet to be an effective member of a business team, one must be able to view superiors' criticism as constructive, as an opportunity for learning and—above all—as impersonal.

Other undernourished women spoke of reacting to upsets at work with rage. Before we examine the example of Laura, let's put her work into perspective by reviewing her formidable professional strengths. Laura—in spite of her frenetic manner —is one of the most brilliant talents in the magazine industry. Her nose for a hot story, knack for inventing catchy headlines, and eye for a sensational photograph make hers a best-selling women's magazine. By her own admission, however, her "greatest professional weakness" is her bad temper. "I'm impatient," she explained, "because I expect people to deliver their best. Most people don't tackle a job with one hundred percent of themselves. Most people compromise. My staff editors and the printers and photographers I deal with often want to quit working when the job they've done is only half-assed. And sometimes I go bananas. I scream and yell and alienate everyone. I did it just the other day." Laura leapt up from her wicker chair and headed to her desk for a cigarette. "The printer had nearly cut off the head of a model in a fashion layout. He said he didn't have the press time to reprint before my deadline. I began screaming, 'I don't publish pictures of headless women in my magazine! I don't publish pictures of headless women in my magazine!' After he left my office, I found myself shaking with rage. I could hear that stupid phrase I'd repeated ringing in my ears. Finally I said to myself, 'Lady, you went overboard again.' "

At this point, it's worth remembering that, in the basic business of being a mother, Laura's mother didn't come through. She reneged on her most basic responsibility: protecting a helpless child from harm.

"Fathers who beat their daughters usually have the mothers' tacit approval," Dr. Bernstein finds, "or else the mother is too feeble or dependent to interfere. Their daughters harbor feelings of anger and betrayal throughout their lives."

Today, Laura can't tolerate people who she feels have let her down. One touch from a potential traitor, and her inner dam of fury bursts. Rather than finding an effective way of eliciting quality work from her colleagues, she, in her own words, screams and yells and alienates everyone. Thus, she not only sees her co-workers as betraying her the way her mother did, she also reacts to them in the way her mother might have. That she earlier used her depiction of herself to describe her mother is no coincidence ("She was always screaming and yelling about how much she hated every minute of her life").

Katharine also has a problem controlling her temper. "I get mad and mouth off all the time," the financial analyst said. "The man I report to doesn't manage well, and as a result, I'm often besieged by last-minute requests. I can't tell you the number of times I've had to cancel plans because he suddenly needs a report 'tomorrow.' Then, the next day, he doesn't even look at my work.

"The other night, I blew up when he asked me to stay late to finish a report for him. I had worked late the previous two nights and I needed to get home. So here's what I mean by my mouthing off. I said, 'Do you want to know what my problem is with staying in the office tonight? I have three Pekingese, and if I don't get home and walk them soon, they're going to pee all over my rugs.' "

As our interview progressed, Katharine seemed to find it less of a chore, probably because she realized I enjoyed her company. She frequently made me laugh with her tales of impertinent behavior, but her words to her boss were clearly off-the-wall. Rather than try to work out her problems with him, she let her frustration build until she reacted unprofessionally and with a disproportionate anger, while the real source of her fury went unacknowledged.

"In a boss, I need someone who always knows what I'm working on and who cares about the work I do," she explained. "My present boss doesn't know and he doesn't care. All that matters to him is how soon I can get the work done. Getting work done on time is not my forte. I'm a very good financial analyst but I need to take my time. He's the worst boss I've ever had."

Katharine wants the same special consideration and warmth from her employer that she wanted from her mother. When her boss asks that she set and meet deadlines, these reasonable requests are greeted by anger.

Katharine's behavior also imitates her mother's. She thinks of her job as a "pain in the butt," just as her mother felt that her life as a housewife was a thankless task.

Lastly, our women warn that having an office affair can damage a woman's career. The subject of office affairs is meaningful to people who spend the greatest part of their lives at work and have little opportunity to meet romantic partners elsewhere. These relationships also have a tempting excitement all their own, because working alongside a lover can be an adventure.

About a third of the women surveyed confessed to having had one or more office affairs, the married women being the least likely to have indulged. Almost all of the women who had affairs dallied with men at higher levels. And, to my great surprise, the women said that the affairs had had no effect on their careers. Why, then, did nearly all of them (93 percent) advise women to steer clear of office affairs? And why did over half (55 percent) agree that "women always suffer more than men do in these situations"? Because office trysts present the *potential* for serious danger to women's careers.

Recently the *Harvard Business Review* received a flood of publicity for its article "Managers and Lovers" (September/October 1983). The normally staid periodical felt so strongly that managerial women should be warned of the hazards of office affairs that it took a stand on the issue. Author Eliza G. C. Collins argued that "love between managers is dangerous because it challenges—and can break down—the organizational structure." Romance between executives upsets a company's internal balance of power by tying two top people together in an intimate way. Collins advised chief executive officers to "deal with the romance as they would any business problem." The CEO should "persuade the couple that either the person less essential to the company or both have to go." And here's the rub: Since most women have affairs with superiors, the women are fired. The obvious example of how even the rumors of an affair can ruin an executive woman's career is the story of Mary Cunningham and William Agee. Bendix's board of directors gave Mary the option of resigning or being fired. Agee's job, of course, was never in jeopardy.

Most of the women I interviewed who had office affairs were very discreet, which explains why their relationships didn't overtly harm them. Nevertheless, all found that the affairs had been destructive. "At first, being lovers and working together was thrilling," Sara said of her romance with the former head of the marketing department at her computer company. "We were convinced that we were more productive since getting involved, but the more involved we got, the less productive we became. Whenever we fought, facing each other at work was a huge ordeal. Finally—thank God!—he left the company. He did so after a breakfast meeting in which he shot down one of my ideas. I wanted to create a series of video games for girls, because all the existing games appealed to boys. I said that girls needed tools to help them develop their hand-eye coordination. Since I have a daughter, the project meant a lot to me. My lover knew that, but was mad at me for some reason and denounced the idea as unmarketable. I was so furious I threw a Danish pastry in his face!" Sara guffawed. "That action was the most unprofessional thing I've ever done. I knew at that point that either the affair or the working relationship had to end."

From age twenty-six to thirty-one, Katharine dated, traveled with, and slept with her boss, the head of the research department at the Boston investment firm she began with. He was the man who pushed her to take her career seriously, but he was also married and a father. "When you're working that closely and sharing the excitement of an affair, life can be exhilarating. He's the only man who ever made me feel beautiful, and I wrapped my entire life around him. But he could never seem to ask for a divorce. Typical! First, he was going to tell his wife after their vacation one year. Then he thought it best to wait until his son graduated from high school. You may laugh"—

Katharine looked at me as if to say, "Please don't"—"but I believed his promises for five years.

"Finally I left him, left the job, fled the state. I came home to Illinois and lived with my mother for a while. I never breathed a word of what was going on to her; she never would have understood. I moved to Chicago, and Donna hired me, and I was just starting to feel okay. Then one of my friends called and told me that he'd had a heart attack. I flew to Boston and booked a room in a hotel by the hospital. I could only go to scc him when I knew his wife and kids weren't there. After five years, I had to be furtive at a time like that. It was agony." Katharine's pretty hazel eyes filled with tears.

CAREER PRIORITIES

To confirm the trends that were emerging from my data, I asked the women I polled how much emphasis they attached to different parts of their lives. The majority rated the following aspects as "very important":

1. "Doing the job as best I can" (80 percent)
2. "Being the best that I can be" (77 percent)

"Having enough time for family activities" (36 percent) and "developing close personal friendships" (13 percent) ranked far below!

A 1983 study by the American Management Association (AMA) corroborates these responses. The AMA polled male and female executives and found that 60 percent of the women got "the most satisfaction in life" from their jobs, as opposed to just 37 percent of the men. Nearly twice as many men (48 percent) as women (28 percent) said that their hearts were with their "family and home lives." Of course, since nearly all executive men are married and fathers, they *have* more "family and home life" than women executives do. But another reason for the discrepancies is the women's lopsided focus on their careers.

When we look at the priorities our women stress in their jobs, their lack of sociability becomes glaringly obvious. Top billing was given to their solo performances (doing and being the best they could). Much less importance was placed on their work relationships. Only half said "knowing who is in power" (47 percent) was important to them. Less than half placed priority on "understanding the needs of colleagues" (44 percent) or "being part of a business team" (44 percent). The lowest-ranked priorities were one-on-one work friendships—"developing close business friendships" (11 percent), "having a mentor" (10 percent), and "being a mentor" (10 percent).

Our women also don't stress the "classic" success priorities: goal setting, risk taking, and visibility. Only 37 percent made a habit of setting goals, although having both short- and long-term aims is the only way to get exactly what one wants from a career. As an example, a corporate vice president might decide that within five years she wants to be a senior vice president, to make enough money to pay off her mortgage, and to publish an article in *Business Week*. She can then try to be seen by and known to the people on the board of directors, indicate to her boss that she hopes for a promotion, take on new responsibilities, demand salary increases, and make the time to write an article.

Gloria Steinem has observed that women's problems with career planning stem from their never having had any power. Financially dependent on husbands, women enjoyed neither the means nor the license to map out their own futures.

Laura learned the hard way to set objectives: She stayed too long in the position of staff writer at a women's magazine. "Men ran the place," the black-haired editor said disdainfully. "They didn't want me to advance, because I was useful to them as a writer. They told me I was the best writer they had; they said they needed me in that job. Finally I said, 'This is bullshit! I'm going nowhere.' That's when I became a barracuda. I gave myself two years to become the senior staff writer. I figured out what I needed to do to get promoted. I was helpful to the other writers, I wrote better articles than they did, and I bombarded my bosses with story ideas. I began asking for raises and stipulating the exact amounts. Within a little over a year I was the senior staff writer."

"Taking risks," our women said, is not a high priority (39 percent), nor is "taking a stand" (29 percent) on a controversial issue or project. But taking chances is *essential* to a successful career. The adage "nothing ventured, nothing gained" is nowhere truer than in business.

Women hesitate to gamble their security because they are raised to be emotionally dependent on mothers and financially dependent on men. One risk most of our women have avoided is switching companies: A startling 60 percent have worked for their present employers for over ten years. All senior managers know that major financial gains are made by changing companies; in business jargon a classic route to the top is called zigzagging (rapidly switching companies).

Other career risks are: backing unpopular projects, taking high-risk/high-reward assignments, and accepting a job one doesn't quite feel ready for. Katharine was once offered the challenge of an undefined position. "A few years ago I was seriously considered for a job as a strategic planner for a brokerage firm," she told me. "I tried to force the CEO to pinpoint my duties, but he wanted a creative planner; he wanted the job open-ended. At the time, I was afraid of the responsibility, but now I could kick myself. I could be making twice the money I do."

A high profile is important in business, but only 37 percent of our women make "being visible" a priority. Business socializing is one way to be seen, as is staying abreast of all upcoming meetings and planning which of them to attend. In my experience, women wait to be invited to join meetings rather than assuming that they are welcome to do so.

Visibility in one's field at large is a key component to success, but our women don't participate in professional conferences and business travel nearly as much as they should: They spend an average of only thirty-three days a year out of town. Korn/Ferry's men travel an average of fifty-two days a year. Because these men are at higher levels than our women (more are senior vice presidents), they are undoubtedly required to travel more, but the difference between them and our women is still far too great.

Why don't our women make more of an effort to be in the public eye? The answer is that while they want more money and the authority to do the best job they can, they aren't very interested in being VIPs. Just four in ten want to "be a leader" in their company (38 percent) or to "be prominent" in their field (41 percent). Many more put high priority—again—on "being independent" (60 percent).

The nourished women give more weight than the under-nourished women do to both their personal and their professional relationships. And because their confidence allows them to dream bigger dreams, they show greater interest in achieving eminence in their company and field. The nourished women also try to take more risks. Annie's and Sara's experiences show how handsomely business gambles can pay off.

When I interviewed Annie, she had just bought the TV rights to a very provocative book—"on the surface, a prime-time disaster," she explained with a laugh. "The plot involves homosexuality and rape, but the book is extraordinary. I hounded my bosses until they gave me the green light to buy it. I know this project is going to fly." (It turned out to be extremely successful.)

"I recently published an article on a touchy issue in my field that brought me national recognition," Sara said. "Right now, just about anyone with decent computer equipment can get access to your bank records and credit card bills. The question is, Has the computerization of business posed dangers to our civil liberties? Should the FBI be able to use in court the fact that a suspected drug smuggler charged trips to South America to his credit card? Does a person with shady business interests have the right to know your bank balance? I had strong feelings on the issue when the leaders in my industry were wishy-washy. I believe we've got to work vigilantly to protect ourselves from computer abuse. I wrote a cover story for a major trade journal that called for specific new safeguards, and I created shock waves."

Sara's capacity for risk taking is even better illustrated in the following anecdote. "A year ago, my manager in charge of video products resigned, and I was desperate to find an exceptional person to fill his shoes. The longer the position remained open, the more vulnerable my biggest money-making division became. I knew it would be difficult to find a good person, but I was lucky and within two months had interviewed someone with superb qualifications. There was a wrinkle, however; Andrew had another seductive offer and needed to make a decision within a few days. I needed the agreement of two other people in my company to hire someone so senior. It was Tuesday, and I had until Friday to convince them that Andrew was the right candidate. My boss saw Andrew at eight A.M. on Thursday and seconded my recommendation to hire him at a high salary.

"The other person was difficult to get to. Tom had been out of town on business all week and would be flying in late Thursday night. I told my secretary to talk to Tom's secretary and arrange a time on Friday for Tom and Andrew to meet. Since Tom was booked all day, the secretaries decided—unbeknownst to me—to give Andrew Tom's home phone number. Andrew called Tom at seven-thirty on Friday morning and woke him up. Tom had had only a few hours' sleep.

"That afternoon, Tom called. 'I don't like Andrew. He's too pushy.' He was in a lousy mood, and I knew it was pointless to argue with him. It was panic time! I had exactly two hours to make Andrew an offer. I picked the phone up and offered him a hundred thousand dollars. I was sure he was right for the job. I spent the rest of the day developing a plan to get Tom to change his mind.

"Monday morning Andrew called to accept a job that wasn't yet his to take. I had to act fast. I had learned that Tom was free for lunch that day. I asked Andrew if he'd have lunch with Tom, telling him Tom's seal of approval was needed as a formality. He agreed.

"Now I needed to convince Tom to meet with Andrew. I knew Andrew had worked with someone Tom greatly respected, and I gambled on that person's giving Andrew an excellent reference. I had no time to check. I asked Tom to make the call that morning, and luckily he did. Shortly thereafter, he told me he was willing to reconsider Andrew. Trying to sound casual, I asked if he were free for lunch. I knew Tom well enough not to push too hard. The lunch was set.

"My nerves were on edge all afternoon. I couldn't concentrate on my work, so I mechanically made lists of things to do. At three P.M. Tom called and said, 'Hire the bastard'—his way of saying, 'I've changed my mind.' I grabbed my jacket and went outside and walked off my tension. Today Andrew is one of the best managers in the company, and recently Tom congratulated me on my choice."

All executive women are—as Sara said—strangers in a strange land. Our nourished women were better than the undernourished ones at adapting to the alien culture of the executive suite, but all the women had considerable difficulties. What is most striking about our women, however, is the degree to which they cut themselves off from their colleagues. In the next chapter, we'll explore some unsettling new reasons for this phenomenon.

CHAPTER
=VII=
WORKING WITH MEN

A woman with a chip on her shoulder is shunned by the vast majority of successful men, both bed- and boardroom partners alike.

—FROM "UNSEXED BY SUCCESS,"
by Dr. Srully Blotnick,
Harper's Bazaar, September 1985

Today's executive women are vastly outnumbered by men, so how they relate to male colleagues greatly influences their careers. I asked our women about these relationships and was shocked by the passion in their replies. The women said that their professional interactions with men were often unproductive, for three reasons:

- They resent the men because they find it's easier for them to get ahead.
- They believe that many of them are unfeeling egomaniacs.
- They think that other of the men deserve to be put on pedestals.

We're going to start with the women's most fervently held belief: that men don't have to try as hard as women do to succeed. *One hundred percent* of those surveyed tell us that "men have more opportunities to advance in business"; that when a man and woman are equally qualified, the man is generally given the edge when it comes to receiving plum assignments, raises, and promotions. Fifty-five percent of the women think that their job opportunities are just "somewhat equal" to men's, while 45 percent see them as "not at all equal."

141

In light of these astonishing responses, it's not surprising that the women find that the greatest stumbling block to their progress has been their gender in and of itself. Eighty percent say "simply being female" has caused major setbacks in their careers. No wonder the women feel a need to hide their femininity! Every woman I interviewed had a story to tell about being discriminated against.

"In business, you learn very early that you're inferior in some men's eyes," Sara said. "When I was made supervisor of the think tank, I was given a lower starting salary than my male predecessor, although the two of us had come to the job with the same amount of experience. I wouldn't have known I was being cheated if my mentor hadn't tipped me off. I demanded parity and got it, but I was scared as hell to complain."

Lines of anger creased Sara's normally serene face. I asked her if she'd like more wine. "I'd love some." She laughed gratefully. "I was the only woman in the think tank," she continued, "and the staff frequently met to kick around ideas. When I spoke, some of the men ignored or interrupted me, which could have seriously harmed my career *and* my self-esteem. Luckily, I had a supportive mentor and I was very stubborn and strong-willed. Otherwise, I would have been so stepped on that I wouldn't have had a chance to compete with the men."

Jennifer's sex also held her back. "I became an art director because the head of the art department happened to like me, but since I was a woman, I stayed on that level a long, long time. The top honchos promoted the male art directors ahead of me, and since I wasn't competitive, I didn't raise a fuss. It was generally acknowledged that I was the best artist in the company, but my talent was irrelevant. It was plain to see that the senior men were more comfortable working with other men. Now I'm ten years older than most of my male peers."

Since our women believe that the deck is stacked in men's favor, it follows that they think men don't have to work as hard as they do. A staggering 97 percent agreed that "women have to work harder than men to reap the same rewards"—the same salary, authority, status, perks, and bonuses. Sara gave a disquieting example of how she brought in large profits for her company but wasn't compensated as a man would have been.

"I pulled off a great coup for my company a month ago," she said proudly. "I designed and oversaw the production of a new computer software program for a specialized group of doctors that allows them to make diagnoses with remarkable accuracy. We've received a flood of orders from medical suppliers. I've been profiled in the popular science magazines and interviewed on TV talk shows." As Sara continued speaking, the happiness she had shown while talking about her coup drained from her face. "Two days ago I was sitting in my office when I realized that if I were a man, I would have gotten a huge bonus. I've seen men get ten thousand dollars for lesser accomplishments. And then the anger came." Sara's green eyes grew hard. "The top brass must have figured that because a woman had created the program, it couldn't be as spectacular as the press had made it out to be."

I asked the women what it took for a man to be an executive. Again, they said, men don't have to be anywhere near as "hard-working" or "disciplined" as women do. Nor, they added, do men have to be as competent—not *half* as "smart," "intelligent," "talented," "creative," "well-educated," or "well-read"! Men can be less "concerned with others," less "loyal," and less "accessible." They can be less "likable," less "thoughtful," less "outgoing," and less "cheerful"—and still be more successful! And while our women often have to fight to control their emotions at work, they believe that men barely need to hold their tempers and tongues in check.

Two groups of women have extremely low opinions of the men, the first being the women in the high-income group ($95,000 and more), who have had the most experience competing with men.

"In a recent management-committee meeting, I volunteered to think up concepts for TV movies whose themes reflect modern social trends," senior vice president Annie told me. "To give you an example of what that task involves, one of the ideas I came up with was for a show about a single woman who decides to have a child on her own. A male peer offered to be my partner on the project. I was excited about it, so I worked through the weekend and presented him with a list of ideas on Monday morning. Rather than helping me or adding suggestions of his own, he challenged every one of my assumptions. He immediately took on a superior role, although he hadn't done a lick of work! As I listened to his comments, I recalled his telling me that the only books he read were those condensed by *Reader's Digest*. What the hell did this guy know about social trends?" Annie cried. "And what on earth got him so far?"

"Ten years ago, I worked for a computer company as a member of their planning department," Sara said. "I had done very well and had been made a vice president. At staff meetings I often substituted for the director of the department and I had also taken on a number of administrative functions. At this point, the company began reevaluating the staffing and management of the planning group, and a management consultant was called in. He suggested that an associate directorship be created, and because the director was female, he recommended that the position be given to a man. He reasoned that if two women ran the department, it would be seen as weak and wouldn't attract good men in the future. I was told that if the choice was based on merit alone, the job would be mine. A less qualified male colleague, who had what we delicately referred to as 'personality problems,' got the job. The hope was that he'd rise to the occasion, but he never did. The pressure got to him, and he became a liability to the company. Fourteen months later, he was fired and escorted out of the building that same day. At a dinner earlier that week, he had gotten drunk and insulted a sober client. Stories also came out that he had made sexual innuendos to his female staff. He kept a list where he ranked the women in the company as the most and least fuckable." Sara took a swallow of her wine. "He got the job over me—and he was a sleaze!"

The highly paid women I interviewed expressed what William Blake called "honest indignation." Like Annie's and Sara's, their allegations of inequities were always grounded in actual experience, and consequently they always rang true. The second group of women that saw great gaps between themselves and their male peers was the never-married women. Their complaints were far less rational.

Common sense tells us that the perceptions of women who are married are more realistic because they are in a position to see the time and effort men give to their jobs. Rose has been married for twenty years and has a lenient view of her male colleagues. "No question about it, women in business get a raw deal." The New Jersey executive shrugged. "The old-boys' network is alive and well, and women have to be better qualified. Still, I work with some terrific men."

Katharine has never been married. "I know brilliant executive women who work for dummies," she sneered. "Men give one another the best jobs no matter how good the women are. Men also prefer male clients so that they can write off golf and boating trips. Sometimes I think that men are all selfish babies. I *loathe* my boss. Sometimes I wake up at night with my muscles tensed to kill. I'm always fantasizing scenes where I tell him what I think of him once and for all. When I'm really mad, I stay out of his way. I'm afraid of opening that Pandora's box."

A second factor creates more problems between the women and the men. Our women believe that their male co-workers have completely different outlooks on life, and in fact, their priorities *are* dissimilar. Our women worked hard at school and in their careers to win respect from mothers, husbands, and bosses. They didn't chart their career paths or take the risks that could speed their growth because they weren't acting on their own initiatives. Emotional rewards, such as praise and affection, meant more to them than such tangible prizes as money and titles.

Executive men enjoy being leaders, as books like *Iacocca* and *Yeager* readily show; even as teenagers, they were often class presidents and captains of sports teams. They entered the business world armed with goals and—our women now report— work not to gain approval from others, but to win money, power, and prestige for themselves.

I asked the women which aspects of life were "much more important" to their male peers than to themselves. "Taking risks" was far more often a male prerogative (71 percent), the women replied, as was the wish to "be a leader" in their company (63 percent). They believed that men stressed "being visible" and "knowing who is in power" much more often (57 percent) and that they put more priority on "developing close business relationships" (that is, friendships that could help them get ahead), "taking a stand," and "being prominent in their field" (50 percent). Finally, a number of the women found that the men "set goals" (40 percent) and "acted as mentors" (33 percent) much more often than they did.

Now I asked our women which life priorities were "much more important" to *them*. Startlingly, the women said that family and friendships mattered more to them than to their male peers! Such concerns hadn't been the women's personal priorities, but they took on sudden significance when the women compared themselves with men.

In an earlier question, the majority of our women had said that excelling in their jobs was their number-one interest in life. By contrast, many executive men told the AMA that their families came first. Flying in the face of these facts, our women now insist that "having enough time for family activities" is *much* more important to them than to their male peers (70 percent)!

The women also believe that they care more about the people they work with than do men. In the last chapter, we saw that "understanding the needs of colleagues" and "getting to know co-workers" were not our women's priorities. When they contrast themselves to men, they sing a very different tune. A majority (75 percent) say that "understanding the needs of colleagues" means much more to them than to their male peers, and 60 percent say "getting to know co-workers" matters far more. What do our women mean by these contradictions? That regardless of how work-obsessed and businesslike they are, they are much nicer, much warmer people than their male colleagues!

Ironically, while this data makes clear the women's disdain for their male colleagues, it also tells us that some of their bitterness is unwarranted. The women admit that they don't use the tactics men do to get ahead, yet they resent the men for advancing faster.

The wives saw the fewest differences between the sexes' priorities. Annie is happily married, and she judges men fairly and compassionately. "Men strategize in their jobs more than we do, but that doesn't mean they don't care about people. The men I work with aren't always as smart as I am, but most of them are extremely nice." Annie chuckled. "I'm the only woman on the management committee, and recently we went on a three-day conference. We had a wonderful time! We went on a hike in the mountains, and at night we sat around a fire drinking and boasting about our kids. We also played poker, and I won a hundred and sixty dollars. Can you imagine *me* with a poker face? What I learned from the experience was not just that my game is good but that it truly matters to men that they get to know the people they work closely with. I've always gotten along well with the guys, but now my relationships with them are a lot stronger."

The never-married women perceived their male colleagues as ruthless operators.

"The first time I went overseas on business was to help my [investment] firm open a London branch," Katharine said. "I was the only woman in a group of men and was very excited about the trip. I thought we'd all go out for wonderful meals and then take in wonderful shows. The night we checked into our hotel, all the men went off together without saying a word to me." Katharine cupped her chin in her hand and stared moodily at the rug. "The next night, we went to a cocktail party held in our honor at the Ritz Hotel. I figured surely somebody would approach me at the party to ask if I'd made dinner plans, but I looked around the room at one point and everyone I worked with had gone. I went back to my hotel room and cried like a baby. The next morning at breakfast, one of the guys said, 'Say, Katharine, where have you been?' He *looked* very innocent," Katharine said angrily. "Maybe the men felt uncomfortable socializing with just one woman. Still, they should have gone out of their way to include me. How can men treat people so shabbily?"

Laura has also never wed. As she told the following story, she became even more wrought up than usual. "A few years ago this guy did me in like nobody's business. At the time, I was heading up the group responsible for all the magazine's articles on health and fitness. I was understaffed and could barely handle my work when a memo arrived from this damned boss telling me he'd like me to take on the entertainment section as well. He probably figured that by not hiring a new person, he could save money and make himself look good. Soon, I was covering books, movies, concerts, and plays with a staff strained to the breaking point. God damn him!" Laura exploded. "My people worked night and day, and two of them quit. I *killed* myself to get the work done! I had no personal life for six fucking months. My lisp came back! For the first time since I was a teenager, my lisp came back! I *hate* that fucking guy." Laura's hands shook violently as she lit a cigarette. "I was going to have a nervous breakdown. I *knew* it! I went and told him so, and he had the gall to say, 'Why didn't you tell me six months ago that you couldn't handle the entertainment section?' " Laura's dark-blue eyes bore into mine. "A man will do anything to get ahead—steamroll right over you, stab his best friend in the back."

Laura's and Katharine's problems were due more to their own lack of assertiveness than to men's chauvinism or insensitivity. Each of Katharine's peers made sure he was included in the group's activities, but her timidity kept her from doing the same. When Laura received her memo, she could have immediately told her boss that she needed more staff or that she couldn't take on more work without jeopardizing the quality of the magazine. Instead, she lived through six months of hell and blamed her boss for her predicament.

When our women *do* like and respect male colleagues, the working relationships are often inappropriate and immature. Forty percent of them had severe "difficulties relating to male superiors." The interviews showed that these problems usually stemmed from the women's being overly deferential. Feelings of awe in the face of men in power is the third and final factor that creates trouble between executive women and men.

"My need for male approval is tremendous." Annie grinned sheepishly. "I'm very bothered by this problem, because I don't stand up for myself the way I should. Recently, I worked for a very gruff man who didn't get along with many people but made it clear that he liked me. And although I have a position of authority and importance in my company, I found I acted like a little girl around him. When he spoke to me, I got nervous. I hadn't had jitters like that since I was in math class and the teacher called on me. That man is a friend now, and a week ago he invited me to dinner. I told him I was busy, so he asked me for dessert. I said I had a late meeting, and he said, 'Boy, when you worked for me I'll bet you would have come for dessert!' I said, 'Are you kidding? I would have come for dinner!' "

Being daunted by men in higher positions also prevents Annie from getting to know the men who have the most influence on her career. "I don't think I've been very smart. I've been reluctant to befriend the big guns at [the parent company that owns the network]. I don't want to take people out to dinner just because it might get me ahead. Those guys make me nervous!"

"I'm a sucker for paternal men." Katharine giggled nervously. "The boss I fell in love with was fatherly, and I worshiped him. Long before we were lovers, he praised me and called me his 'favorite girl.' I treated him as if he were the daddy who could solve all my problems. I asked his advice on *everything*. When I started working for Donna in Chicago, I was afraid to do anything on my own."

Whether our women regard their colleagues as gods or as devils, they create big problems for themselves. When they don't like or trust their male peers, they don't ask for their advice or support. When they idolize their superiors, they don't assert their needs for raises and authority. Without such help, the women's jobs are more difficult than their male peers'. They keep on working harder . . . and get angrier and more withdrawn.

CHAPTER
=VIII=
AT HOME

You can have deep love, true friends, money, fame, satisfying days and nights—anything you *want* when you apply [yourself] *seriously.*
—HELEN GURLEY BROWN,
editor of *Cosmopolitan* magazine,
from her book *Having It All*

As our women talk about their private lives and the sacrifices they have made for their careers, the violent anger they feel toward their male colleagues resurfaces. No wonder: Marriage hasn't been in the cards for a good number of the women, and a lasting marriage has proved elusive for many more. Meanwhile, nearly all their male peers go home at night to the same wives they have been married to—presumably happily—for years (Korn/Ferry). Adding insult to injury, only half of our women are mothers, and a third of those mothers are single. All the men they work with are fathers, and not one raises his children alone. Imagine the frustration these women live with day after day!

As if the differences between their lives and the men's weren't irritation enough, the media's version of the women's private lives is galling. In any given month's selection of magazines for working women, a short biography of a woman with a successful career, a good marriage, and happy children appears. Advertisements repeat the image: Young and slim in a business suit, the executive woman holds a briefcase in one arm and a baby in the other as she strolls by her husband's side, laughing delightedly at some shared joke. This woman (real or fictional) appears to have struck a happy balance between the traditional roles of wife and mother and the newer one of careerwoman, but the truth about successful businesswomen is far different. My survey shows that the woman who "has it all" is the exception to the rule: Only one in three of our women has both a husband and children! And if we continue to believe that having a high-powered career doesn't involve serious sacrifices, we'll feel the same kind of anxiety our mothers felt from the media's portrayal of the "perfect housewife"—an ideal to which many of our mothers aspired but few came near.

I asked the women which aspects of their lives have suffered significantly because of their success. Their account of the personal costs of being executives is dumbfounding.

Ninety-three percent report that they forfeit a huge amount of time for hobbies, sports, and other leisure pursuits. The women I interviewed corroborated this fact, telling me that they rarely have the chance to see a movie, read a book, or even luxuriate in the bathtub. Sara, as disciplined as she is, never has extra time. "Not one hour of my life is improvised. I have two homes to run—an apartment and a beach house—a daughter I'm very close to, and a staff of thirty people. I never get up later than six A.M., and all my good times are carefully planned. If I go windsurfing with my daughter, I have to keep an eye on my watch because I have to save time to read through the contents of my briefcase and get the food shopping done. If I were irresponsible even once, the whole house of cards would collapse."

Nine in ten of the women have almost no time for their friends. "I have no social life, no real friends," Annie said with her usual honesty. "I'm out five nights a week on business. The other two nights I want to be with my husband and kids."

In spite of curtailing or even eliminating their availability for friends, *90 percent* of the women don't have enough time for their family obligations. "I'm always a month late with a birthday gift," Laura said. "It's embarrassing."

"My husband resented how much time my job took," Jennifer said. "My working so hard was one of the reasons we got divorced."

The vast majority of women (88 percent) tell us that they've had to renounce the comfort and convenience of living in an organized home. "If it weren't for my housekeeper, my apartment would be a pigsty," Laura declared. "Still I don't have time to keep track of when I need toilet paper and soap, and I never manage to pick up my dry cleaning when I need the clothes for a business trip. As a result, my home life is as crazy as my office life."

Eighty-three percent assert that executive women must forgo the right to have as many children as they'd like. Some believe that they can't have even one child. "To me, it was career or children," Jennifer said evenly. "Obviously, I chose my career."

An amazing 86 percent of our women are pro-abortion. In most surveys of the issue, women divide down the middle, with half being "pro-life" and the other half "pro-choice." Our women say that they *need* the right to choose how many children to have, that since no method of birth control is completely effective or safe, the option of abortion must be available. They have given too much of their lives to their careers to threaten all they have worked for with the responsibility of an unplanned child.

The final pleasure to be offered up at the altar of success was love life. *Sixty-eight percent* of the women tell us theirs has been damaged by their careers. Of our six women, only Annie is content with her love and sex life. Here are the other women's capsule reports on the state of their romantic affairs.

"I haven't been to bed with a man for over five years." (Katharine)

"I'd have to see a psychiatrist before I could let go and enjoy sex." (Rose)

"My love life is pitiful." (Laura)

"I'm too busy to get seriously involved with a man." (Sara)

"I haven't yet found a man who could deal with my success." (Jennifer)

Now I asked our women to compare their sacrifices with those made by their male peers. They acknowledged that the men were forced to give up some pleasures, but adamantly believed that they themselves abdicated more.

Eighty-one percent feel that the men can live in smoothly run homes, which is only logical since the men have wives who run their homes for them. Only 5 percent of Korn/Ferry's men have spouses who work full-time; nearly all of them have wives who take complete charge of their homes. By contrast, half of our women are single, and nearly all the wives' husbands have full-time jobs.

A majority (79 percent) say that executive men can have as many children as they like. Again, they speak from experience, because the men have bigger families. Only 8 percent of our women have four or more children, whereas over three times as many of the men do (28 percent according to Korn/Ferry).

One out of two (50 percent) of our women believes that her male peers have more time for their families—not surprising, since the men don't waste time doing housework. Half also feel that the men have more hours for hobbies and fun, and a third maintain that the men have better love lives.

Only 40 percent of the women generally take all the vacation due them, and many work for years without taking any break at all. "I didn't take any vacation for ten years," Laura informed me. "I was a workaholic, and it was very bad for my nerves."

"I still feel guilty about how hard I worked when my children were small." Rose gripped her delicate teacup with both hands. "Summers when their friends' parents were renting beach houses, I was staying at the office until eight P.M. Sometimes we'd go away for a weekend, and I'd come home alone on Saturday night. I was too anxious about my work. I couldn't enjoy myself."

Magazine stories that depict executive women as happy "jugglers" do ambitious young women a gross disservice. The article "Superwomen of the Financial World," for example, profiled five Wall Street executives. All were married and mothers; all ostensibly had peaceful, pleasant lives. The author of the piece shared a discovery she had made while conducting her interviews: In the "success subculture, many women . . . use the word 'problem' only when it is preceded with a 'no.' . . . When their guards are down, they admit to being tired at times, to worrying once in a while, but they don't dwell on these things. . . . They are 'problem solvers or problem avoiders or persons who deny problems exist.' " The author didn't elaborate on the problems the women were denying, nor did she speculate on the anxiety that such constant repression must evoke.

Other articles that whitewash the serious sacrifices executive women make stress the "richness of [the women's] lives outside work." One woman *Savvy* magazine profiled in their "1983 Roster of Outstanding Women Executives" has a high-pressure job, a husband, and young children, yet she "sits on numerous boards of professional, community, philanthropic and cultural groups." *Vogue*'s article on twenty-one successful women, "Life at the Top," also makes us think that the women have "rich," satisfying lives. One woman said she worked out on the Nautilus, bicycled, played tennis, swam, gardened, cooked, and knitted in her "free time."

How do they do it? By reading the articles closely, one soon finds out: The women with the "richest" lives sleep the least— usually four to five hours, while a few boast of getting by on just three hours' sleep. The "superwomen" shown us as paragons are extreme overachievers; and instead of being typical, they are anomalies. The majority of the women I surveyed sleep seven hours a night, the amount doctors agree is necessary for good health. Yet so strong is the media's attachment to the idea that women can "have it all," that we almost never hear about the truly typical executive woman—the one who has no time at all for hobbies, exercise, or friends; who goes through the agony of divorce while maintaining her career; who raises children alone while carrying on her stressful job; or who longs to share her life with a man but realizes she never may.

To allow these women's stories to be told, I tabulated all the responses in my survey separately for the women who were married, single, and divorced. Just as when they talked about working with men, the greatest differences in opinion on the subject of their private lives were between the wives and the women who have never wed (if you visualize a diagonal line, the "divorced" women's answers were in the middle and the "married" and "never-married" women's were at the two extremes). We'll begin by examining the 48 percent of our women who are married.

THE MARRIED EXECUTIVE WOMEN

Who are the men who have married the most successful businesswomen in America? Are they as outstanding as their spouses are? Are they CEOs? Jet-setters? I asked the women if, in their judgment, their husbands were as "successful" as they. I purposely left the meaning of the word *successful* ambiguous for each woman to interpret as she wished. Half the women (50 percent) replied that their husbands were as successful as they, but a nearly equal number (45 percent) had spouses whose achievements were inferior to theirs. Only one in twenty (5 percent) of the women has a husband she believes is more accomplished.

When income is our sole criterion, the numbers of husbands who are as successful as their wives dwindles from one half to a mere one third. Two thirds of the wives are the major breadwinners, bringing in well over 50 percent of the household income. And in a complete reversal of traditional roles, 10 percent of the women entirely support their mates!

Do executive women buck the longstanding national trend for women to marry men at higher career levels? Evidence exists that some of them do "marry down." *Fortune*'s article "How Harvard's Women MBA's Are Managing" reports that one executive "married the summer substitute doorman of her apartment building," but this pattern wasn't the norm among the twenty-five women I interviewed. The majority of those women married men whose career status was equal to or higher than theirs; only gradually did they surpass their husbands' levels of income and responsibility. Moreover, as the women grew more successful, their husbands often became the "anchor" member of the partnership. In the largest and most comprehensive study of American couples ever done (*American Couples,* by Dr. Philip Blumstein and Dr. Pepper Schwartz) the authors found that a marriage stood the best chance of surviving when one spouse served as an emotional anchor, devoting more energy to the relationship than to a career. "Something had to give," Sara said to explain the phenomenon in her own marriage. "We couldn't both be traveling and putting in twelve-hour days. My husband became more available to my daughter and me. He was there to drive us to work and school and take care of us if we got sick. Executive women don't need husbands," Sara said only half-jokingly, "they need wives!"

Most of the wives I interviewed felt uneasy about earning more than their husbands. "While consciously they may be comfortable with the role reversals they are living out, their unconscious perceptions reflect the thinking of their parents and grandparents," Dr. Bernstein says. "The cliché that a good man should be able to provide for a wife and that a good woman should be able to find a man who can take care of her nags at them." Three quarters of the wives I interviewed—after admitting that they brought most of the bacon home—assured me that "next year" or "soon" their husbands would make as much money as they.

A well-meaning Annie did more harm than good as she rushed to her spouse's defense. "If my husband hasn't been as successful, it's only because he hasn't settled down in any one field yet. My stability allows him to try different things, different businesses. He's very creative, very unusual. He's the one who was behind my success." Annie paused for breath, then blurted out: "He's an excellent athlete!"

Rose assured me that one day her husband would be rich. "My husband is a professor of biology," the small woman said proudly. "He's very involved in genetic-engineering research, and eventually he's going to patent something or win a Nobel prize." Still, Rose often resents being the major breadwinner. "Twice, my husband has taken time off from teaching to do research. Once he was on sabbatical and received partial salary, but the next time he had no money coming in, and I supported him. By the end of that second year, I felt like the weight of the world was on me. Because I was the sole provider, I became insecure in my job. I gave all my energy to my work and I had nightmares about being fired. I realize now that I was furious at my husband." Rose smiled weakly. "I couldn't stand all that responsibility. Because my mother told me I'd be taken care of by a husband when I grew up, I never expected to support him and two children by myself."

So emotionally packed is this issue that *The Wall Street Journal* and Gallup (in a joint poll) revealed that executive women who earn less than their husbands are happier than those who earn more! My own survey showed that another factor figures into the wives' dissatisfaction—whether or not they do more housework than their husbands do. The unhappiest wives contribute more money *and* more energy to their homes. Unfortunately, many of the wives perform this double duty.

Sixty percent of the wives I surveyed have either "major" (40 percent) or "more" (20 percent) responsibility for the household chores! Even the richest women—those who make at least $125,000—do more housework than their husbands in 50 percent of the cases! Doing housework (for men, anyway) doesn't come with the responsibility of being the anchor. Luckily, our women can afford to hire part-time (50 percent) or full-time (10 percent) household help. Even so, the women must make sure that their homes are neat and efficiently run. They are the ones who do the light housecleaning and who hire, fire, and supervise their housekeepers. They see to it that household supplies are in stock and they cook more often than their husbands do. Their spouses aid them occasionally by shopping for food or scrubbing pots. Helping around the house, though, doesn't cause much stress. Having the ultimate responsibility for running the household does.

Mary-Lou Weisman, in an article on the degree to which husbands help their wives, asks the rhetorical question "Could kinder, more altruistic words come from the mouth of man than 'Sure, I'll help'? " She responds: "They sure could. They would be 'It's my turn to take charge.' Man the Helper agreeably drips hollandaise into the blender but does not chip the centrifuged egg yolk off the cabinet doors. He will vacuum but he never changes the filter bags. . . . He puts dishes into the dishwasher but he does not unload them. He carries groceries into the house but he doesn't put them away. He shops for groceries but he will not make a list. He will play with the baby but he has no sense of smell."

Weisman is a funny writer, but the situation doesn't amuse executive wives. After our interview concluded, Rose invited me to stay for lunch, and I offered to help her prepare the meal. As we chopped the ingredients for a chef's salad, her husband entered the kitchen. "Where are the black olives, Rose?" he demanded. Rose opened a can, added olives to the salad, and started slicing hard-boiled eggs. "No, no, no, no!" her husband cried. Rose winced. "Don't slice them lengthwise—the yolks fall out!" He never helped, but continued to give Rose directions until the meal was served. "Sometimes he drives me crazy," Rose confided when she walked me to my car. "He writes out shopping lists for me and then expects me to find every item on them." Her eyes widened helplessly. "I'll come home exhausted, and he'll insist I cook his favorite meal."

Why don't our women—who are professional delegators—demand that their husbands pull their weight on the domestic front? *American Couples* found that wives are often ineffectual at getting their husbands to help because men so hate housework that the more they do, the unhappier they are and the greater the chance they'll divorce their wives. But "women who stay married to such unreasonable men are very dependent. Their need for their mother's approval has been transferred to their husband," Dr. Bernstein says. "They fear they'll be deserted if they demand standards that are fair, so they keep their mouth shut and take on the brunt of the work themselves." And they build up anger toward their husband in the process.

There's another reason why our women do more of the housekeeping. "When my husband and I first married, he cooked all sorts of lovely meals and did all kinds of cleaning up," Jennifer said sarcastically. "Then he stopped helping completely, and I was shocked out of my mind. But I wanted to be a 'good wife,' so I made all the meals and did most of the cleaning up myself. I was much less confident then; I badly needed to be loved. After acting tough in the office, I believed that I should be humble and sweet and feminine at home so that my husband would be attracted to me."

"If a woman suppresses her femininity at work, she will naturally harbor insecurities about her womanliness," Dr. Bernstein asserts. All day, Jennifer was careful not to be feminine. She didn't feel at all pretty in her "uniform suits." When she came home to her husband, how was she to be sure that she was appealing? By overburdening herself with traditionally "feminine" tasks.

The fear that a "manlike" commitment to a job diminishes her sexual attractiveness is often at the root of the "superwoman syndrome." Jennifer became a gourmet cook solely to please her husband. "I took cooking lessons twice a week because it made him happy. At the time, I was working seven-day weeks to complete a major ad campaign. I was pulled

in so many directions that I had constant tension headaches."
Two pink spots on her cheeks betrayed the anger she still
felt. "I baked my own bread and grew my own herbs. What
a sucker!"

Only the undernourished wives went to such extremes. Because they lacked a strong, consistent sense of their femininity,
they had a hard time switching from the role of executive to
wife and had to look to outside sources to show them how to
be womanly. They were also influenced by their mother's actions in the home. Jennifer's equating being "sweet and
humble"—that is, being deferential—with being feminine indicates not just that she attached a negative meaning to the
word, but that *she didn't know how to be feminine without being a
martyr and a stereotype*—a meek, subservient, unhappy "good
wife."

The nourished women could be affectionate, giving, empathetic, and nurturing without behaving masochistically. And
since they weren't out to prove how competent they were as
wives, they were more flexible than the undernourished women:
They took less responsibility for the housework and were much
more likely to hire housekeepers. "I completely rely on my
housekeeper," Annie said. "I also have a great husband. We
have a weekend home where we do all the cooking and cleaning
ourselves, and whatever chores need to be done are split fifty-
fifty between us. When the kids were little, I'd come home from
work and play with them while he made dinner. Come to think
of it"—she winked—"my husband has always done a lot more
of the work than I have."

Recently, I watched a Phil Donahue show on two-career couples and housework. Donahue approached a man in the audience and asked if he and his wife both worked.

"Yes," the man said.

"Who comes home first?" asked Donahue.

"I do," the man replied.

"Who makes dinner?" pressed Donahue.

There was a moment's hesitation, then a soft, embarrassed,
"I do."

The result was a thunderous standing ovation from the mostly
female audience.

THE EXECUTIVE MOTHERS

The conflict created when a woman tries to balance motherhood and a career is the most difficult problem facing working women today. A generation ago, most women left work soon after becoming pregnant and returned only when their children were in school, if they came back at all. Now women are combining full-time jobs with the responsibilities of raising children and are often finding this dual burden formidable. With the long hours and pressures involved in an executive career, the fact that over half our married women are childless (52 percent) is understandable. Those who do have children normally have just one (17 percent) or two (23 percent). A few have three (10 percent), and even fewer (8 percent) four or more.

The difficulties of being both an executive and a mother can instantly be seen in the fact that only 27 percent of the mothers polled took maternity leaves of absence, that is, time beyond the six weeks' leave supposedly enlightened companies offer new mothers. Many went back to work a few short weeks after giving birth—and some did so not just once but twice or more.

Their prompt return reflects, in part, the harsh realities of this nation's maternity policies. Only 40 percent of America's working women are granted six weeks' paid disability leave. Longer, unpaid leaves are even rarer, and these last only two to three months. In most European countries, the minimum paid leave, by law, is fourteen weeks, and women are *usually* given five to six months' paid time off. On top of that, most of the countries allow at least *one year* of unpaid but job-protected leave, a practice almost unheard of in the United States. And a few countries, such as Sweden, Norway, and Finland, offer leaves to new fathers as well.

Because the United States has no laws entitling women to maternity leave, policies vary widely from company to company. Since many of our women work for large corporations, they are offered better-than-average leaves, but they rarely take advantage of this privilege. Rose explained why she hurried back to work after giving birth. First, she described being pregnant when she was twenty-six and the assistant to the director of marketing at her chemical company.

"I didn't tell anyone at work I was pregnant until I couldn't hide it anymore, and I didn't show for five months because I'm so small," she said proudly. "Afterward, I hid my stomach as best I could. I spent a lot of time behind my desk, and I didn't wear maternity clothes until my final month—I just wore looser dresses. When I was forced to wear maternity clothes, I wore dark, businesslike dresses and tried to minimize my pregnancy in whatever ways I could. If I had shown any sign of weakness, my job would have been in jeopardy. I never spoke about being pregnant and I kept on traveling with my boss no matter how uncomfortable it became."

After delivering her son, Rose took four weeks off, although she was allowed to take eight weeks' paid time. "And during those four weeks, I held meetings at my house. I was working on a campaign to promote a new painkiller to hospitals. I had my office mail delivered by messenger every day. The point was not to let the baby get in the way of the job; I had to prove to management that I was as effective as before. I didn't want to be denied opportunities because they thought I couldn't handle the work."

Rose's fears were justified. Several women I interviewed, after becoming pregnant, were given less responsibility because their superiors assumed that they were going to quit. Others, after becoming mothers, were stripped of some of their authority because their bosses believed that they would now devote less time to their careers. The women were therefore careful to downplay not only their pregnancies but their status as mothers. The conviction that they had to hide their maternity is part of the reason why the trait "nurturing" was rated one of the least conducive to success.

Annie has four children. "The woman who won't stay until the end of a late meeting because she has to pick up her kids from the baby-sitter is seen as not being dedicated to her career," she has found. "So is the woman who takes a three-month maternity leave or who misses her children while she's at work."

When Rose returned to work after her maternity leave, she displayed no pictures of her son on her desk and was careful not to get excited when she spoke about him. "If someone asked, I said, 'He's fine,' and left it at that. When I took him to the pediatrician, I lied and said I had a business appointment. I didn't like lying, but the people I worked with wouldn't have understood."

Annie's and Rose's beefs were echoed by nearly all the mothers I interviewed. Yet not even the women's fears of repercussions in their careers prepared me for the fact that just 40 percent of the mothers supported legislated maternity leave. It is not that the women who gave birth and returned to work in a few short weeks found the experience easy. Without exception, the mothers I interviewed who took short leaves suffered extreme hardships. "The physical act of childbirth is incredibly draining," Rose said. "So is the constant worry about whether or not the baby's okay when you've left him in someone else's care. And only a woman who's gone through it can understand what working all day and then dealing with a newborn child is like. I was shocked by how exhausted I was."

Our women don't demand legislated leave for the same reasons they don't take all the leave allowed them: They don't want to call attention to their femaleness. They want to prove that motherhood won't slow them down professionally.

Having been nourished makes our women no more inclined to support legislated leave, but it does make them more apt to take extended leaves. Sara took six months off from work after giving birth. "My job was technically secure," she explained, "but I was only paid for a month of my time off. I had saved up because I wanted to be with my baby." Sara also took a long leave so that she could find a nurse she trusted for her daughter. "As any working mother knows, getting someone to care for children on a full-time basis is tough. No matter how much money you have, you're going to have problems because that kind of labor—'women's work'—barely exists anymore. I saw friends go to pieces when they lost a good baby-sitter, so I looked very hard and finally found the right person. She and my daughter loved each other."

When Sara returned to work, she found that some of her duties had been taken over by others. "I had expected problems, so I handled the situation in stride. One by one, I demanded my responsibilities back. Soon I had all of them and more." Sara rolled her eyes. "Only I missed my daughter. Those months with her were the best period of my life."

Sara was confident that she could return to her level of previous performance, but her taking a long leave was also influenced by how happy she was as a mother. Rose's hurrying back to work was as much a personal preference as a fear of losing professional momentum. "Quite frankly, I didn't know anything about babies." Rose smiled self-consciously. "The nurse I hired was a lot smarter about them than I was. I was relieved to let her take over the care of my son. I couldn't wait to get out of the house and go back to work. I'm not the type to stay home. I'm too wrapped up in my job."

Rose's identity is so focused on her career, and her fear that she'll lose all she's strived for is so strong, that she worked nonstop through her child's first weeks of life! She was more comfortable professionally than maternally because she was unsure of how to be a mother. Her own mother hadn't set a good example for her. "The single most important indicator of what kind of parent a woman will be is the way in which her mother raised her," Dr. Bernstein says. "The adage that the apple doesn't fall far from the tree is true." Indeed, when we contrast what Rose, Annie, and Sara have to say about being mothers, the degree to which each replicates her own mother's behavior is striking.

When Rose's son entered nursery school, she gave birth to a daughter, Rachel. This time around, she took just two weeks of maternity leave. Because she returned to work so quickly, she was unable to find a satisfactory nurse for Rachel. "My son had a wonderful nanny," she said regretfully, "but she was unavailable when my daughter was born. The woman I hired for Rachel didn't pay enough attention to her, and as a result, my daughter had problems. She was very dependent on me. She screamed whenever I left the house; and when I went away on trips, she threw temper tantrums. Michael, my son, was such a good baby," she sighed.

As Rachel grew older, Rose felt a distance between them. "We sometimes spent Saturdays together," Rose recalled. "We'd shop and go out for a nice lunch. My daughter loved those occasions, but she was very moody. She was always a difficult child." Rose found herself liking her son better as her children grew older. "Michael and I have always had a stronger relationship. When Rachel was young, she wanted to play at her friends' houses, whereas Michael wanted to bring his friends home." Rose sipped her tea and was silent for a moment. Then, in a careful voice, she said, "I made a huge mistake with my daughter, one I'll always regret. She had a little bump on her nose; nothing major, just a little bump. When she was thirteen, I told her that if she wanted a nose job I'd pay for it. And now when Michael comes home from college and the whole family is together, she's always saying, 'Can you believe Mom wanted me to have a nose job?' I just thought she'd look prettier without the bump!"

"Rose's suggestion that her daughter get her nose fixed is a good example of a narcissistic mother's behavior," Dr. Bernstein says. "Rose wanted her daughter to look pretty because she felt Rachel was a reflection on her, and because Rachel reminded her of her own teenage insecurities. She broached the subject of an operation, although she must have known she'd hurt her daughter's feelings. Rachel became the target for Rose's projections, and her son became the favorite." Meanwhile, Rose's daughter must have been as jealous and hurt by her mother's preference for her son as Rose had been by her mother's.

As part of a minority of the women surveyed, Annie didn't begin her career until all her children—three boys and a girl —were in school. She enjoyed being a mother and began working only because she and her husband needed money. "My four were wonderful." Annie beamed. "Funny and adorable. I'm very thankful that my life turned out the way it did. If I had begun my career before having kids, I would never have had all four. I *might* have had one. *Might.* As it is, I've had the best of both worlds.

"I relied very heavily on my mother's help in raising the kids. After my father died, I persuaded her to move near us, and I paid a big price for that because she practically lived in my house. When I had my third child, I realized I was much too dependent on my mother and I forced myself to stand on my own two feet. Now I love her tremendously, but I don't feel dependent on her at all."

Although her husband is a caring, available parent, Annie often insists on shouldering the burden for their children's care. "My husband spends more time with them than I do," she said as she poked bobby pins into her wobbly-looking bun. "He's an extremely devoted father, but sometimes children just want mommy. Recently, for example, my son had an accident at school, and he called me. My husband was playing tennis at his club, and I was in an important meeting, but the call came to me, and I'm the one who took my son to the doctor. Don't get me wrong," she warned. "I *want* to be the one they call. I'm their mother, and I'm happy to be."

Dr. Bernstein says, "Mothers often assume most of the responsibility for child care. They want to hold on to their children just as they held on to their mothers. Separation problems work both ways."

Annie's relationship with her daughter is particularly intimate. "Cindy and I are very close," Annie said warmly. "She's a delightful person. But it's funny; as we talk about her, I'm reminded of my relationship with my mother. I'm seeing all these parallels." Annie laughed and hugged her blue-jeaned legs to her chest. "This interview is like being on an analyst's couch! Seriously, I've just had a revelation. My daughter is in college now, and she calls me every day. I did the same thing. I called my mother every day."

On a hunch, I asked Annie if she'd seen the movie *Terms of Endearment,* in which a mother who dotes on her daughter loses her to cancer. "Yes!" Annie responded before I had time to finish my sentence. "I certainly did, and I loved it. My husband and I went to a screening and when we walked out of the theater, I vomited, I was so upset."

Sara's relationship with her daughter also approximates hers with her mother. "When I'm with Julie, I'm all hers," Sara said of her twelve-year-old, "and I never renege on my promises to her. We have a ball together. We watch TV, pig out on popcorn, and scratch each other's backs. I taught her to windsurf, and we do that every chance we can, but I don't believe I should be home with her every night or weekend day. I've made an effort to let her know I'm not the sole source of love in her life, so that she hasn't become overly dependent on me. She spends a lot of time with her father, and she often visits my parents out East. Many people love that girl, and she knows it."

A moment later, Sara was at my side with her opened wallet,

showing me a photograph of a blond, tanned girl with a radiant smile. "Julie is very creative." Sara's pride was obvious. "She loves to put together interesting clothes combinations." Sara's daughter was wearing a breathtaking cherry-red sari. "And I respect her taste, even if it's too avant-garde for me. It's important to me to let her be an individual, the way my mother let me be myself." Before returning to the couch, Sara bent over to touch her toes a few times. "I'm going to do something differently from the way my mother raised me. I think my mother pushed me to go to college a little too hard. I want Julie to live her own life and make her own choices, so I'm not going to insist on college for her. She wants to travel, and whatever she does, she'll be fine. Sometimes I can't believe I'm lucky enough to be her mother."

"Letting go [of a daughter] . . . implies generosity, a talent a good mother needs in abundance," Nancy Friday says in *My Mother/My Self*. "You cannot leave home, cannot grow up whole, separate and self-reliant, unless someone loved you enough to give you a self first, and then let you go." Sara's mother did these two things, and Sara is returning the favor with her own daughter. "Because Sara had an exceptionally good relationship with her mother, she is comfortable raising her child in some ways differently from her mother's ways. Daughters more narcissistically tied to their mothers seldom deviate from their patterns," Dr. Bernstein notes.

Happily, to judge from the interviews, our women's husbands were very accessible to their children. Still, the women worried that they themselves were negligent as parents. A full half of the mothers polled said they didn't have the time they *needed*, let alone wanted, to spend with their children! (The nourished mothers were more apt than the undernourished mothers to say they had sufficient time.)

"I felt very, very guilty about my daughter," Rose said anxiously. "I was made associate marketing director just after I had her and I couldn't spare much time to be with her. Thank God, my husband was wonderful." Relief entered Rose's voice. "I know he seems a little gruff when you meet him, but he has a very tender side, and he lavished a lot of love on the kids. Still, I was the mother, and I felt terrible.

"Mornings when my children were young and I had to go to work, I'd head for the door, and Michael would shout, 'Don't go!' At that, Rachel would run and cling to my legs and sob. I would feel such pain and conflict. I loved them, but I resented their making my life so tough. Did I feel guilty?" Rose looked at me with a haunted expression. "I wrote the book on guilt."

If Annie suffered less guilt than Rose, she avoided it by making severe sacrifices. "When I began working, I was promoted very quickly and I had to do a lot of business socializing. I only had a couple of nights and the weekend to be with my kids, so I spent every free second with them."

Again and again in the survey, the mothers told us that they longed for more personal time. Of all the women, they felt most intensely that they sacrificed hobbies. They also said that they desperately wished for "time to be alone" (78 percent) and to occasionally "read a book or magazine just for fun" (80 percent). The nourished wives were twice as likely as the undernourished wives to find such time for themselves. The experience of motherhood was far more fulfilling and less stressful for our nourished executives.

THE DIVORCED EXECUTIVE WOMAN

Like the married women, the divorced executive women—over half (57 percent) of whom have children—struggled to make time for their families and careers—only to go through the shattering disappointment of divorce. Frequently (50 percent of the time), they found that their career caused problems in their marriage. *American Couples* found that husbands resented ambitious wives, and that breakups often stemmed from men's beliefs that their spouses spent too much time on the job. My facts support that theory. The more money our women made, the more often they cited their career as a factor in their divorce.

"The bottom line in any divorce is that the development of the partners diverges rather than converges," Dr. Bernstein believes. "When two people marry, they share the same expectations, but the advent of housekeeping and parenthood brings forth unimagined behaviors and needs. Maturation and age change people in unforeseen ways. One spouse's success radically alters patterns in a couple's life, and not all partners are willing to adapt to new routines and bring their needs and wishes into realignment. Sadly, few people are willing to accept that marriage—even childless marriage—requires more work than the most successful career."

Jennifer and Sara are divorced, and their experiences help us understand why a woman's success is often a casualty to her marriage.

"When I was really booming away, my husband was very threatened," Jennifer said. "He perceived my promotions and raises as proof of his own failure. He couldn't bear that I was more successful than he. He criticized my work at every possible opportunity.

"Once I was asked to give a speech at a well-known art school. I thought I wrote a good speech, but my husband picked it to death, and I stayed up half the night making the changes he recommended. The speech was a disaster. My rewriting had ruined it, and I felt tired and insecure delivering it."

Jennifer's lip trembled, but she kept her feelings under control. "My husband deeply resented the time I gave to my career, although I had told him from the start that my job came first. When something came up at the office and I had to cancel plans with him, he'd become furious. And to think that when I was home, I cooked all those lovely meals for him!"

Jennifer's husband's refusal to cook or do housework created obvious conflicts between them and had a less obvious, but very destructive, side effect. "We had sexual problems," Jennifer said coolly. "I was working so hard at the company and doing so much around the house that all I wanted to do when I got into bed was sleep. My husband badgered me, and his demands made me desire him less."

"I see this problem all the time in the marriages of the executive women I treat," Dr. Bernstein says. "The women are tired sometimes, but their lack of desire is more often an expression of their rage toward their husbands and men in general. It's also related to their overidentification with their career. After 'playing man' all day, they find it hard to be sexual women at home. I tell my patients to set aside special times for their husbands and to invite them along on weekend business trips. The wives who don't take these measures deprive themselves of basic pleasure and give their husbands a signal that the job is more important to them."

Jennifer believes that the greatest factor in her divorce was that she "changed enormously" during her marriage, while her husband "barely changed at all. I used to be very quiet, insecure, and compliant. Now I'm much more outspoken; my career gave me some self-confidence. Remember, when I first married, I thought I should act like a sweet wife. Now I think that idea is a bunch of crap."

Many elements contributed to Jennifer's divorce: her husband's hurt at coming in second in her life, his laziness around the house, their sexual problems, and her own psychological and professional growth. However, Jennifer's relationship with her mother was the greatest cause of her marital problems. Jennifer wed someone who couldn't enjoy her success because his ego was too frail. When she rose above him, he stepped on her. Still, Jennifer was a "good wife" to him, just as she'd been her mother's "good girl." "People often marry people with whom they can reenact family psychodramas. Jennifer married a narcissistic mother," Dr. Bernstein observes.

Regardless of how happy a marriage was, divorce is a major trauma. Coping with its emotional upheavals while maintaining an executive career causes overwhelming stress. Extraordinarily, 40 percent of our women have suffered this ordeal!

"After fourteen years of marriage to an unsupportive man, I expected to feel euphoric after he moved out," Jennifer stated. "Instead, I felt alternately numb and nauseous. I kept thinking that I was a failure, that no man would want to live with me and that I was doomed to spend the rest of my life alone. Going to work was torture." Jennifer quickly shook her head. "All those people making demands on me when all I wanted to do was put my head on my desk."

Two years after her divorce, Jennifer is "sort of frantic about finding a man. The *right* man. I couldn't face another divorce. I've joined my alumni association and a health club, but I haven't met anyone I like." Jennifer pushed her glasses higher on her nose and cleared her throat. "I always used to say to myself that I didn't want to have a child, that I couldn't handle both a baby and my career. Actually, I didn't want to make a kid go through what I went through. I was afraid I'd be too much like my mother as a parent. Now I don't think I would be; I've grown stronger." Our eyes met, and suddenly Jennifer's filled with tears. For the first time in our interview, she was showing her feelings. "I'm thirty-nine years old," she said. "I ache to be a mother. I honestly don't know how I'll live with myself if I can't have a child. I don't condone single parenthood, so unless I get married in the next few years—and I very well may not —I'll never know what it's like to be pregnant and a mother. I'll never have the most beautiful experience that a woman can have. When I think about it too much, I start crying and can't stop."

Certainly, childless women can live fulfilling lives, but some sorrow about not being a mother is inevitable. "We grew up cuddling dolls, baby-sitting, and fantasizing about having children," Dr. Bernstein asserts. "Motherhood is too powerful a part of femininity to be easily dismissed."

Jennifer has learned to fill her inner void with work. "My job has become my refuge. When I don't have a date, I work straight through the weekend." The need to turn to work as a solace is one reason why the divorced women are the least likely to take their full vacation time.

Sara told me that her husband was a "loving and caring man"; nevertheless, her success changed her in ways that he couldn't accept. "Harry made me believe I was wonderful. When I started advancing in my career, I became more confident. I'd always felt good about myself, but now I began to realize that I had rights that were being trampled on because of sexism. Here I was, a vice president in a major corporation, and after I had specifically requested that I wanted a credit card in my name, the company had it engraved with my husband's moniker. I began to see the world in new ways. I read everything I could on the women's movement, joined NOW, and became an outspoken feminist. I sounded off at stuffy parties. Gradually, my husband withdrew from me," Sara said regretfully. A moment later she snorted with laughter. "I'm the first to admit that I could be obnoxious in those years! Once, I had a passionate argument with the hostess of a dinner party because she made a denigrating remark about homosexuals. I had become sensitive to discrimination of all kinds. I relentlessly tried to get her to accept the concept of sexual choice, but she was rigid, totally convinced that gay people were sick. I harangued her for a good half hour, and when I finally looked across the table at my husband, his face was chalk-white. Today, I can argue for what I believe in without getting hotheaded, and I can give up the fight when I see I'm not getting anywhere. Then, I was metamorphosing; and in the process, a rift developed between Harry and me."

Sara found splitting up with her husband "almost unendurable. Since I asked for the divorce, I found the lawyer and initiated the proceedings, which were time-consuming, expensive, and emotionally trying. Then, neither Harry nor I could afford our apartment alone, so I began looking for apartments for both of us. We were having a heat wave, and I spent months tramping around the city apartment-hunting after working my usual twelve-hour days. And when I went home"—Sara rolled her eyes skyward—"I had to coax my husband to help me decide how to divide our property. Who should get the lamp we bought on our honeymoon?"

Sara also had to deal with the guilt of separating her daughter from her father. "We both thought Julie would be happier with me; so, thank God, we didn't argue over custody. Julie tried to be a little trooper, but she missed her father terribly. Just looking at her face—" Sara broke off her sentence abruptly. She stood and walked to my window; darkness was falling. "To compensate for my guilt," she said, fingering her necklace, "I encouraged Julie to see and talk to Harry as often as possible. I also made sure I never discredited him to her."

Since Sara was making more money than Harry, she didn't ask for child support. "I never expected to be so frightened of bearing the sole responsibility for a child. Suddenly, my job became extremely important to me. I barely took any vacation in the first few years after the divorce because I was so concerned about getting good raises."

Today, six years after the divorce, Sara still finds her life very difficult. "I do believe I spend as much time with Julie as she wants and needs, but sometimes I worry that I'm being selfish when I want to be alone with a man. I have so few free nights. Business dinners and late meetings take up four nights out of my week."

The single mothers I interviewed had immense responsibilities. All told stories as harrowing as the following. "At times, my job and my daughter's needs pull me in opposite directions," Sara said. "Recently, Julie was brushing her teeth when a glass fell in the sink and gashed her face. The bathroom rug was soaked with blood in no time at all. She needed stitches, and I had a ten A.M. flight to Washington, D.C., to make a pitch for more research money for the computer industry. I had no husband to take Julie to the hospital. I went with her, caught a later flight, and kept an auditorium full of people waiting for a solid hour. I'm normally a calm person, but I was in a cold sweat."

THE NEVER-MARRIED WOMEN

When all our women were asked to think back to when they were twenty-one and to disclose how important both marriage and a career had been to them, most gave their careers the edge. When we contrast the wives' responses to those of the women who have never wed, the differences are startling: To the never-married women careers were twice as important and matrimony five times *less* important than they were to the wives. However, a closer look at the survey data reveals that the never-married women's choice of career over marriage wasn't as deliberate as it seems. Many factors made them unlikely to have married—whether they wanted to or not.

As teenagers, they dated less than the women who wed and viewed themselves as more self-conscious and less attractive. They were "brains" who took their education very seriously, and many more of them graduated from college than the women who married (80 percent versus 50 percent). Not coincidentally, both their parents were better educated than the married women's, with their fathers being particularly so (50 percent of their fathers graduated from college, compared with just 23 percent of the wives' fathers). By having at least sixteen years of education, the never-married women placed themselves in the category of women whose chances of marrying are slimmest. The Census shows that the greater a woman's education, the greater the odds she'll never wed.

Well-schooled—but not in the art of romance—our never-

married women were highly motivated to succeed professionally. Over the years they worked hard—to their minds, much
harder than their male peers. Their anger at these men tar-
nished their overall views of men and further reduced their
chances of marrying.

The never-married women's tunnel vision literally paid off,
for they earn more than the divorcées and wives (an average
of $77,000, $74,000, and $69,000, respectively). On another
positive note, they rate themselves as the most intelligent of all.
However, they view themselves as the homeliest and the most
unfeminine—and only 23 percent believe that "men are generally attracted to successful women," compared with 43 percent of the wives. Since they also see themselves as less outspoken
(35 percent versus 50 percent), assertive (45 percent versus 60
percent), competitive (50 percent versus 63 percent), and aggressive (23 percent versus 38 percent) than the wives, they are
the most timid and the most insecure.

Laura illustrates the route that many of the never-married
women took in their lives. As a teenager, she had a very poor
opinion of her looks. She was uncomfortable with boys and
devoted herself to her schoolwork. After college, she gave little
thought to marriage as a goal. "Before all else, I wanted to make
it in my career. I spent my twenties doing nothing but working.
I worked night and day; I worked *constantly*." Then a point
came when Laura wanted more out of life than her career; she
wanted to enjoy herself and share her hard-won success with a
man. She wanted to change her priorities . . . but solid patterns
had been set. She had never learned how to open up and be
comfortable with men.

"One day, I turned thirty, and I spent that entire birthday
in bed, crying. I felt so old and so alone." Laura's eyes were
wide; she looked uncharacteristically vulnerable. "It had never
occurred to me that I might grow old alone. In the back of my
mind, I had just assumed that I would marry someday. Afterward, I made a conscientious effort to date. I bought a new
wardrobe; I got rid of all my preppy clothes. I began to like
shopping and trying to look pretty. Now I'm thirty-six and I'm
just learning how to relax and enjoy being with men. Wouldn't
you know." She laughed bitterly. "By the time that happened,

there are no men left on earth for me. Now every man I meet is either married, crazy, or gay."

Part of Laura's problem finding an eligible man lies in her too-high expectations, which are based on her idealized view of her father. No man, to her mind, is as handsome or funny as he, and Laura's years in the workforce have further embittered her toward men. But another reason for Laura's difficulty is that society has placed today's woman in a double bind. Encouraged to pursue a career, Laura put off thoughts of marriage until she believed she could handle both marriage and a job. By the time she felt ready, the chance for marriage may have passed her by.

Most of us know that women outnumber men in America. Because there are over a million more single women than men between the age of thirty and fifty-four, men are more in demand than supply, and those who are good "catches" are hotly pursued. "The men it would be appropriate for me to marry enjoy the largest possible selection of mates," Laura stated. "They can marry a Cristina Ferrare or a nineteen-year-old secretary."

As women get older, the odds against their marrying increase because men who divorce or are widowed remarry sooner and in greater numbers than their female counterparts. Men also die sooner, which further thins their ranks. Women age sixty-five and over outnumber men almost two to one.

As women rise higher in the corporate ranks, they must often fish for marriage partners in the pool of men junior to themselves in age and/or socioeconomic status. Many of the women I interviewed found this notion difficult to accept—and no wonder. "There is nothing unaccustomed about a male Ph.D. marrying a woman who has only a B.A., or a doctor marrying a nurse. But the reverse is viewed, and felt, as socially deviant," as a writer for *Savvy* magazine remarked.

Even if they ignore social stigmas and date men who are younger or less successful, our women often find that they don't enjoy themselves. "I want to be a woman when I'm with a man, not a mother or a mentor," Sara said. "I don't want to date someone who's still finding his way in his career." Katharine found her conversation going over the heads of the men she used to date. "I remember shopping with a guy and trying on a dress that made me look huge. The saleslady went on and on about how nice the color was on me. I whispered to the guy, 'The lady doth protest too much,' and he didn't know what the hell I was talking about."

The never-married women are also subject to society's prejudice. While the career mother is viewed as "having it all," the never-married woman is seen as "someone who is un-something, as someone who has missed out," as a *Ms.* magazine article says. A bachelor in our culture has dignity, because he has power: the power to propose. He may be quirky, but his female counterpart is seen as pathetic; to our minds, no man has chosen to marry her. The only terms that exist for her (spinster, old maid) are pejoratives. This truth lends a chicken-and-egg logic to the women's low self-esteem: The lack of confidence that led them to avoid men was aggravated by the social consequences of being single. "At least you're divorced," a friend who never married complained to me. "I wish I could just marry and divorce so that it looked like someone had wanted me!"

The women's insecurities and relative lack of family obligations combine to make them the most workaholic. They believe as passionately as the wives that they have no time for their homes, and are more likely to hire household help. Naturally, they feel much more strongly that they have missed out in the area of romance, but they also say that their time for friends is just as meager. "These women get caught in a vicious cycle," Dr. Bernstein finds. "They so neglect friendships in their zeal to succeed that they finally have nowhere to turn except to work for gratification."

The never-married women are the unhappiest. Only 40 percent tell us they are happy, compared with 65 percent of the wives. Every study on modern American women shows those who are both married and working to be the most content, because working wives have a better chance than other women at receiving both ego strokes and emotional support.

"Work is my *raison d'être*," said Laura. "Most of the men I meet are creeps, so although I've finally managed to walk away from the job long enough to date, I've lost faith that I'll meet Mr. Right." Laura slowly rose from her wicker chair; our interview was ending, and she was tired. She took a cigarette, slumped into her desk chair, and swiveled to the window to sit with her back to me. "You know," she said pensively, "if I had it to do all over again, I would have gone to Europe after college. I miss the fact that I never traveled." Laura sat quietly for a moment. "If I could do it all over again, I would have lived in a foreign country. I would have taken some more risks." Laura inhaled deeply on her cigarette. "I was a very conservative, very good little girl all my life. I did everything by the book, one step at a time. Now I wonder what I really achieved." Laura laughed in a short burst. "I have a very prestigious position. I have a lot of money for a woman. I've dated a movie star—a handsome, vain, stupid man." She turned in her chair to face me, her eyes challenging me to guess who he was. Suddenly she was vulnerable again; her shoulders drooped, and she looked deeply into my eyes. "Lately, I have been going through that classic dark night of the soul. I've been extremely upset. I've come to realize that being successful doesn't mean that much. So I'm the top banana here. So what?" Laura's mouth was a twist of pain. "What the hell has that done to make me happy?"

Katharine has "given up on men." "Men hurt," she declared, "and I don't want to be hurt anymore. Oh, I know it was wonderful to get the phone calls." Katharine's voice became singsong. "It was wonderful to go out on dates, and wonderful to be in love!" Katherine sighed. "But I always ended up being hurt and feeling worthless afterward." Slowly, a mirthless smile crept over her face. "Do you know what a career is? A career is school extended. Getting raises and promotions is just like getting A's. Once, my grades were the sole source of my self-esteem. I still can't get along with people, and now nobody appreciates my work."

Our women tell us more than once how they prize their independence. They work hard and make agonizing sacrifices, not for personal glory, they say, but so that they can live their lives as they please. Yet few of the women are at peace with the choices they have made. The married women worry about being too feminine at work and about being unfeminine at home. The mothers hide their maternity at the office. The never-married women have lost touch with their human needs.

Society restricted our mothers from doing and being all that they could. Our women—true mothers' daughters—have found ways to shackle themselves.

CHAPTER

=IX=

ALONE
AT THE TOP

I've noticed that women who feel least sure about themselves as women—in the shadow of their mothers' self-
denigration, those mothers who didn't feel good enough
about themselves to love a daughter strongly—are most
likely to fall into the superwoman trap, trying to be Perfect
Mothers, as their own were not, and also perfect on the
job. That female machismo, passed on from mother to
daughter, hides the same inadmissible self-hate, weakness,
sense of powerlessness as machismo hides in men.
—BETTY FRIEDAN,
The Second Stage

A year ago, I was in my office when I saw a woman in the
hall who had just been made a vice president. I had known
Bernadette for years and admired her for her talents and seeming confidence. Since the trauma of my hysterectomy, I had
been reaching out to my female colleagues, and she and I had
become friendly, though not as close as I'd have liked. Now, as
I congratulated her on her promotion, I sensed that something
was troubling her. "Come in and have a cup of coffee." I ges-
tured for her to sit on my couch. Bernadette slowly moved to
the couch, sat, and burst into tears. "I'm fifty years old and I
haven't done one thing I've wanted to do my whole life. I can't
stand it anymore," she sobbed. "I feel like I've lived every moment as other people wanted me to—first my parents, then my
husband and children. Now I'm doing only what this company
wants me to do.

"Looking back, it seems that all I've ever done is work. I wanted this promotion so badly, but now I don't know how I'll handle more work. I'm afraid I'll go crazy! I don't get along very well with the men I'll be reporting to, and then there's my husband. We got married twenty-five years ago and began our careers with the same dreams. I felt survivor's guilt when I succeeded and he didn't, so I took care of the house and cooked for him. Now I'm mad at him for not helping me, and he's angry because he thinks I neglect him. We're strangers to each other." Bernadette's crying grew hysterical. I put my arms around her, and she clung tightly to me.

Early the next morning she came to my office, tight-lipped and tense. She greeted me, then peered out my door to make sure my secretary wasn't within earshot. "Please forget what I said to you yesterday. Everything is all right now; I've worked my problems out." She turned and left the room, and we never mentioned the incident again.

Bernadette feels completely helpless and alone. After years of hiding her problems, she can neither open up to others nor admit to herself how lost she is. Isolated from her own emotions and—for reasons we have only begun to explore—from other women and men, she is typical of those I interviewed.

ISOLATION FROM ONESELF

Because women raised in a male-oriented culture sense that they aren't worthwhile, they learn to hide their feelings and desires and be whom others want them to be. Predictably, 60 percent of the women I surveyed said that "being liked by others" was much more important to them than to their male peers.

As our women advanced in business, their need for acceptance—and consequently, their self-denial—intensified. Many of the interviewees adopted what Betty Friedan calls a "female machismo." Rose returned to work exhausted after her two-week maternity leave, yet "worked harder than ever, to prove that being a mother wasn't going to slow [her] down." Jennifer told no one about the "terrible headaches" she suffered from. Laura "paid no attention to the colds and flus" she often caught in the ten years she worked without taking a vacation day.

Similarly, the women who get only a few hours' sleep a night never confess to being tired. Instead, one woman who sleeps four hours says she's "a very high-energy person" (*Vogue*, "Life at the Top"), while another claims, "I only need three to five hours' sleep. After my husband and children are in bed I can sit down and get a lot done." (*Savvy*'s "1983 Roster of Outstanding Women Executives").

What happens to someone whose life is marked by constant self-denial, whose energy is invested not in being herself and meeting or communicating her own needs but in pleasing others and maintaining a facade? Looking at two undernourished women's experiences gives us a good idea.

After years of overwork and loneliness, Laura had a near breakdown. Her every instinct was telling her that she had to change her life, but she paid little heed to her feelings. Appearing successful and competent was more important to her than her own well-being. Today, she is still a workaholic. Most of her socializing is business-related, and she has no interests outside her work. On weekends, she spends her time poring over competitive magazines and thinking up new story ideas.

Laura dates occasionally, but deprives herself of the chance to be loved. "I can't fall in love with an average-looking nice guy. I've met plenty of guys who want to treat me like a queen, but I only fall for the handsome bastards. Maybe I'm looking for the perfect guy to show off to my mother."

Laura pays so little attention to her innermost drives that she often doesn't satisfy the most basic need of all: hunger. "If I gain two pounds, I hate myself and starve myself," she told me. "I never eat ice cream or what I really like." Laura can't reward herself because she thinks she must constantly prove her worth. After our first interview, on a Friday, she and I shared a cab home. I had just found out that Channel F on cable showed old movies on Saturday mornings. "Tomorrow I'm going to make a big breakfast and watch *Bringing Up Baby*," I told her.

"Won't you feel guilty?" Laura asked.

"At ten o'clock on a Saturday morning? Why on earth should I?" I wondered.

"You mean you can actually do nothing without feeling guilty?" she replied.

Rose, too, is remarkably divorced from her feelings and desires. After twenty years of marriage, she still doesn't have orgasms. Her sexy look is a ploy for attention, not a reflection of how she sees herself. She makes no sexual demands on her husband and puts up with his bullying because she wants to preserve their relationship at all costs. The costs, of course, are her sexuality and her very self.

A life-style that affords a woman no opportunity to express herself is a one-way ticket to disaster. There comes a time when the lid on all that repression must blow off. Self-denial will lock us out of the boardroom as surely as if a law were passed to keep us from getting in, because it ultimately forces us to self-destruct.

ISOLATION FROM WOMEN

Carol Kleiman, the associate financial editor of the *Chicago Tribune*, recently said to a fellow journalist, "The opening comment by 90 percent of the businesswomen I interview is 'I'm not a feminist.' These women are not comfortable being woman-identified, so they're trying to tell me they're like men. [They're trying to make] an alliance with the men who still, for the most part, control their destinies."

If women don't want to be "woman-identified," they will not just curb their warmth and liveliness, they will steer clear of women's issues . . . *and women themselves.*

I have been struck recently by a major difference between my male and female colleagues. Men, when they drop by my office, open the conversation with a pleasantry; they talk about a recent news event or a restaurant they have discovered. Women come right to the business at hand, and a simple query about their weekend elicits a suspicious look and a vague reply.

Most of the women I interviewed agreed with my observation. "Even in the privacy of their offices, women won't talk about a child's problem or a favorite recipe," Sara said. "Meanwhile, men's laughter rings through the halls as they discuss a recent football game."

I asked the women I surveyed to describe the interactions of the businesswomen they knew, and the resulting picture was disturbing, to say the very least. Many said they believed women felt "understanding" for one another (60 percent), but that this understanding seldom translated into active support: Only 34 percent find that women are generally "supportive" of each other.

Early in Jennifer's career, she sought an executive woman's help. "I was in a meeting with two men when one said to the other, 'What does she know? She's only a woman.' I was so upset, I made an appointment to talk with a senior woman in the company. I said, 'I'm sure you've had similar experiences and I'd like to know how you handled them.' She acted aghast at what happened to me: 'I can't believe a man said that!' She believed it. She didn't want to make waves, to antagonize the men in power by being prowomen."

Nearly two thirds of our women found female networking "not very effective" (64 percent). "Networks are a joke," said Laura. "I've stopped going to the luncheons held by [a prestigious New York network]. It's a status symbol to belong. They don't help other women; they exclude those who aren't yet at high levels and could actually use some help in their careers."

"Most women's networks are nothing more than social clubs," Sara agrees. "The women don't want to offend the male power elite by backing issues like the ERA or showing special support for women employees."

Only 40 percent of the women polled considered themselves feminists, a fact that blatantly contradicts their views on major feminist issues (in addition to the statistics we've seen, 75 percent favor the ERA). I was thunderstruck by the responses of the interviewees when I asked if they were feminists. "I'm not a feminist because I've never felt that being female hurt me," Katharine said. Earlier in our talk, she had supported feminist ideology and had railed about men's giving men the best jobs.

"I would go to war on the front lines for the right to abortion." Laura's blue eyes blazed. "Any fucking man who tried to tell me what to do with my body . . . ! But I don't want anything to do with those feminists."

Not surprisingly, our women are much more likely to have read best-sellers on business than books that deal with women's shared experiences. Two thirds (66 percent) read *In Search of Excellence*, by Thomas J. Peters and Robert H. Waterman, Jr., a book that traces similarities in America's best-run companies. Over half (55 percent) read *Megatrends,* by John Naisbitt, which details upcoming changes in American business because of new information technologies. An equal number (55 percent) read *The One Minute Manager,* by Kenneth Blanchard, Ph.D., and Spencer Johnson, M.D., which outlines a quick way for managers to increase productivity, profits, and morale.

The "women's book" read by the largest number of women (46 percent) was *The Managerial Woman,* a study of the careers of twenty-five executive women. Only 38 percent read Betty Friedan's classic *The Feminine Mystique,* which many credit with launching the modern feminist movement and galvanizing a generation of women to take control of their lives. And I was further dismayed to see that only a third (34 percent) read Nancy Friday's groundbreaking book, *My Mother/My Self.*

The clearest signal that our women won't take a stand for female solidarity is the fact that only 16 percent of those surveyed take part in feminist organizations or activities. While Jennifer, Annie, and Sara described themselves as feminists, only Sara works to promote women's rights. She belongs and is a financial contributor to several women's organizations, has trained women in assertiveness, and was instrumental in creating a day-care facility at her company.

The problem of withdrawal from women and women's issues becomes much more serious with the undernourished executives. "Years ago, my boss hired a woman to assist us," Rose confided. "She was a nice, smart, outgoing person whom everyone liked. She had a lot to learn about marketing, but she often had excellent ideas. One of her concepts for a direct-mail campaign was chosen over mine." Rose's eyes anxiously sought mine. "I can't tell you how uncomfortable I was having to work with her! I lost my appetite and I couldn't sleep nights! After a few months, I told my boss that she had to go or I'd quit, and he fired her. I think I would have handled the situation differently had a man been involved."

Two thirds of our women (68 percent) observed that their female colleagues were often "unnecessarily competitive" with one another. These women are nearly always undernourished, and the mold for their behavior is set in early childhood.

"At about age four, a girl enters the Oedipal phase and grows very curious about her father," Dr. Bernstein explains. "For the next few years, she'll actively seek his love. If a mother wants her daughter's undivided love, she'll feel threatened and try to keep the father and daughter apart. Many women remember their mothers saying, 'Leave your father alone. He's busy.' Others remember only silences and glowering looks."

But "the contest between mother and daughter isn't only for daddy," as Nancy Friday explains. "It is the girl's struggle for recognition, for the limelight, for her place in the world with or without daddy's presence." A non-nurturing mother casts a pall on her daughter's attempts to shine, and can become particularly oppressive in the daughter's adolescence. "Many mothers won't let their teenage daughters have nylon stockings or bras when they want them," Dr. Bernstein reports. "One patient of mine wouldn't allow her fifteen-year-old daughter to wear the color red. She said it was because her daughter was busty and she didn't want her getting 'the wrong kind of attention.' Actually, the mother couldn't bear that her daughter was sexual; that she was becoming an adult and would soon go off on her own."

Such mothers intrude into their daughters' privacy, saying, in effect, "What's yours is mine." "Many mothers read their teenage daughters' letters and diaries or listen in on their telephone calls," Dr. Bernstein finds. "Others become overly close to their daughters' boyfriends and friends.

"To maintain the tie to her mother, a girl will rationalize her mother's invasiveness. But if a mother prevented her from doing what she wanted most in life—from her right to win her father's love to her rights to be independent and sexual—she is going to feel angry. If she can't express her anger directly, it may easily emerge in her interactions with other women. Because they transfer their feelings for their mothers onto other women, *many women, deep inside, are furious at other women.* Another woman will always present a threat to their happiness."

Our women told us that "feeling threatened" by one another was pervasive among the professional women they knew (74 percent). Annie isn't the only woman I interviewed who once almost lost her job because of a female boss's fears of being usurped.

When she was forty, Annie was a vice president of movie

development for her TV network. She worked well with others and was perceived as the department's rising star. Her boss, Joyce, ran the department. Joyce, at fifty-five, was the only woman on the board of directors and was nationally respected for her expertise. Annie was her protégée, and the two had developed a close business friendship.

After they had worked together for five years, Joyce came to Annie's office late one afternoon to ask if she was free for dinner. She said she thought they needed to have some quiet time to discuss the department's budget. Annie agreed. Joyce chose an elegant Italian restaurant where the women talked and relaxed over antipasto and wine. Then the main course arrived, and Joyce confessed she'd been thinking about something more important than the budget.

"I've been thinking about your career, Annie, and I've come up with a wonderful idea," she said. "I think you would be terrific in publicity. And moving to promotion would broaden your knowledge of the industry." Annie laughed; she thought Joyce was joking. Publicity was way outside her experience; and as Joyce knew, she loved movie development. But Joyce wasn't joking. In fact, she was so serious, she had already discussed the idea with several people in top management who would have to sanction the move.

At the time, Annie says, she was too naive to comprehend Joyce's motives. At first, she felt only stunned by what Joyce had done. Then she burst into tears and told her she could not, and would not, change departments. Annie stayed on and continued to work effectively in movie development, and months later, Joyce admitted that she'd been trying to get rid of her. "I thought the men in management liked you better," she confessed. "I was afraid they had lost interest in me and would eventually put you in my spot."

I asked Annie if she knew how Joyce had gotten along with her mother. "*Terribly,*" Annie said. "She hated her mother. She referred to her as 'my mother, that bitch.' "

Joyce told Annie that she feared the men in authority preferred her not just because she was smart, but because she was pretty and younger. Being "fearful of younger, more attractive women" is common among women in the workplace (60 percent), not only because our culture places so much importance on a woman's looks but because after years of corporate life, many women forget how to be attractive. "Joyce didn't like herself as a woman," Annie observed. "She hated her body and dressed dowdily. When she complimented me on a blouse, she'd have a pained expression on her face. She finally decided to make herself over, but she had no idea of how to do it. Her new haircut and clothes did absolutely nothing for her."

Sadly, our women report that as a result of their fears, women frequently "manipulate" one another at work (64 percent), as Joyce tried to do with Annie. "Manipulation is often learned from a controlling mother," Dr. Bernstein finds. "The mother tells the daughter that a suggested action is 'good for her,' that she's only forcing the daughter to do it out of motherly love. The daughter suspects her mother's motives aren't pure, but can't react assertively because her mother has tricked her with protestations of love."

Some of our antifeminist women are anti*woman*. "I am not, and will never be, a feminist," Rose told me. "I have always hated women's organizations, hated women in general. No, not hated women," she hastily corrected herself, "just hated being with them. I find being with men much more interesting. I hate going to parties and getting stuck talking to women about babies and shopping and making roast beef."

To Rose, anything that smacks of being female is dull, degrading, detestable. She has no female friends ("My husband is my only friend") and offers no support to her female colleagues. "I managed to climb to my position without any special help. I can't see that women should have concerns beyond those that affect men." (Minutes before, Rose had said she worked twice as hard as her male peers.) "Women's groups have formed periodically at my company to try to change certain policies. I always took the position that I wouldn't support just women *or* men. The women resented me. They figured that since I had some clout, my backing them would make a difference. They were right; I could have helped them, but I chose not to."

Dr. Bernstein believes that unconscious fury at their mothers is often the reason women don't support legislated maternity leave. "*I* did it," Rose said angrily. "I gave birth to Rachel and came back to work within two weeks. It was tough, but if I did it, why can't other women?" "*Let them suffer,*" is the message she conveys.

Since Laura believes in feminist goals, she could give no logical reason why she wasn't a feminist. "I have never been comfortable around those committee-clubby-feminist-women types. They don't have senses of humor; they take themselves so seriously. I used to feel intense dislike for Gloria Steinem. I was on a plane with her a few weeks ago. I could've sat beside her, but I sat behind her. I wasn't interested in talking to her."

To counter Laura's charge that the women weren't funny, I told her that Gloria Steinem had once described women like us as having "grown up to be the men we wanted to marry." Laura burst out laughing. "That's very funny! Oh, that's terrific!" She paused in thought. "Gloria Steinem is skinny," she confided, narrowing her eyes, "but in the face, especially around the eyes, she looks like she's been through some *stuff*!"

Clearly, not all women are unsupportive of each other, and not all their working relationships are destructive. But because women often bring emotional baggage to their interactions, their working liaisons run to extremes. Kathleen V. Shea, a psychologist who wrote a seminal study on the emotional health of executive women, "commonly [saw] disasters or roaring successes" in the women's relationships with their female assistants.

"Working with a woman can be better than working with a man," Sara said. "For a very short time, I worked for a woman named Nanette. It was wonderful, because I could be myself. I could tell her I had cramps or that my daughter was sick and know she wouldn't think I was trying to make excuses for something. I could act warmly toward her and not have my motives misinterpreted."

A third of the women I spoke with, however, said they preferred working with men. "With a man, I always know what to expect," Jennifer explained. "I have worked for a manipulative man, but his actions were less covert, less sugar-coated, than those of the women I've worked for. I know this sounds terrible, but I hope I never work for a woman again."

Women's undue competitiveness is a major stumbling block to their success. It keeps them awash in anger and fear when their energies could be used more constructively; sets a negative example for lower-level women; creates difficult working conditions for the women who are its targets; diminishes the effectiveness of teamwork; and, in some cases, actively inhibits career progress. Nearly a third (30 percent) of the women surveyed reported that "the jealousy of female colleagues" had seriously hindered their advancement.

"For sad if obvious reasons," Gloria Steinem says, "women . . . are the only discriminated-against group whose members seem to think that, if they don't take themselves seriously, someone else will." Let's stop kidding ourselves. Men won't change the policies that keep us from having fulfilling careers unless we, together, demand they do.

ISOLATION FROM MEN

In our culture, boys and girls tend to play in same-sex groups and as they grow up, they rarely establish close, nonsexual friendships with one another. As a result, when men and women interact, a subtle sexual charge is often in the air. Playfulness and even flirtatiousness between men and women is natural—and nice.

Bending over backward not to act feminine leaves us at a loss as to how to act around men. If we feel we have to ignore our sexuality around them, our relationships become overly reserved and strained.

"One night my former boss, Joyce, and I were at a business dinner where I laughed and flirted innocently with a guy in top management," Annie said. "Both he and I were happily married; our joking was all in fun. The next day Joyce told me she was 'horrified' by the way I'd behaved. She succeeded in humiliating me, but I was very angry. I remember saying, 'Damn it, I'm a grown woman! My own mother wouldn't talk to me this way!' Later, Joyce admitted she was jealous of me. I had friendly, sometimes teasing and bantering relationships with the men. Her working relationships with them were all substance, no levity."

Many of the women I interviewed felt uneasy socializing with male colleagues. "I dread having drinks with the men, because when I drink, I can get sort of vulnerable." Jennifer cleared her throat. "If I let my hair down, they might not take me seriously. I completely avoid the office celebrations."

Interestingly, Rose, for whom no bells toll in her sex life, is afraid of what might happen if she loosened up around her male colleagues. "The men I work with socialize all the time," she said. "They have dinner parties and cocktail parties, but I never go. My husband works nights a lot, and I don't want to go alone." Rose smiled apologetically. "I know this sounds ridiculous, but I suspect I'd flirt with the men and I'm afraid that things might go too far. I don't want to do anything to jeopardize my marriage."

Women who don't get to know their male colleagues in relaxed settings miss tapping an essential source of business intelligence, not to mention fun. In informal gatherings, men learn about each other's areas of expertise. They pick up hints on how to relate to each other (for instance, what someone's special interests or favorite sports are) and exchange clues about upcoming changes in management. Women who cut themselves off from this flow of news are unable to predict corporate shake-ups. They can't effectively plan for their growth because they don't know who'll run the company or what the philosophy of the management team will be.

Our women are as isolated in their personal lives as they are from both men and women in the executive suite. Katharine is alarmingly alone. She has stopped dating and has only a few female friends. "Once I had a lot of girlfriends, but I got burned in those relationships too. Girlfriends always seem to betray me or hurt my feelings. I'm just not a people-person. Maybe it's because of my weight, but I feel that people are always judging me. After the work week, I'm too tired to be nice and put on a smile. I often spend the weekend in bed just reading or watching TV." How's that for a day in the glamorous life of one of America's top businesswomen? And a good number of those I interviewed spend their days off similarly!

When an executive woman's life is as empty as Katharine's, her emotional well-being depends heavily on her job. Professional failures are shattering to her—and if she lacks a support team, business disappointments and even disasters are inescapable.

Mary Cunningham's life until the time she left Bendix provides a stunning example of how lonely the lives of executive women can be, and of the harrowing consequences such solitude can incur. Her story shows how the forces in a female achiever's life can conspire to render her incommunicado.

In *Powerplay: What Really Happened at Bendix*, Mary begins by describing her childhood. When she was five, her mother left her father, and the family had to live on a very small income. Mary recalls her reaction to seeing her mother cry in those difficult years. "I vowed . . . I'd always be strong. I'd never show sadness or give her reason to think she'd done the wrong thing." To please her mother and an uncle (a father figure), Mary got excellent grades in school, and her social adjustment was extremely poor. Before she went to her first dance in the seventh grade, she felt so awkward she made a list of "topics [she] thought normal people talked about: the weather, the teachers at school, the neighborhood." She was alienated from boys and uncomfortable with her sexuality. Once she became aroused while slow-dancing at a party, but "as soon as the music stopped [she] decided [she'd] better go home." Another time, when she finally summoned up the courage to ask her mother for a bra, she burst into tears of embarrassment.

Mary loved her mother, but believed she was too strict and too much in her own world. "All of the parents of the kids in the honors class, which I was in . . . socialized. It was a social town. But my mother didn't participate in any of that. We weren't part of a social network. . . . [She] was not a social woman." Her mother would sometimes ask Mary why she spent so much time on her homework. " 'I really enjoy it,' I'd tell her. And it was true. . . . But often I was tempted to tell her what was also true: 'There's such a gap between me and the other kids because of what you think is acceptable behavior that it's just easier to sit up here and work,' or 'Why go to a party at seven-thirty when you'll only have to be picked up at ten-thirty while everyone else stays till midnight? It makes more sense to stay home and study.' I wouldn't tell her this. At all cost I wanted to avoid fighting or arguments of any kind."

At Wellesley, Mary was "well aware that [she] had too little balance in [her] life. . . . I could already see people's eyes glaze over when I started to talk about theology or ethics. 'Did you actually let him up to your room?' someone would say, divulging the details of her latest exploit, and I'd contribute an observation about human nature gleaned from Aquinas."

In her senior year of college, Mary met Bo, a black student at Harvard Business School who, like her, felt an outsider. After she graduated, the two married and moved to New York. Soon Mary went to the Business School herself, while Bo stayed behind in New York. After graduating from Harvard, she was offered $55,000 to start at an investment bank in New York; instead, she went to work for William Agee in Detroit, a city she and her husband had already decided they didn't want to live in, for a salary of only $34,000. Why? Because William Agee had relentlessly pursued this introverted overachiever (who confessed that she felt lonely, sometimes even when with her husband), had promised her a high-profile, fast-track job, and most important, had convinced her that he desperately *needed* her. Mary liked feeling needed, as we all do. Soon, however, she would be so devoted to him that she would completely give up her personal life. Mary moved to Detroit; her husband again stayed in New York.

Mary had initially decided not to take the job because the members of Agee's (all-male) executive staff had been unfriendly during her interviews with them. Agee convinced her to ignore her instincts, but from the start Mary had problems with these men. When, at Agee's request, she began fielding his phone calls, the executives who could no longer reach their boss deeply resented her. "Had I been more judicious, I might have politely refused to field those calls," she now realizes. At the time, she felt, "my job was to help the chairman, and I decided, even if it cost me a few allies, at least I was doing my duty."

Soon Mary was estranged from her husband and "too busy to live. My entire life was devoted to Agee. . . . I'd try to round out my life, to make plans to see someone for dinner, and then Agee would say, 'Mare, I really need you for this one, could you please just cancel that?' " She spent her Christmas vacation formulating a strategic plan for Bendix and her evenings thinking up improvements for the plan. Agee held her up as an example to his staff: "Even a twenty-eight-year-old woman can do more analysis and show more energy than you seasoned executives who've been here ten or fifteen years." The executive men's resentment grew.

After Agee promoted Mary to the position of vice president for corporate and public affairs, she flew to Washington, D.C., to meet with Nancy Reynolds, the only other executive woman at Bendix. It was soon apparent that Mary wasn't going to get along with any of her peers, male *or* female. Reynolds, who was in her fifties, would now be reporting to Mary, who was in her late twenties, and Mary sensed that Reynolds didn't like the idea. However, Reynolds gave her what sounds like very good advice: "If I were you, I wouldn't spend too much time being seen with Agee. Those things have a funny way of landing in the press." Mary interpreted Reynolds's suggestion as jealousy: "Her tone was about as motherly as Don Corleone's. . . . I had no idea of what the past relationship between Reynolds and Agee might have been, or why she seemed so intent on distancing me from him." Whatever happened, the relationship started off badly and deteriorated from there. Later, Mary would conclude—with some justification—that Reynolds had fanned the flames of gossip that resulted in Mary's having to leave Bendix.

Mary didn't have even one friend in the company.

Top management shied away from me but gradually a group of younger people, middle-level managers and recent Business School graduates, started dropping by. Usually the invitation was for lunch or drinks. I rarely had time for either, which I suppose made people think I was cold or aloof, but when I tried to attend social occasions I felt uncomfortable. My visitors seemed to come in two groups: the just plain curious and those trying to pump me for confidential information about Agee. I felt impatient with the first and uncomfortable with the second. It was clear that my choice was between being loyal to Agee and being one of the guys.

Friday nights were "the only times [Mary] had real doubts about [her] job. At five the place emptied out," she explained.

"Good night," the secretaries would sing out. "Good night," I would respond in my cheerful, businesslike voice. "Are you sure you wouldn't like to come out and have a drink with us?" a few would ask. "No, thank you," I'd say. . . . Sometimes I worked late to avoid the prospect of going home. . . . Back in my empty apartment, I'd look at the clock and wonder if it was too late to call my mom. "Hi, Mom?" "Why, hello, Mary. How are you?" "Oh, fine." It usually took her only a few minutes to root out the truth. "Mary Elizabeth, how are you really?" "Lonely."

Mary's promotion to the executive level riled a lot of people at Bendix. Soon the board of directors began receiving anonymous letters accusing Agee and Mary of having an affair and insinuating that Mary was unqualified for her job. The rumors spread and then exploded in headlines across the country. Mary lost her job, and lost almost the only meaningful thing in her life. Her strong religious faith was badly shaken, she grew emaciated, and was depressed to the point of being suicidal. With a psychiatrist's help, she was able to heal physically and emotionally, but we must wonder whether she would have recuperated so well had she been older, with even more of her life bound up in her job. "There is no data base yet for how soon after retirement executive women die of heart disease," Dr. Bernstein says. "I suspect that the statistics won't differ from those for male executives. With only one investment in life, one loss means the loss of everything."

In her book, Mary Cunningham exhibits a high degree of self-awareness. She realizes that she should have listened to her feelings before taking the Bendix job. More important, she recognizes how strongly her isolation figured into her crisis. In recent writings, she advises women to cultivate balanced lives and to build strong business friendships. Mary learned from her mistakes, but the learning was a living hell.

CHAPTER

══X══

SORROW, ANGER, AND LITTLE GIRL LOST

If you want to know what I regard as the principal crux of female despair, it is this: in the Greek myth of Oedipus and Freud's exploration of it, the son's desire for his mother is admitted; the infant daughter also desires its mother but it is unthinkable, either in myth, in fantasy or in fact, that that desire can be consummated.

—EDNA O'BRIEN

Years of pushing pleasures and needs aside take a powerful emotional toll, but the sorrow and rage our women feel are often fueled by deeper conflicts. A little-discussed but profound reason for grief in all women is that they must lose their mothers as well as motherly love. Boys, even when very young, know that when they grow up, they can marry and, through being held and loved by a woman, reexperience the blissful early bond with their mothers. Women must forever relinquish the chance to be loved by a maternal, nurturing person. Because of the different ways in which the sexes are socialized, "there is an unequal emotional exchange between men and women, and the emotional caretaking is not reciprocal," as Luise Eichenbaum and Susie Orbach say in *Understanding Women*. Women reconcile themselves to this loss as best they can, but often remain starved for love throughout their lives.

Even if it was inconsistent, mother's love was the tenderest, most unselfish, most idyllic we knew. Even Katharine's martyrish mother could make Katharine feel cherished. "The happiest I can remember being as a child, oddly enough, is when I was sick. My mother hated to see me suffer. She read to me, sang to me, and stroked my hair. She brought me soup and ginger ale and made me feel safe and adored." How do women deal with the irretrievable loss of such love? "Some women divert their thoughts," Dr. Bernstein finds. "Women's frequent envy of men ('If I were a man, my life would be easier') often disguises intolerably painful feelings of yearning for maternal love. Every woman must eventually face these feelings and mourn for herself—admit to her sorrow, cry—so that she can let go of her grief. Avoidance of the pain makes it linger."

The undernourished women can rarely confront their sorrow, because their grief seems bottomless and because they've built up an arsenal of psychological defenses. "No infant or child can fathom the lack of response to his or her needs by a mother or father," says Dr. Alexander Lowen in his book *Narcissism: Denial of the True Self*. "The main effect of too little nurturing on a child is the suppression of the feeling of longing, specifically, longing for contact with the mother's body, which represents love, warmth and security. The feeling is suppressed because it is too painful to want desperately something one cannot have."

How does a child stanch the unbearable ache for a mother's love? Frequently, with a wish-fulfillment fantasy. Rose had a very common girlhood fantasy. "I was sure my identity was confused at birth. I thought I was secretly a princess. I was a *princess*." Rose smiled dreamily. Jennifer had a recurring dream about a loving mother surrogate. "A good witch held me close in her arms and flew me to a beautiful field of flowers."

When we get older, we have more sophisticated ways of hiding our sorrow. Laura claimed not to love her mother, but her feelings were transparent. "I have never felt much affection for my mother," she said haughtily. "However, she's my mother, so I'm obliged to deal with her. Recently, she got a promotion, and I flew to Milwaukee to surprise her with a diamond pin. I had planned to spend the night, but I went back home the very same day. All that matters to her is what movie stars I've interviewed for the magazine! She doesn't care about how I feel or whether or not I'm happy. Because I get panicky when I'm with her, I told her I had to get back for a meeting in New York. I spent four hours in the airport waiting for the next plane."

Katharine's utter hopelessness was painful to see. At the end of our interview, I asked her if she had any goals. "I'd like to lose weight, except that men would start asking me out again. I can't handle men. I'll probably stay fat." A defeated look crossed her face. "I guess I don't have any goals. I hate my job, but I can't quit because I'm in debt. When I feel stress, I eat, yell, and spend money. Now I'm just stuck in this crummy life."

The most transparent symptom of our women's sorrow—and most women's sorrow—is the "undue grief they display over someone else's suffering," as Dr. Bernstein says. "Women who always cry at other people's woes are usually crying for themselves. They never cry for the right reason—for their own terrible feelings of loss—so their tears spill out at the slightest provocation." One of my friends—an executive for a well-known brokerage firm—cries if she sees a news story about poor people, if she drives past a dead animal on the road, or if she hears a song about life's fleetingness or love lost. At sad movies, her sobbing becomes uncontrollable.

Women who haven't resolved their need for nurturing are those most apt to act immaturely in their relationships. In the workplace, such women are almost compelled to hand over their power to men—and, in so doing, rob themselves of authority and credibility. I can't count the number of times I've seen a competent businesswoman act so silly and giggly around a male superior I half-expected her to crawl into his lap.

Such women also act like juveniles in their sexual relationships. Laura falls madly in love with men she doesn't even know. When she does become involved with a man, she swings wildly from ecstasy to despair. Her vocabulary is symptomatic of her sophomoric behavior—her last lover, she told me, was "darling" and "cute."

"When my husband gets angry with me, I crumple," said Rose (who makes twice her husband's salary). "I rub his back, bring him goodies, do anything to get on his good side. I also turn into a big baby when he's out of town. I'm a grown woman with grown children, and when he's gone, I can't sleep nights."

Women who yearn for maternal love are *very* inclined to behave childishly with other women, especially women in positions of authority. Annie's relationship with her ex-boss, Joyce, is a good example. Annie loved but was dependent on her mother well into adulthood; she also leaned on Joyce for many years. Because she had been nourished and had high self-esteem, she was able to loosen her emotional and professional ties to Joyce, but the undernourished women I spoke with were never as fortunate.

"A woman who's angry at her mother and wants to control other women creates obvious problems in the workplace, but she must have a willing victim," Dr. Bernstein warns. "It takes two to play the mother-daughter game. A dependent woman often seeks to play the role of the child in a relationship and, if she's very lucky, she finds a nurturing woman to mother her. If she isn't so lucky, she finds a manipulative woman. This duo is a human Molotov cocktail."

One of Jennifer's bosses was a "bad mother." Because Karen was as inconsistently affectionate as Jennifer's own mother, she pushed the normally cool Jennifer's emotional buttons with ease.

"We had a sick relationship," Jennifer said tersely. "I put Karen on a pedestal and would do anything for her. She wanted to know all about my private life and would be angry if I kept anything from her, so I entertained her with all the salient details of my love life. She was very seductive and charming. For example, I would be in my office and would hear her voice coming from hers. 'Jennnnnyyyyy.' I hate being called Jenny! 'Jennnnnyyyyy, could you come and help me find my checkbook?' I'd go in, and her desk would be overflowing with papers. She'd give me a sweet look and say, 'You're so nice to me.' Then the next day I'd make a mistake, or she wouldn't like my work, and she would reprimand me and make me feel two feet tall. She knew just how to get to me and get what she wanted out of me." Jennifer shook her head. "A couple of times she humiliated me in front of a roomful of people. She pointed out my flaws in a teasing, condescending tone. Karen switched very quickly from being a friend to being an enemy. I spent so much time worrying about whether she loved or hated me that I don't know how I did my job."

Earlier, Katharine told me she had "loved" and "adored" Donna, the Chicago boss who hired her after she had fled from Boston and her painful affair. Now Katharine said she also resented her. "Donna was a great mentor, but she constantly ordered me around. Everything had to be done her way. For a while, I did do everything her way; that is, before I saw her mistakes. At one point, she called me in and said that management had suggested moving me to a department where I could gain new experience. They were trying to hold on to me, to get me away from Donna, but she had told them that I didn't want to move. She hadn't even consulted me!" Katharine said indignantly. "Then she proceeded to tell me the reasons why I should stay with her."

Years later, with Donna retired, their relationship goes on nearly unchanged. Katharine has been unable to bring it to a close. "We're still friends, and she still bosses me around. She says I act like a child, which is probably true, but I don't want to be lectured by her. I'm forty years old! She also drinks a lot and is awful on the rare occasions that I have dinner parties. She insults people. She falls asleep with her head on the table. She makes me furious!"

The price they paid for being mothered—the loss of their independence—enraged Jennifer and Katharine. However, the factor most responsible for their anger was sorrow. They wanted love from their female bosses, and their disappointment was unendurable. Wishing for affection and being incensed when they don't get it is the story of their lives. "Anger keeps the women alive," Dr. Bernstein states. "Without their wrath, they could be immobilized by depression. Anger frequently serves as a defense mechanism to block out feelings of yearning and loss, because those emotions are much more painful than anger."

Throughout this book, we've seen situations where our women's ire is justified. Let's take a moment to look at those circumstances, and applaud the women who express indignation over them.

After her confession that she wanted to have a baby, when she realized that I empathized with her, Jennifer began revealing more and more about herself. She still rarely allowed her emotions to register on her face, but her voice lost much of its detachment and cynicism. Now she spoke with undisguised hostility. "Somehow, we are supposed to have interesting careers, husbands, children, *and* be gorgeous. I'll never forget being in bed with my husband when he slapped my fanny and said, 'Not bad! Lose a few pounds and you'll look great!' I was furious. I looked good and I was healthy and fit. I didn't look like a model, because I worked twelve hours a day and then cooked and did the housework. I didn't have hours to plan my diet and do the stupid Nautilus. Yet women who fall short of perfection are judged with such a critical eye. Every time I see that ad for diet soda on TV where the woman says, 'I like myself and so I drink these carcinogens,' I see red. We should poison and starve ourselves so we can weigh one hundred twenty pounds? And doing so is supposed to be a mark of our self-respect? It's ludicrous!" Hear, hear, Jennifer!

"Five years ago I applied for a loan to buy a beach house," Sara said. "My credit rating was superb, and I had plenty of money. The all-male officers of the bank decided I was overextended." Sara's voice took on a steely quality. "If I'd been a man, they would have fallen all over themselves to give me a loan. Because I was a woman, they thought I couldn't handle money."

"I was *so* tired after I had my daughter," Rose said. "Anyone in his right mind would have seen how much I needed a kind word, but every one of my male colleagues acted like it was business as usual." Rose got up and gave the logs in the fireplace a fierce poke. "It was unbelievable! Couldn't *one* of them have said, 'Oh my God, Rose has a brand-new baby at home as well as her four-year-old,' and shown just an ounce of compassion for me?" Indeed!

"The men in the office all have wives who cook for them and take care of them," Jennifer said bitterly. "I was exhausted for over a decade while I tended to my husband, home, and career. I don't know how I managed or how I lived with those awful headaches. How in hell do men expect us to do it all?"

"Throughout my childhood, I dreamed of meeting my Prince Charming. I had all the dreams every girl has, all the dreams every girl is *fed*," Katharine said. "I thought I was going to be loved by a wonderful man who would take care of me if I wanted to quit working. Then, when I was thirty-five, I realized I might never get married. Suddenly work became something I had to take very seriously. All the women's magazines had said that having a career would be glamorous. Ha! They neglected to say that careers involve *work*—sheer, hard work. I feel like I was sold two shoddy bills of goods. I entered adulthood armed with only a couple of worthless fairy tales."

Some of the women's anger toward their mothers is valid. "For all her enlightenment, my mother believed that the most important thing in a woman's life was getting married," Annie said. "If you were a brain surgeon, she still thought you hadn't accomplished anything until you had that ring on your finger. I followed those rules and, luckily, married a terrific man. But I wasn't ready for what happened when my husband couldn't pay the bills anymore. I had no work experience, and I had to go out and get a job. I had to get a baby-sitter to be there when the kids got home from school. That was years ago, when very few women with children worked. People thought I was a monster for going off and leaving my kids. I felt mad, and I think that helped me break my dependence on my mother once and for all. I realized she didn't have all the answers and that I'd have to find my own way."

The undernourished women's fury toward their mothers is excessive and, at this late stage, entirely unreasonable. "My mother never told me anything to help me cope with my life. She's the most apathetic—" Katharine exhaled exasperatedly. "I could never ask for her advice, and I still can't to this day. She didn't tell me how to catch a man, because she wasn't happy being a wife. She didn't give me pointers about work because she herself didn't work. Now if I tell her I have a problem, she says, 'Life is full of problems.' She doesn't want to be bothered. She lives completely in her own world."

"My mother was a miserable person who made the family miserable. It's a wonder I've achieved even half of what I have," Laura said hotly. "My mother always used to say how much she loved being a mother and wife, but she obviously hated every single second of it. She always looked as if she'd barely managed to drag herself out of bed, and her life was one long headache, one long complaint. When I dream about her, she's in one of those ugly housedresses with the laundry basket and those unhappy lines all over her face. Ohhhh! I wake up and want to punch someone! The minute the last kid was in college, she went out and got a job, and now she's happier than she's ever been. She should've left the house years ago! We all would have been better off. I knew a long time ago that I would never, ever, *ever* have kids. Women are supposed to become just like their mothers when they do. I couldn't stand to make a child suffer the way I did. I'll bet the real reason I'm not married is that I'm afraid my husband would want kids."

"Non-nurtured women hold on to their anger for their mothers for their own reasons," Dr. Bernstein finds. "First, they fear they might drown in their sorrow without the life raft of their anger. Staying angry also helps them stay psychologically close to their mothers. In their mind, the emotions they feel for them—anger and love—are twined. They're afraid to let go of the anger because they fear losing the love."

Laura falls in love with "bastards" not just because her father was cruel but because, to her, love and unhappiness are linked. When she says she's bored by nice men, she's not kidding. She doesn't feel anything with them because she isn't conditioned to feeling love without pain.

Anger is a constructive force when it makes us aware of a problem and spurs us to take action, but the undernourished women's constant rage traps them. "Anger shifts the responsibility for ourselves onto someone else," Dr. Bernstein says. Rather than focusing on what needs of ours aren't being met, we divert our attention to the people we see as standing in the way of our fulfillment. If we always point the finger, we don't look at how we need to change.

Laura is angry all the time—at bosses, men, women, everyone. I met her for a second interview; this time, we were to talk over lunch. She looked breathtaking in a deep-blue flapper dress that hugged her body and flared out in a series of ruffles at the hips. Her black hair had been braided through with strips of tiny diamonds and pulled away from her face into a chignon.

We left Laura's office to take a taxi to the restaurant. Outside her building, a cabbie stood parked by a curb. He was writing in his fare book and his On Duty lights weren't on. Laura ran up to his car and banged on his window. "Open up!" she hollered. "Are you free or not?"

The cabdriver gave her a weary look. "Please, lady."

"You're supposed to have either your On or your Off Duty signals on," she yelled. "I can take you to court for this offense." As he sped away, she told me she had taken three such cabbies to court. We caught another cab and soon stood at the restaurant's bar waiting to be seated. The maître d' approached, and Laura gave him her name. A few minutes later, a well-meaning waiter asked Laura if he could help her. "What is this?" she screamed. The waiter's face went scarlet. "Somebody just asked me that question!" Not coincidentally, I believe, we were seated at a cramped table near the kitchen door, prompting another scene from Laura. The last I saw of her, she was reentering her office building through a set of revolving doors. "Oh, hurry up, for God's sake!" she was yelling to a woman in front of her.

Laura shows her anger in countless everyday ways . . . but she may eventually do so in blind acts of self-destruction, as so many other executive women seem to do.

Shortly after being made a vice president, Bernadette (my colleague who had seemed so self-controlled until the day she burst into tears in my office) began acting strangely. Twice, she quit her job; twice, she returned. First, she walked out after learning that a raise wasn't up to her expectations, although she hadn't previously told management how much money she wanted. After she and her superiors negotiated a compromise, she came back to work. She quit the second time when management refused to let her hire a new staff member. When she realized she had put herself and her family in financial jeopardy, she ate humble pie and resumed her position.

Many of the women I interviewed were so filled with rage that even a small problem in the office could set off a tantrum. These flamboyant scenes gave them quick relief from their tension, but hurt their prospects for promotion and threatened their job security. Why didn't they check their behavior when they had to have known they were sabotaging themselves? Because, secretly, they wanted out of the corporate game. Their sacrifices, pressures, and loneliness had become too much to bear. They were either unconsciously hoping to be fired or were trying to move themselves to the sidelines of the corporate action so that they needn't struggle so hard anymore.

Bernadette eventually admitted to herself that she couldn't continue on the path she was on. Her angry outbursts were becoming more frequent, and the need to maintain good relationships with her superiors had become too much of a strain. She began looking for another profession, one that didn't require her to build strong, long-lasting bonds with those in upper management. When she quit for the third and final time, she had a source of financial support: a job in idea generation for a food manufacturer, where she worked relatively autonomously.

Annie's ex-boss, Joyce, wasn't as smart as Bernadette. She also played with fire, but let the fire get out of control; she lost her job and ruined her reputation in the television industry. Joyce had no husband or close friends, and career frustrations loomed large in her life. "She was always ready to fight management," Annie told me. "Once, after a year of dismal profits, general budget cuts were announced. That meant that a couple of the movie properties she'd optioned would have to be shelved. Joyce was fit to be tied." Annie rolled her eyes. "Immediately, she wanted to call a meeting with top management. I pleaded with her to wait until the atmosphere was more upbeat; business wasn't very good, and everyone was under the gun. She was blind to the needs of others and had no sense of timing. I learned as a kid that you have to develop that sense. There are certain times you shouldn't ask your mother to bake you an apple pie, and if you ask her three times anyway, you're going to get smacked. Joyce wanted to meet with the president and his five top deputies. What did she expect to gain? They had just told her that they didn't have any money. She saw the budget cuts as a personal rejection, so she threw a scene to get attention. She was unable to step back and see that she was only hurting herself. Everyone shied away from her until she became ineffectual at her job." Sympathy for her once-loved boss showed on Annie's face. "She finally left in a huff, and after that, no one would touch her. The word was out that she was a troublemaker. She's selling real estate in Florida now."

Finally, why did Marie Luisi take part in the scandal that ruined her professionally? Had her emotional conflicts turned her career into a battle . . . a battle that didn't seem worth fighting anymore?

CHAPTER

=XI=

ACHIEVING
EXECUTIVE
SUCCESS

If it wasn't for the women's movement, I wouldn't be where
I am today.

—SALLY RIDE

W hat does the future hold if executive women continue on
their present course? While we can't know for certain, we
can get an idea from the survey data. The characteristics that
distinguish the youngest (thirty to forty-five) and oldest (fifty-
five and up) women reveal how social changes may alter wom-
en's lives. The differences between the women who are best
educated (attended graduate school) and those who are least
educated (high school only) also allow us to speculate, because
American women are becoming better educated every year.

Let's look first at the youngest women. Are they the best able
to juggle multiple roles? The friendliest with male colleagues?
Female colleagues? To find out, I compared them with the two
groups of older women (those forty-five to fifty-five and those
fifty-five and up) and focused on the dramatic differences between them and the "oldest" group. We'll start by examining
how their childhoods varied from the older women's.

Predictably, the youngest women's mothers often worked outside the home and were the most apt to have seen their jobs as
a "career." Happily, tomorrow's executive women will have
working mothers as models. The oldest women were the most

likely to have been their fathers' favorites, which corroborates my theory that only the first generation of executive women felt a special kinship with their fathers. The youngest women's mothers were no more apt to favor daughters than the older mothers—a bad sign for the women of the future.

Following the national trend, our youngest women are the best educated. The majority (75 percent) graduated from college, in contrast to only 36 percent of the oldest women. At the age of twenty-one, they very much wanted both marriage and a career, because society promised them that they could have it all. Since their expectations were so great, however, they suffered bitter disappointments. Although the youngest women make the most money and are the most apt to be senior vice presidents, they are the least satisfied with their salary and degree of authority.

The youngest women are the most inclined to embrace "male" behaviors—and to do so at the expense of their femininity. They viewed themselves as more outspoken (52 percent versus 33 percent) and twice as assertive (65 percent versus 32 percent) as the oldest women and were much more likely to recognize the importance of assertiveness and competitiveness to success. Out of all the women, they assigned the least priority to the traditionally feminine traits!

Most of the youngest women had mentors early in their careers—a good omen, even if their mentors were rarely women. "Female colleagues' jealousy" often hurt their careers, which suggests that negative competitiveness among women is on the rise as more women compete for top jobs. The women's relationships with men were strained as well. They believe as strongly as the older women that they have to work harder, be better qualified, and make more sacrifices than their male peers.

Disillusionment and confusion reign in the women's private lives. They are the most apt to have married *and* the most apt to have divorced. They have the fewest children, and many of the wives are childless. Those who are mothers feel they have the least time for their children.

Out of the three age groups, the youngest women take the least vacations; yet, in spite of their pressures, they are no more liable than the older women to hire household help or to have spouses who assist them with the housework! Since their husbands were raised in the era of women's liberation and are probably the least opposed to doing housework, we can safely assume that the youngest women are straining toward superwomanhood. The theory gains credence when, in a sudden turnabout, they say they don't have to make as many sacrifices as the older women. "I can, too, do it all!" they seem to say.

Hearteningly, the youngest women are the most apt to be feminists and to be familiar with feminist literature, but they only rarely (19 percent) get involved with feminist causes.

From this evidence, tomorrow's executive women will be much the same as the women in this book. They won't find it easier to combine marriage, motherhood, and a career. While they'll make more money and—very slowly—more inroads into upper management, their success will leave them angry and alone.

Will women's becoming better educated improve the picture any? Our best-educated group (those who went to graduate school) includes many women with M.B.A.'s, a number with law degrees, and a few with M.S.'s or M.A.'s. Did their schooling prepare them for the business world? Are they more adept at setting goals than the other women are? Less professionally isolated? More assertive when making demands on co-workers? We'll begin by regarding the achievement-oriented homes in which they were raised.

Ninety-five percent of their fathers had at least some college, with 58 percent having gone to graduate school. Just as remarkable, a near majority (70 percent) of the mothers went to college. Both parents were upscale in terms of job status as well. The fathers were often professionals, with many being doctors or lawyers. The majority of the women's mothers worked, with half of them having not jobs, but "careers."

The best-educated women had fewer siblings than the least-educated women and were much more apt to have been only children. Their fathers—presumably preoccupied with their careers—didn't set much stock on family values. They were described as twice as "distant," "demanding," "selfish," and "angry" as the least-educated women's fathers, and their relationships with their wives were seen as devoid of affection.

Every one of our best-educated women was an "excellent

student" as a teenager; she was also far more cloistered, particularly from boys, than the other women were. Today, she doesn't see herself as sociable or feminine, but has confidence in her knowledge and professional skills. She views herself as much more creative, talented, demanding, smart, well-educated, intelligent, and well-read than the least-educated woman sees herself, and she believes that women succeed primarily because of their education and intelligence. However, she radically underestimates the importance of people-skills to success and places scant priority on her work relationships. What most sets her apart from the least-educated women (and all the women) is the strikingly low importance she assigns to "loyalty." Her years in graduate school, rather than honing her communications skills, seem to have made her even more of a loner than the average executive woman.

The best-educated woman makes almost double the salary of the least-educated woman ($94,000 versus $54,000), but is far more dissatisfied with her earnings and amount of clout. As with the "youngest" woman, her professional hopes have been dashed. She invested time and money in her education and, at age twenty-one, was far more interested in success than marriage. Now she finds that the men on her level are *much* less qualified than she. Her male counterparts probably got ahead faster than she did, because men with graduate degrees often rise to the topmost corporate rungs (Korn/Ferry). This woman believes not only that her superiors discriminated against her but that her male peers played dirty when competing with her.

Conflict mars the best-educated women's private lives as well. Nearly all the wives have husbands who are "less successful" than they are, and one in four is married to a man who is "*much* less successful." Still, these wives—the most unsure of their feminine appeal—are the most likely to take on the brunt of the household chores!

Out of the three groups of women who either went to high school, college, or graduate school, the best-educated women take the least vacation time. They feel they make the most sacrifices in their personal lives and believe that "anxiety from too much pressure" has greatly damaged their careers. Their dissatisfactions (and educations?) make them twice the feminists the least-educated women are, but no more apt to fight for women's rights.

Outwardly, our best-educated woman is the most successful of all the women, but she is the angriest, tensest, and most cut off from others.

Women with challenging, high-paying careers don't necessarily have to be miserable. By taking the following steps, we can greatly improve our own and other women's chances for achieving *true* success—the positions, responsibilities, and salaries we seek and the satisfaction we want from our lives.

Our first task is to *understand the profound impact of the mother-daughter bond* and how it affects our relationships with our daughters, women, and men. A non-nourishing mother was the most potent force deterring our women from getting paid what they felt they deserved and from being happy both profession-ally and personally.

The majority (74 percent) of our undernourished women and—alarmingly—half (46 percent) our nourished women told us they were unable to "openly discuss most things with [their mothers] today." Since beginning this book, I have learned that an amazing number of my female friends and acquaintances have similar problems communicating with their mothers. The trouble lies, in part, in their refusal to look at their feelings for them. When we talk about my research findings, the subject of Nancy Friday's book *My Mother/My Self* often comes up. Over and over again, women tell me they began reading the book but abandoned it after only a chapter or two. Woman who aren't afraid to handle multimillion-dollar budgets fear confronting the truths in Friday's book!

Women who do face up to their anger and love for their mothers can change uncomfortable or adversarial bonds with them into mutually supportive relationships. "Before I got en-gaged, I stood up to my mother for the first time in my life," a thirty-eight-year-old friend who recently married said to me. "She never liked the men I dated, and I finally decided I didn't want to hear her crap. I said, 'Mom, I'm hoping to marry this man. I don't care if you like him or not, and I don't want to hear your criticism.' She was miffed, but she laughed, and I could immediately hear a new respect for me in her voice. That's all it took to change our relationship. I had never dared assert myself. No wonder she treated me like a child!"

"I have recently found I could get angry with my mother and that it would not destroy her or me. The anger that separated me from her also put me in touch with the real love I have for her. Anger broke the pane of glass between us," Nancy Friday wrote in *My Mother/My Self*.

As Jennifer discovered, the key to becoming closer to your mother is recognizing not only your individuality and individual rights but hers. Two years ago, she entered psychotherapy and was able to acknowledge her need for her mother. "My mother and I shared a passion for classical music, but I held such a grudge against her that I never brought the subject up when we spoke. I always expected her to challenge my taste and I wanted to avoid getting mad. After going into therapy, I started talking about music to her. Sure enough, she tried to blast my opinions, but by then I had learned it was okay and even fun to defend myself. We wound up respecting each other and discovering some shared tastes. We began going to concerts together and we both enjoyed those times immensely." For the second time in our interview, Jennifer's light-green eyes welled up. "My mother had a fatal heart attack a year ago. I'm so glad we made peace before she died!"

The woman who "breaks the pane of glass" can stop blaming her mother and let go of the rancor she directs against herself and others. She must learn not only to be honest with her mother, however, but to see her as someone with sorrows of her own. Our mothers, too, were reared by mothers who were second-class citizens. If we can empathize with them, we may be in for a wonderful surprise. "The woman who reaches out to her mother usually finds that all the mother ever wanted from her was love," Dr. Bernstein says. "Often, this daughter will be rewarded with the maternal love she has always craved. Few mothers want to fight with their daughters. Like daughters' anger for mothers, mothers' anger for daughters is often a smokescreen for their own yearnings for love."

Unless we *raise our daughters in loving environments,* the next generation of women will be no more successful than we are.

In addition to the data we've seen, one survey finding shows the astonishing impact that an attentive, caring mother has on a woman's life. I contrasted the Protestant, Catholic, and Jewish women and discovered that the Jewish women's mothers were the most emotionally available to their daughters. They weren't perfectly "nourishing" mothers, but simply being there when their daughters needed them made an immense difference. Let's compare the women by religious upbringing, starting with the 60 percent of those surveyed who were raised Protestant.

The Protestant woman is the "average" woman described in the book, but she differs from the Catholic and Jewish women in a few notable respects. She was the most likely to have grown up in a rural area, and her family was comfortably middle-class. Her mother was often perceived as "conservative," which fits our stereotypical view of Protestants.

At age twenty-one, the Protestant women placed the least emphasis on their careers, perhaps because their mothers were the least likely to have worked. This early lack of enthusiasm may account for why they make less money than the other women—an average of $68,000. The Protestant women vigilantly read business-related best-sellers, but pay almost no attention to books about and for women. Doing what men do, they believe, leads to success.

The Protestant women often cited two obstacles as having slowed their progress: "not controlling their emotions" and "not being demanding enough." The Puritan influence on American Protestantism, with its credo of self-control, may be responsible for both the women's fears of overreacting emotionally and their reluctance to make demands.

Our Catholic women (23 percent of the sample) come from the least-educated, lowest-income families, and their families were also the largest and most traditional. Their mothers were seen as "authoritative," and were the most likely to have worked before marrying, with most of them working at "just jobs."

A huge 70 percent of our Catholic women felt favored by their fathers! However, in another illustration of how women idealize their fathers, the Catholic fathers were portrayed as being as distant as the other fathers were. The Catholic men, like their wives, played a very traditional role. Protective and highly authoritative, they were easy to romanticize.

As teenagers, the Catholic women felt the least attractive and the most uncomfortable with boys. Because they weren't less nourished than the Protestant women, their inhibitions obviously relate to their religious upbringing.

The Catholic women, like their parents, are the least-educated of their peers, with only 49 percent being college graduates. Nevertheless, at twenty-one, they were very interested in having careers and the most likely to view marriage as "not at all important." Many of the Catholic women never did marry, either because they remained leery of men and sex or because their mothers worked so hard at home that they themselves couldn't imagine having both a family and a career.

When the Catholic women do marry, they have more children than the other women. They are the least likely to favor abortion (73 percent as compared to the 86 percent average); but, surprisingly, a near majority do. Happily for the Catholic wife, her husband often does half the housework. She is especially lucky to have such a spouse, since she almost never hires household help. Does she refrain from doing so because her relatives worked in people's homes? Lack of money isn't the reason, because she makes an average of $80,000 a year. From the start, she was more motivated to work than the Protestant woman, and she may have worked harder to make up for her lack of schooling. No doubt because she came from the humblest roots, she is the most satisfied with her salary.

The Catholic woman doesn't believe that being "well-educated" is integral to success, but she places very strong emphasis on "loyalty." As proof of her fidelity, she has been with her company longer than any of the other women. She sees the widest differences between the priorities men and women stress, and her upbringing helps account for this phenomenon. In lower-class homes, men and women tend to have clear-cut sex roles and, therefore, disparate concerns. The mother takes care of the family, cooking, and rearing the children. The father looks after the family "business," earning and managing the money.

Finally, the Catholic woman presents herself as a "good girl." Unlike the other women, she is well aware of who in her company has power. The most important things in her life, by far, are "doing the best work she can," "being the best she can be," and "being better than anyone else" at her job. While she isn't always happy with her personal life, she is pleased with how well she lives up to her professional priorities.

Our Jewish women (10 percent of those polled) came from the wealthiest, most educated families, no doubt because education and self-improvement are prized in the Jewish heritage. They were often raised in cities (66 percent)—hubs of cultural and intellectual activity—and, as with the "best-educated" women, had fewer brothers and sisters than our average woman.

The Jewish women's fathers were three times as likely as the other fathers to hold graduate degrees (44 percent), and they often worked as professionals. They were the least "conservative" of all the fathers. Perhaps their education made them broad-minded, or the Jews' history of persecution made them antiauthoritarian. Probably because of the prejudice Jews face, the Jewish fathers were the least confident.

The mothers of our Jewish women were better educated than the other mothers (they went to college three times as often as the Catholic women's mothers). Most of them stayed home to take care of their children, but nearly all of them pursued careers once their children were grown. The Jewish women presented their mothers as very complex people. Of all the mothers, they were seen as the most unhappy, worried, and insecure. Still, they were dubbed the most intelligent, attractive, outgoing, and affectionate—*and not a single Jewish woman described her mother as distant.* Traditionally, Jewish mothers made it a priority to be close to their children, and these mothers were no exception. Their angst probably stemmed from being Jewish in a Christian society and from the ambivalence they, as educated women, felt about being housewives.

Our Jewish women themselves felt confusion in their teenage years. They believed they were more popular than the other women and were more comfortable both with boys and girls. In a seeming contradiction, however, they said that they weren't "social." My guess is that they felt well-liked by their circle of friends but thought they weren't generally accepted because they were Jewish. Another sign of the conflict they felt is that while they often thought they were attractive, they were the most apt to have been overweight. They also report having been the unhappiest! Why? Coming of age is probably toughest for women from minority groups. The women may also have felt pushed by their parents to achieve, for while they were excellent students, they didn't like going to school as much as the other women did.

The Jewish women are the most educated, with 90 percent being college graduates. Nevertheless, the Jewish woman is very different from the "best-educated" women and, for that matter, from all our other women. Unlike the others, she grew happier and more confident after adolescence. Today, she is very "outspoken," has close business friendships with both women and men, is frequently a mentor, and refuses to be a workaholic. She is much more in tune with her femininity than the other women, viewing herself as very affectionate, empathetic, giving, generous, and understanding. She is twice as likely as the average woman to say she is attractive (60 percent versus 32 percent) and even more apt to feel sexy (26 percent versus 8 percent).

Like her mother, however, she has an anxious streak and she tells us that she isn't as "healthy" as she'd like to be. Because "tension from too many pressures" has slowed her advancement, she may fear that stress has taken a toll on her health. She also appears to watch her weight more carefully than the others do. Once the chubbiest, she is now the slimmest.

The Jewish woman makes the most money—on the average, $91,000. She is the most apt to be a senior vice president, but —like her best-educated peers—is very dissatisfied with her salary and level of authority. She admits she is partly to blame for not having the money and clout she wants: She doesn't believe she is as visible as she should be or that she takes sufficient risks.

The Jewish woman tells us that her education, talents, creativity, people-skills, and ease with making demands got her to where she is today. She is the least likely to say that "loyalty" helped and has changed companies more frequently than the other women. Because she belongs to a minority group whose members feel a responsibility toward one another, she believes that connections play a role in success.

While the Jewish women fiercely believe that their job opportunities aren't equal to men's, they get along well with the opposite sex. They see the fewest differences between what it takes for a man and what it takes for a woman to reach the top, and they depict their male peers as talented, smart, and diligent.

They are twice as likely as the others to think that men are attracted to successful women, twice as likely to have had office affairs, and the least apt to see negative consequences arise from such affairs (they often told us that their own relationships had been "exciting"). At age twenty-one, they placed high priority on marriage, and nearly all of them married. Today, they are the most likely to have spouses who are as successful as they. They have the highest household incomes and hire full-time housekeepers more often than the other women (ten times more often than the Catholic women!).

The Jewish women have fewer children than their peers—and since they generally don't believe that executive women must limit the size of their families, they probably don't want more children than they have. Of all the women, they feel the guiltiest about having minimal time for their children; in part, because they compare themselves to their accessible mothers. They also place a high premium on their personal time. They often take all their weeks of vacation and they feel the most keenly that they must sacrifice hours for hobbies, friends, and love life.

The Jewish women are the most apt to call themselves feminists. They read a lot of "women's books," but almost no business best-sellers. Every Jewish woman polled favored the ERA. Several factors may account for the women's feminism: (a) Their religious background has sensitized them to discrimination of all kinds; (b) they saw that their mothers were troubled and wanted better lives for themselves; (c) they are the least afraid to speak their mind; and (d) they have the strongest sense of their femininity.

Out of all the religious groups, the Jewish woman came closest to having it all—a happy home life and a successful career. While she felt discrimination and was displeased with aspects of her job, she was the least alienated from women and men and—more important—she liked herself!

Besides being good mothers to our daughters, we must *be mentors to the women in our companies.* That executive women don't see mentoring as a priority is tragic for ambitious junior-level women. Women have many problems in business that men can't help them with—how to plan for maternity leave, how to react when a client insists on working with a man—yet the women who have grappled with these issues are rarely available to give advice. Lack of time was the reason cited by most of the women I interviewed for why they don't take on protégées, but this excuse doesn't hold water. Being a mentor doesn't take a significant amount of time. Mentors don't need to take their protégées out to lunch or get deeply personally involved with them. Mentoring is a matter of recognizing that a staff member is worth spending an extra few moments with at a business-social function or after a meeting concludes.

One woman wrote in on her questionnaire that she was the "sole role model for three thousand women." Let's hope that, rather than remain a passive exemplar, she acknowledges a few women's outstanding performances and lets them know she's available to answer questions and give advice.

We can't gain ground in the corporate world without *actively and successfully fighting for the legal rights that allow us to compete with men.* Only in retrospect do we realize how effective the Civil Rights Act, whose Title VII barred discrimination against women on the job, has been since it was passed in 1964. In 1965, according to the *Harvard Business Review,* both the male and the female managers they polled "rejected the suggestion (men by 71 percent and women by 55 percent) that the new law would expedite progress toward equal opportunity for women." In 1985, "only 16 percent of the men and 26 percent of the women polled believed such legislation has had no impact on equal opportunity for women." The men and women surveyed in 1985 *saw* the huge difference that the law had made. Precisely because of the Civil Rights Act, women's numbers in middle management doubled between 1965 and 1985.

Administration officials are presently trying to abolish some affirmative-action ordinances, including the law that refuses government contracts to companies found guilty of sex discrimination. The ERA, by guaranteeing us the same constitutional rights as men, will protect us if such laws are taken off the books.

Even more essential to our progress is legislated maternity leave. How can anyone justify the fact that women make up half the workforce yet jobs are structured to fit only men's needs? Or see the choices women are forced to make as a result of inadequate maternity policies as anything but unconscionable? The argument that maternity leave is reverse discrimination is inane. Men don't *need* paternity leave. Since women get pregnant, give birth, and nurse, they do require maternity leave.

Anne Jardim, who co-wrote *The Managerial Woman,* finds it "mind-boggling" that most companies don't try to accommodate high-level women who want to have children. "Either some of the brightest women in this country aren't going to reproduce or the companies are going to write off women in whom they have a tremendous investment," she comments in *Fortune*'s article "Why Women Aren't Getting to the Top." "In the end," however, "the burden of easing the working-mother bind" doesn't belong to individual companies but to "a [society] that has encouraged women to pursue careers yet still expects them almost singlehandedly to raise the next generation," as Anita Shreve writes. National legislation that guarantees new mothers paid, job-secure time off from work has been proposed to the House of Representatives. It will not be enacted unless women insist that it is.

We must *stop blindly following men's ways—not only their policies, but their behavior.* "Female managers who try to be fear-inspiring figures of authority are rarely acting from the heart," Sara believes. "My management style is very different from my male peers'. I think it's important to create a positive business climate, and unless I'm in conference, my door is always open to my staff. Being a mother taught me to see things from another person's point of view, and that ability has served me well in my career."

For years, Annie reined in her exuberance and warmth, but she eventually found her own manner of being executive. "I was too self-conscious, too controlled. In time, I realized I was more effective when I was relaxed. I have good gut feelings and I like to blurt out my opinions. When I decided that my candor and enthusiasm were strengths, I began to love my work. My intuition makes me good at my job. Men are often afraid to make decisions that aren't supported by facts; for example, if last year's TV movie on domestic violence was a bust, they don't want to risk doing another movie on the same theme. My bosses know that when I start talking *much* too fast, I've got a winning screenplay." Annie laughed. "I also used to think that as a manager I had to be stern and a little aloof, but I've abandoned that philosophy. I love my staff, and I'm protective and motherly toward them—even toward the women I hire who are older than I am. My people matter to me, and they're glad I show I care."

Finally, we have to *stop being martyrs*. If we don't set priorities and bargain for the time we need for them, our business gains will be won only at an excruciating price. Our women said that their careers always came first in their lives, but their unhappiness and guilt tell us that personal concerns should sometimes have taken precedence.

Most of the men I work with consider their vacations important and well-deserved and take them with no apologies (although they may work harder than usual for a month before they go). They can also recognize that a home situation is going to demand a lot of their time and communicate this fact to their superiors. As an example, a male friend was offered a promotion at a time when a child of his was extremely ill. He told management he wanted the promotion but that he couldn't give his all until his child had recovered. His bosses respected his frankness and promoted him anyway.

Our women found it very hard to assert their personal needs. Rose couldn't leave work to relieve the baby-sitter; Katharine couldn't tell her boss that she needed an evening off. Let's look at two women who *were* able to set priorities. Before Sara began work on the software program physicians use as a diagnostic tool, she realized she would have to work fourteen-hour days and six-day weeks to meet her deadline. She planned to complete the project in two months and warned her bosses that for a two-month period she would be unavailable to take on new assignments. Recognizing the importance of the program, her bosses asked for her assistance on only one short-term project, one she was able to delegate. Her diagnostic program has been the crowning achievement of her career.

Recently a very successful woman I know was offered a job

in a major advertising agency. She negotiated a contract that allowed her to choose her working hours for the first year of her baby's life and guaranteed that her business entertaining would be cut to a minimum during that year. Making such demands took guts and intelligence. The company accepted her terms, and she will have a relatively stress-free first year with her child.

We must draw boundaries in our personal lives as well. Gloria Steinem offers a simple solution to the problem of uncooperative husbands: "Divide the housework as you would if you were living with another woman, and then don't lower your standards." If you want a career, a husband, and your sanity, you'll have to.

Occasionally, special work projects demand our full attention. If we let our loved ones know that, for a period of weeks or months, we can commit ourselves to only limited amounts of time with them, we will avoid their unhappiness and ours. "When I worked on the diagnostic program, I told my daughter that I was going to disappear for the greater part of two months, but I promised her I'd always have breakfast with her and I'd always save Saturday night for her," Sara said. "She adjusted her expectations accordingly, and we had no problems at all."

"When the network decides on its programming schedule for the sweeps, my workload doubles," Annie said. "Still, my husband knows that, no matter what, I'll spend Friday night with him. Those months aren't easy, but oh, some of those Friday nights!"

A sad and frightening—but not uncommon—example of a high-level woman who made inordinate sacrifices appeared in a book aptly entitled *Too Smart for Her Own Good*. "[Ms.] Lane, a thirty-eight-year-old [single] woman, recently was made a partner in a Chicago law firm," authors Karen Levine and Dr. Conalee Levine-Shneidman begin.

> She recollects a conversation that, in retrospect, she identifies as "pivotal" between herself and a senior partner in the firm. At the time of the conversation, Lane was an associate being considered for partner, and the senior partner was a man she proudly identified as her mentor.

"He came into my office just before I came up for partner and said, point-blank, that he thought I was a brilliant lawyer with a terrific future in the firm, but that I had some very critical decisions to make," [said Lane]. "And he said that it was only because he cared for me on a personal level that he was even addressing me on this level, but he wanted me to understand that the hard work—the late hours and weekends—didn't end when someone became a partner. In a sense . . . a very real sense . . . the responsibilities increased. . . . He warned me that it would be hard to find a man who'd be really sympathetic to the kind of schedule I'd have to keep . . . and he went so far as to admit that *he* personally could never be married to such a woman. He needed someone, like his wife, who could be available to him and really offer support.

"I was very touched by his concern," [Lane] explained. "He asked me how much I cared about having children. He said he thought it would be impossible to have both . . . not if I wanted to be the kind of top-notch mother he knew I'd want to be. And, of course, he talked about what a big sacrifice it would be for someone like me to give up having kids. He hadn't been as involved with his kids as he would have liked, but he said the involvement he *did* have was important to him.

"Finally, he urged me to assess it all, to think long and hard about the partnership and then tell him what conclusion I came to. And if I wanted to be a partner, he assured me that I would be. Obviously, I opted for partnership . . . and I did it with my eyes open. I can't always say I'm happy about the way my work limits my life, but that's the way it is. In fact," [Lane] concluded, "just a few months ago, I had a similar conversation with another woman associate who's coming up for partner. I'm still waiting to hear what her decision will be."

Was Ms. Lane's choice between a career and a personal life so black-and-white? Of course not. That an intelligent woman could listen to, and dole out, such advice infuriates me, but perhaps her tale may serve a cautionary purpose. Ms. Lane— rather than agreeing with her mentor's limited perceptions— could have told him that she planned to find a husband who accepted her for the hard worker she was. She could have said that yes, her husband or child would sometimes come first in her life—as his family had no doubt in his—but that she had made a great commitment to her career and would act accordingly.

Having agreed to be single and childless must have upset Ms. Lane. Did she hide her feelings? Probably. Martyrs suffer in silence. For their own and other women's sakes, executive women must tell the truth about their lives. We can no longer pretend that we have "no more problems than usual." Tomorrow's women should learn from, rather than repeat, our mistakes.

Writing this book has generated some profound personal changes. I used to look outside myself for clues as to how to present myself; today I'm guided by what feels right for me. I used to feel insecure that I wasn't tough enough as an executive; now I believe my closeness with my staff makes me a better manager (it also makes me happier). I work long, hard hours and make sacrifices in my personal life, but I've also learned to relinquish job opportunities when my family and friends come first. I'm content with my choices and don't feel forced to do anything I do.

I have grown closer to my mother than I've ever been—able to face my anger and fierce love for her and to accept her as she was and is. My mother has worked all her married life and she strongly relates to the data I uncovered. I have shared my research with her and found her highly supportive and enthusiastic.

Over the past few years, I've made an effort to communicate my new awareness to the executive women I know. About a month ago I had a date for drinks with Linda, a friend from another ad agency. Linda stormed into my office at 6:00 P.M. waving a copy of an article from one of the major New York newspapers. The paper had profiled her at length after discovering that she was responsible for a string of successful ad campaigns. The article was flattering; Linda was fuming. She told me that when she had spoken to the reporter, she had refused to disclose her age. He had apparently looked it up in *Who's Who*, for it was printed in the article.

"I'd like to strangle him!" Linda's dark eyes were alive with anger.

I hesitated before I spoke and could immediately see her surprise. Only a few years ago, I would have commiserated with her. Instead, I told her what I felt—that the longer we act ashamed of aging, the longer our aging will be seen as shameful. I said I thought that by doing such seemingly innocuous things as being coy about our age, we were perpetuating our second-class status.

Linda was silent. I could hear my watch ticking as I waited for her to shout at me. Instead, her tense face slowly relaxed into a pleased smile. "You know, Edith," she said, "you're absolutely right." Linda is fifty-two years old.

I hope this book will begin a dialogue among women that will help us break the cycle of attitudes that keeps us from moving forward and achieving personal satisfaction in the business world.

HOW TO EVALUATE YOUR RESPONSES TO THE QUESTIONNAIRE

From reading this book, you already know how to interpret many of your answers; for example, if you were your mother's favorite, you're one of the lucky few and have an excellent chance at achieving both personal and professional satisfaction. Other of the answers were self-explanatory, such as how you're doing on your priorities and how happy you are with your job. This guide will help you analyze your responses to the less-straightforward questions.

Questions 8 and 9. What is your mother's job history?
If your mother worked after having children and considered her job a career, you should be able to regard her as a role model. If you don't (or never have), ask yourself why you've overlooked a helpful source so close to home. If your reason is, "my mother doesn't understand me," have you tried to understand her?

Question 13. How did you describe your father?
If you ranked "intelligent," "healthy," "special," "attractive," "confident," and "authoritative" among the top traits, your view of your father is typical.

If "giving," "affectionate," "nurturing," and "warm" are also among the top ten, you had an unusually close relationship with your father. You probably aren't as inhibited around men in authority as most women are, and you may have an easier time establishing relationships with male peers.

Question 14. How did you describe your mother?

If you ranked "attractive," "healthy," "intelligent," and "nurturing" among the top five traits and "happy," "accessible," "giving," "affectionate," and "warm" among the top ten, your view of your mother is typical. If, in addition to all of the above, you checked "successful" under "most of the time," you will have a relatively easy time reaching your goals.

If, on the other hand, you checked two or more of the following under "most of the time"—"nervous," "insecure," "worried," "angry," "distant," "selfish," or "reserved"—you fall into the "undernourished" category. You may need to work on your relationship with your mother. It's likely that you take disappointments and criticisms too hard, and that you don't assert yourself as strongly as you should.

Question 17. How did you see yourself as a teenager?

If you ranked "liked going to school" and "an excellent student" among the top five items, you are highly achievement-oriented. If you also checked two or more of the following under "most of the time"—"inhibited," "afraid," "nervous," "worried," "self-conscious," or "lonely"—you were, and still may be, too driven. Are your relationships as successful as you'd like them to be? You may need to seek more balance in your life.

If in addition to "an excellent student" and "liked going to school," you ranked "happy," "popular," "social," and "having many friends" among the top ten traits, your ambitions—with a little luck—will get you far.

Question 24. What traits do you feel are most important to a woman's success?

If you ranked "hardworking," "concerned with results," and "well-disciplined" among the top five characteristics, you're either already successful or you have the potential to succeed.

If you didn't place at least three of the following traits among the top ten— "nurturing," "outgoing," "accessible," "concerned with people," "generous," "empathetic," and "thoughtful"—you may wish to reassess your management style.

If "loyalty" is among the top five, you're probably overdoing it.

Question 25. What personality traits do you associate with successful men?

If "hardworking" and "disciplined" aren't among your top five choices, you don't have a very positive—or accurate—view of men.

Count the number of traits you ranked as "extremely important" for women and for men. If the number for men is much smaller, you may be too angry at men. Have a few bad experiences prejudiced you?

Question 26. What are you like?

If you ranked "hardworking," "disciplined," "concerned with results," and "concerned with people" among the top five characteristics, you possess the fundamental qualities needed for corporate success.

If "smart," "talented," "well-educated," "assertive," "competitive," "accessible," and "even-tempered" are among the top ten, you're all set to make your mark in the business world. If you also checked at least two of the following under "very much like me"—"empathetic," "thoughtful," "giving," "warm," "nurturing," "humorous," "fun-loving," or "generous"—you could achieve spectacular success. If, in addition, you checked "feminine" and "attractive" under "very much like me," you are undoubtedly a "happy" person.

Question 27. What are your priorities?

If "being successful," "being a leader," "being the best one can be," "setting goals," and "taking risks" are not among your top ten priorities, you aren't really interested in becoming a VIP.

If either "being liked by others" or "being admired by others" is among the top ten, a need for attention may be what motivates you to achieve.

If "being a mentor" or "having a mentor" weren't among your first ten choices, you're no different from most other women. Getting involved on either end of a mentor relationship is an easy way to improve your chances for success.

Question 28. Men's versus women's priorities.

The more items you checked under "no difference," the more realistic your view of men is and, I'd venture to guess, the better you get along with men.

Question 37. Barriers to your professional growth.

If you checked "lack of confidence," "difficulty relating to superiors," and "not being demanding enough" as obstacles that have hurt you "a lot," you have a serious problem with assertiveness. You aren't alone; many of our executive women shared this problem. Finding a role model who speaks up for herself could make a big difference in your life.

Question 49. What books have you read?

Should you be like most women, you haven't read much "women's literature." The books I consider must reading are *My Mother/My Self* and *The Feminine Mystique*

NOTES AND SOURCES

CHAPTER I: THE STRANGER BESIDE ME

Page 44. WQXR's news flash about Marie Luisi is reproduced from memory.

Page 45. The number of women in the workforce is taken from the 1985 U.S. Bureau of Labor Statistics. The number at the level of vice president or above (5 percent to 6 percent) was reported in Jay Cocks, "How Long 'Till Equality?," *Time*, July 12, 1982.

Page 47. Paul Blustein, "Phantom Ads: How the JWT Agency Miscounted $24 Million of TV Commercials," *The Wall Street Journal*, March 30, 1982. Other articles that helped me understand the Marie Luisi case were: Christy Marshall, "Her Side: A Bitter Luisi Tells How JWT Scandal Blew Up in Her Face," *Advertising Age*, March 18, 1983; Philip H. Dougherty, "Former JWT Executive Files Suit Over Ouster," *The New York Times*, April 8, 1983; Jerry Capeci and Peter Fearon, "Mad. Ave. 'Godmother' in an 'Adscam' Suit," *The New York Post*, April 12, 1983; Richard Morgan, "Luisi's Charges Against JWT Stir Industry's Sympathy," *Adweek*, April 25, 1983; and Christy Marshall, "One Year After Luisi, JWT Looking Ahead," *Advertising Age*, March 14, 1983.

Page 49. The information on how many women are on corporate boards is taken from Basia Hellwig, "73 Women Ready to Run Corporate America: A Working Woman Report," *Working Woman*, April 1985.

Page 49. The *Harvard Business Review* presented its 1985 and 1965 survey results in an article entitled "Probing Opinions: Executive Women—Twenty Years Later," by Charlotte Decker Sutton and Kris K. Moore, *The Harvard Business Review*, September/October 1985.

Page 50. The articles referred to are Judy Klemesrud, "Women in the Law: Many Are Getting Out," *The New York Times*, August 9, 1985, and Ellen Rittberg, "The Pink Parachute: Some Women Who Rise to Executive Heights Find It Hard to Breathe and Are Bailing Out," *Daily News Magazine*, August 11, 1985.

CHAPTER II: WHO IS THE EXECUTIVE WOMAN?

Page 52. The *Working Woman* article referred to is "What Makes an Executive Woman?" by Elizabeth Overton, January 1980.

Page 52. Korn/Ferry International's Executive Profile: A Survey of Corporate Leaders, N.Y., A Publication of Korn/Ferry International, 1979. *Korn/Ferry's International Profile of Women Senior Executives,* N.Y., A Publication of Korn/Ferry International, 1982.

Page 57. The 1985 Census data on income earned by female professionals indicates that there are roughly 5 million executive women in the country.

Pages 58–59. Most of the women surveyed grew up in the 1940s and 1950s. I used the figures from the 1950 Census to compare their mothers and fathers to the "average" mothers and fathers of their generation.

Page 59. My assumption about the average age for men who reach the level of vice president or above is based on personal observation. Since Korn/Ferry's men were at higher levels than our women, I couldn't compare them on issues like age or salary.

Pages 62–63. All the statistics on American women's marriage, divorce, and childbearing rates come from the 1985 Census. All the statistics for executive men are from Korn/Ferry's 1979 study.

CHAPTER III: THE EARLY YEARS

Page 64. Nancy Friday, *My Mother/My Self: The Daughter's Search for Identity.* (New York: Delacorte Press, 1977), p. 91.

Pages 64–65. Margaret Hennig and Anne Jardim, *The Managerial Woman: The Survival Manual for Women in Business* (New York: Pocket Books, 1977), pp. 103–105.

Page 65. While researching *My Mother/My Self,* Nancy Friday uncovered the fact that children often prefer abusive biological mothers to nonabusive foster mothers. Her discussion of the phenomenon appears on page 8 in *My Mother/My Self.*

Page 65. One landmark study of the effects of birth order and favoritism on children was conducted by Dr. Robert Zajonc and his colleagues at the University of Michigan. Its results were published in "Family Configuration and Intelligence," by Dr. Robert Zajonc, *Science,* April 16, 1976.

Page 66. Hennig and Jardim, *The Managerial Woman,* p. 49.

Pages 78–80. An excellent discussion of the early mother-daughter relationship, which helped us solidify our ideas, appears in Luise Eichenbaum and Susie Orbach, *Understanding Women: A Feminist Psychoanalytic Approach* (New York: Basic Books, 1983). We are especially indebted to the authors for helping us understand how sociological and psychological influences conspire to make daughters less independent than sons. Dr. Bernstein guided us on the basic patterns and problems in the early mother-daughter relationship.

For those interested, Dr. Alexander Lowen's book *Narcissism: Denial of the True Self* (New York: Macmillan, 1983) offers additional insight into the personality disorder narcissism.

Page 81. The statement by Dr. Elizabeth Hoppin Hauser came from a discussion with Nancy Friday and appears on page 397 of *My Mother/My Self.* At the time of their talk, Dr. Hauser was a psychotherapist on the staff of the Long Island Consultation Center in Forest Hills, New York.

Page 81. Psychiatrist Mio Fredland, formerly an assistant professor of clinical psychiatry at Cornell University Medical School, is quoted from *My Mother/My Self*, p. 308.

Page 84. This passage is from Kim Chernin's fascinating book *The Hungry Self: Women, Eating, and Identity* (New York: Times Books, 1985), pp. 62, 63.

CHAPTER IV: THE TEENAGE YEARS

Page 85. Mary Cunningham with Fran Schumer, *Powerplay: What Really Happened at Bendix* (New York: Linden Press/Simon & Schuster, 1984), p. 63.

Pages 86–87. Susan Brownmiller, *Femininity* (New York: Linden Press/Simon & Schuster, 1984), p. 25.

Page 90. Nancy Friday, *My Mother/My Self: The Daughter's Search for Identity* (New York: Delacorte Press, 1977), p. 146.

CHAPTER V: THE EXECUTIVE WOMAN TODAY

Page 96. Kim Chernin, *The Hungry Self: Women, Eating, and Identity* (New York: Times Books, 1985), p. 33.

Page 96. Asta S. Lubin, "Superwomen of the Financial World," *Working Woman*, September 1984.

Pages 97–98. The study that found that pretty women were less apt to advance into managerial spots than plain women, conducted by New York University psychologist Madeline Heilman and doctoral student Melanie Stopeck, was published as "Attractiveness and Corporate Success: Different Causal Attributions for Males and Females," *Journal of Applied Psychology*, May 1985. The quote from Betty Lehan Harragan is from her book *Games Mother Never Taught You: Corporate Gamesmanship for Women* (New York: Warner Books, 1977), p. 346.

Page 98. A good explanation of why man-tailored suits don't flatter most women appears in Amelia Fatt's book *Conservative Chic: The Five-Step Program for Dressing with Style* (New York: Times Books, 1983).

Page 102. Kim Chernin also suggests that women's present obsession with slenderness correlates to their need to make it in a man's world. She argues that many women who diet compulsively are trying to get rid of female curves. Adrienne Rich is quoted from her book *Of Woman Born: Motherhood as Experience and Institution* (New York: W. W. Norton, 1976), p. 236.

Page 102. The books referred to are: Charlene Mitchell and Thomas Burdick, *The Right Moves: Succeeding in a Man's World Without a Harvard MBA* (New York: Macmillan, 1985) and Marilyn Loden, *Feminine Leadership: Or How to Succeed in Business Without Being One of the Boys* (New York: Times Books, 1985).

CHAPTER VI: ON THE JOB

Page 121. Betty Lehan Harragan, *Games Mother Never Taught You: Corporate Gamesmanship for Women* (New York: Warner Books, 1977), p. 78.

Page 125. The discussion of Jeanette Kahn is based on a lengthy article about her by Susan K. Reed, "Zap! Pow! Shazzam!" *Savvy*, January 1984.

Page 126. Kim Chernin, *The Hungry Self: Women, Eating, and Identity* (New York: Times Books, 1985), p. 33.

Pages 133–134. Eliza G. C. Collins, "Managers and Lovers," *The Harvard Business Review*, September/October 1983.

Pages 135–136. Warren H. Schmidt and Barry Z. Posner, *Managerial Values in Perspective: An AMA Survey Report* (New York: AMA Membership Publications Division, 1983).

Page 136. Gloria Steinem presents this idea in her article "The Time Factor," which first appeared in *Ms.* (March 1983) and now appears in her book *Outrageous Acts and Everyday Rebellions* (New York: Holt, Rinehart and Winston, 1983), pp. 173–75.

CHAPTER VII: WORKING WITH MEN

Page 141. Dr. Blotnick is quoted from his article "Unsexed by Success," *Harper's Bazaar*, September 1985.

Page 145. The books referred to are: Chuck Yeager and Leo Janos, *Yeager: An Autobiography* (New York: Bantam Books, 1985) and Lee Iacocca with William Novak, *Iacocca: An Autobiography* (New York: Bantam Books, 1984).

CHAPTER VIII: AT HOME

Page 150. The statement by Helen Gurley Brown is from her book *Having It All: Love—Success—Sex—Money . . . Even If You're Starting with Nothing* (New York: Linden Press/Simon & Schuster, 1982), p. 11.

Page 153. The author of "Superwomen of the Financial World" (*Working Woman*, September 1984) was quoting sociologist Cynthia Fuchs Epstein's *Women in Law* (New York: Basic Books, 1981) when she labeled successful women "problem solvers or problem avoiders or persons who deny problems exist."

Page 154. "Twenty at the Top: Savvy's 1983 Roster of Outstanding Women Executives," *Savvy*, April 1983. "Life at the Top," *Vogue*, August 1983.

Page 155. Roy Rowan, "How Harvard's Women MBA's Are Managing," *Fortune*, July 11, 1983.

Page 155. Dr. Philip Blumstein and Dr. Pepper Schwartz, *American Couples* (New York: William Morrow & Co., 1983).

Pages 156–157. The fact that executive women who earn less than their husbands are more satisfied with their personal lives appeared in Helen Rogan, "Executive Women Find It Difficult to Balance the Demands of Job, Home," *The Wall Street Journal*, October 30, 1984.

Page 157. The "Hers" column by Mary Lou Weisman, *The New York Times*, October 13, 1983.

Page 158. Blumstein and Schwartz, *American Couples*, pp. 146, 312.

Pages 159–160. The conversation from *Donahue* is reproduced from memory.

Pages 160–161. The facts on maternity-leave policies in the United States and abroad are gleaned from the well-researched article by Sheila B. Kamerman and Alfred J. Kahn, "Company Maternity-Leave Policies," *Working Woman*, February 1984.

Page 166. Nancy Friday, *My Mother/My Self: The Daughter's Search for Identity* (New York: Delacorte Press, 1977), pp. 36, 68.

Page 167. Blumstein and Schwartz, *American Couples*, p. 311.

Page 172. The fact that better-educated women are less likely to marry was noted in the article by Christine Doudna with Fern McBride, "Where Are the Men for the Women at the Top?," *Savvy*, February 1980.

Page 173. The statistics that explain why marriageable women outnumber marriageable men are taken from the 1985 Census. The book that first made me aware of these patterns was by Marion Zola, *All the Good Ones Are Married: Married Men and the Women Who Love Them* (New York: Times Books, 1981).

Page 174. Doudna with McBride, "Where Are the Men for the Women at the Top?"

Page 175. "Single Living," *Ms.*, November 1984.

CHAPTER IX: ALONE AT THE TOP

Page 177. Betty Freidan, *The Second Stage* (New York: Summit Books, 1981), p. 113.

Page 180. Carol Kleiman is quoted in the "Hers" column by Letty Cottin Pogrebin, *The New York Times*, September 22, 1983.

Page 183. Nancy Friday, *My Mother/My Self* (New York: Delacorte Press, 1977), p. 138. Our understanding of competition between mothers and daughters was greatly enhanced by Nancy Friday's illuminating chapter "Competition."

Page 186. Kathleen V. Shea is quoted from the article "Women and Their Secretaries," *The New York Times*, October 15, 1984.

Page 187. Gloria Steinem's quote appears in her book *Outrageous Acts and Everyday Rebellions* (New York: Holt, Rinehart & Winston, 1983), pp. 199. Her chapter entitled "Networking" was originally published as an article for *Ms.* (February 1982) and was entitled "How to Survive Burn-Out, Reagan and Daily Life: Create Psychic Turf."

Pages 189–192. Mary Cunningham with Fran Schumer, *Powerplay: What Really Happened at Bendix* (New York: Linden Press/Simon & Schuster, 1984), pp. (in order of appearance), 57, 61–62, 63, 65–66, 78, 45, 43, 53. Other sources used were Mary Cunningham, "Power Steering," *Harper's Bazaar*, September 1985, and Betty Lehan Harragan, "Mary Cunningham's Story," *Working Woman*, May 1984.

CHAPTER X: SORROW, ANGER, AND LITTLE GIRL LOST

Page 193. Edna O'Brien is quoted from an interview with Philip Roth that appeared in *The New York Times Book Review* on November 18, 1984.

Page 214. Charlotte Decker Sutton and Kris K. Moore, "Probing Opinions: Executive Women—Twenty Years Later," *The Harvard Business Review*, September/October 1985.

Page 215. Susan Fraker, "Why Women Aren't Getting to the Top," *Fortune*, April 16, 1984.

Page 215. Anita Shreve, "The Maternity Backlash: Women vs. Women," *Working Woman*, March 1985.

Page 217. Gloria Steinem, *Outrageous Acts and Everyday Rebellions* (New York: Holt, Rinehart & Winston, 1983), p. 6.

Pages 217–218. Dr. Conalee Levine-Shneidman and Karen Levine, *Too Smart for Her Own Good? A Modern Woman's Guide to Finding and Loving Real Men* (New York: Bantam Books, 1986), pp. 56–57.

BIBLIOGRAPHY AND RECOMMENDED READING

Bernstein, Anne E., M.D., and Gloria Marmar Warner, M.D. *Women Treating Women: Case Material from Women Treated by Female Psychoanalysts*. New York: International Universities Press, Inc., 1984.

—. *An Introduction to Contemporary Psychoanalysis*. New York: Jason Aronson, Inc., 1981.

Blotnick, Dr. Srully. *Otherwise Engaged: The Private Lives of Successful Career Women*. New York: Facts on File Publications, 1985.

Blumstein, Dr. Philip, and Dr. Pepper Schwartz. *American Couples*. New York: William Morrow & Co., 1983.

Brownmiller, Susan. *Femininity*. New York: Linden Press/Simon & Schuster, 1984.

Chernin, Kim. *The Hungry Self: Women, Eating, and Identity*. New York: Times Books, 1985.

Chodorow, Nancy. *The Reproduction of Mothering: Psychoanalysis and the Sociology of Gender*. Berkeley, Calif.: The University of California Press, 1978.

Cunningham, Mary, with Fran Schumer. *Powerplay: What Really Happened at Bendix*. New York: Linden Press/Simon & Schuster, 1984.

Dollard, John, and Neal E. Miller. *Personality and Psychotherapy: An Analysis in Terms of Learning, Thinking and Culture*. New York: McGraw-Hill, 1950.

Dowling, Colette. *The Cinderella Complex: Women's Hidden Fear of Independence*. New York: Pocket Books, 1981.

Eichenbaum, Luise, and Susie Orbach. *Understanding Women: A Feminist Psychoanalytic Approach.* New York: Basic Books, 1983.

Friday, Nancy. *My Mother/My Self: The Daughter's Search for Identity.* New York: Delacorte Press, 1977.

Freidan, Betty. *The Feminine Mystique.* New York: W. W. Norton, 1963.

———. *The Second Stage.* New York: Summit Books, 1981.

Greer, Germaine. *The Female Eunuch.* New York: McGraw-Hill, 1970.

Harragan, Betty Lehan. *Games Mother Never Taught You: Corporate Gamesmanship for Women.* New York: Warner Books, 1977.

Hennig, Margaret, and Anne Jardim. *The Managerial Woman: The Survival Manual for Women in Business.* New York: Pocket Books, 1977.

Lasch, Christopher. *The Culture of Narcissism: American Life in an Age of Diminishing Expectations.* New York: W. W. Norton, 1979.

Levine-Shneidman, Dr. Conalee, and Karen Levine. *Too Smart for Her Own Good? A Modern Woman's Guide to Finding and Loving* Real Men. New York: Bantam, 1986.

Lowen, Alexander, M.D. *Narcissism: Denial of the True Self.* New York: Macmillan, 1983.

Scarf, Maggie. *Unfinished Business: Pressure Points in the Lives of Women.* Garden City, N.Y.: Doubleday, 1980.

Sheehy, Gail. *Pathfinders: Overcoming the Crises of Adult Life and Finding Your Own Path to Well-Being.* New York: William Morrow & Co., 1981.

Steinem, Gloria. *Outrageous Acts and Everday Rebellions.* New York: Holt, Rinehart & Winston, 1983.

INDEX

INDEX

INDEX

separation from, 78–79, 85,
120, 165, 193
single, 150, 171–172
statistics on, 63, 150, 167
"successful," 74–77, 84
unconscious imitation of, 132,
133, 163
"unsuccessful," 77, 84
widowed, 58
in work force, 59
Ms., 175
"My Man," 119
My Mother/Myself (Friday), 8, 64,
90, 166, 182, 207, 208

Nagel, Madeline, 7
Naisbitt, John, 182
narcissism, 80–81, 83, 89–90,
122–123, 164, 169
Narcissism (Lowen), 194
networking, 181
New York Times Magazine, 43, 97
New York University, 97
"nice," 128
"1983 Roster of Outstanding
Women Executives," 154,
179
"nurturing," 101, 106, 125, 161

obesity, 122, 195, 198, 211
O'Brien, Edna, 193
Oedipal relations, 78, 182–183,
193
office affairs, 133–135, 149
Of Woman Born (Rich), 102
old-boys' networks, 104, 124, 145
Oliver!, 119–120
One Minute Manager, The
(Blanchard and Johnson),
182
Orbach, Susie, 193
"outgoing," 103, 123, 124
outspokenness, 100, 173, 204

parents:
of executive men, 58
of executive women, 57–59, 64–
85, 93, 172, 205, 210, 211

of executive women, education
of, 58–59, 93, 172, 205,
210, 211
of executive women, marriages
of, 69, 76–77, 205
favoritism by, 69–70
see also fathers; mothers
paternity leave, 160, 215
penis envy, 78
Peters, Thomas J., 181
Powerplay (Cunningham), 48, 85,
189
pregnancy, 160–161

racial issues, 57
Reader's Digest, 144
religious issues, 57, 209–213
Reynolds, Nancy, 48, 191
Rich, Adrienne, 102
Ride, Sally, 203
Right Moves, The (Mitchell and
Burdick), 106
risk-taking, 136–137, 138, 145
role models, 112–114, 214
role reversals, 155–156, 174

salaries:
of executive women, 52, 53, 60–
61, 206, 209, 210, 212
of husbands vs. wives, 155–156
raises and, 127–128
sexual discrimination in, 145
Savvy, 154, 174, 179
Schwartz, Pepper, 155
Second Stage, The (Friedan), 177
self-denial, 178–180
sexual discrimination, 141–145,
170, 198, 214
sexual harassment, 111, 144
sexuality:
development of, 91–93, 183
double standard and, 92
of executive women, 152, 168,
180, 187, 195
of men, 92, 98
of women, 91–93, 98, 183
see also office affairs
"sexy," 98, 126